Eye of the MAJESTIC CREAture

Issues 5-7

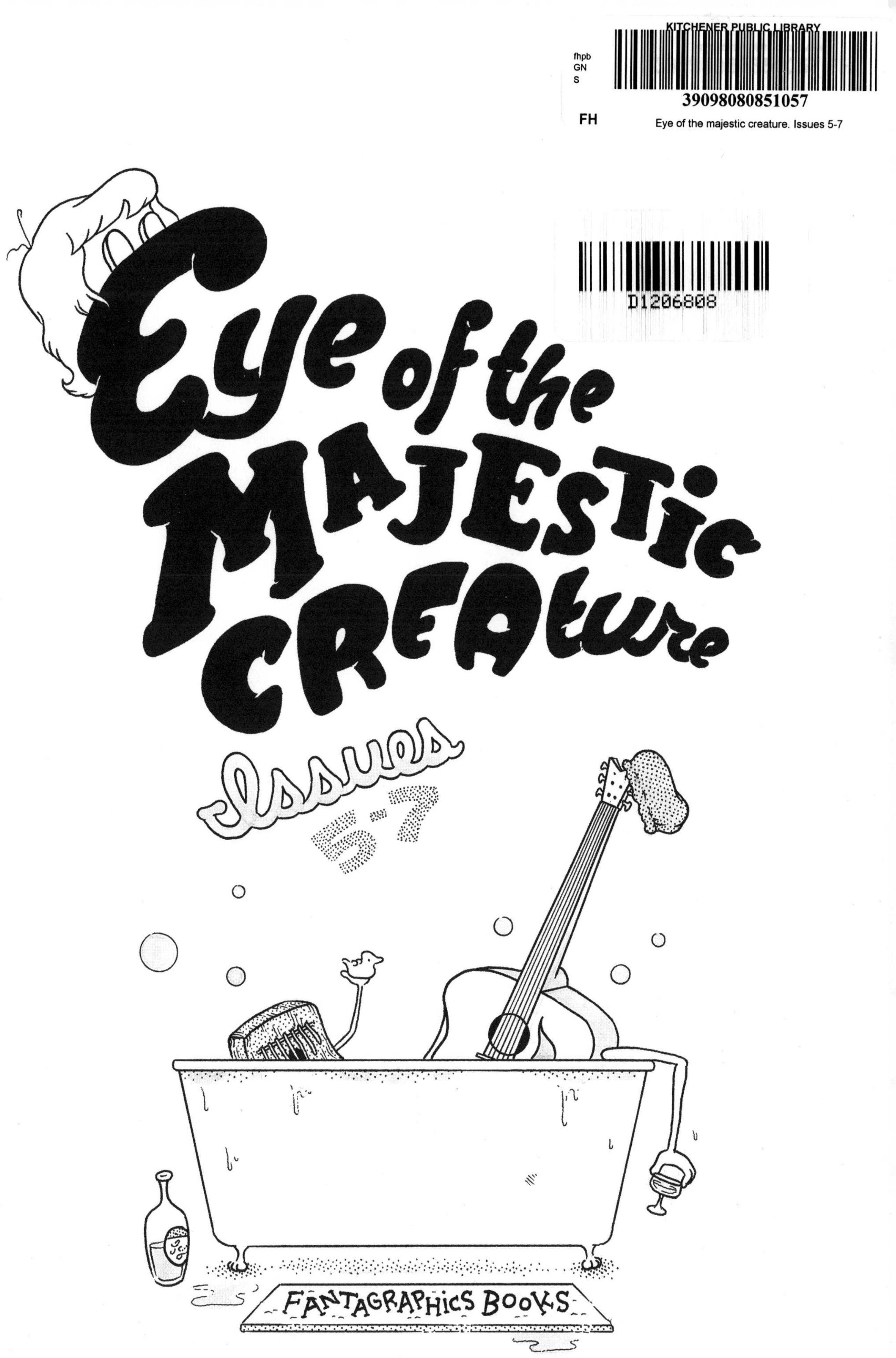
FANTAGRAPHICS BOOKS

FANTAGRAPHICS BOOKS
7563 Lake City Way NE
Seattle, Washington 98115

PUBLISHERS *Gary Groth and Kim Thompson*
EDITOR AND ASSOCIATE PUBLISHER *Eric Reynolds*
DESIGNER *Leslie Stein*
PRODUCTION *Paul Baresh*

To receive a free full-color catalog of comics, graphic novels, prose novels, and other
fine works of artistry, call 1-800-657-1100, or visit www.fantagraphics.com.

ISBN: 978-1-60699-672-0

First Fantagraphics printing: July, 2013

Printed in China

EOTIIC

NUMBER 5   Leslie Stein

All text in black
was written by
Theodore Dreiser
and published in
his 1900 novel
Sister Carrie.

SISTER CARRIE

I.
When a girl leaves home at the age of eighteen, she does one of two things. Either she falls into saving hands and becomes better, or she rapidly assumes the cosmopolitan standard of virtue and becomes worse.
VENTURES
VENTURES

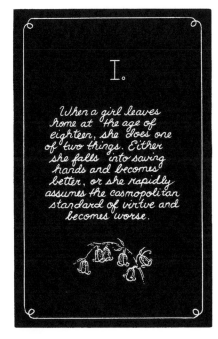

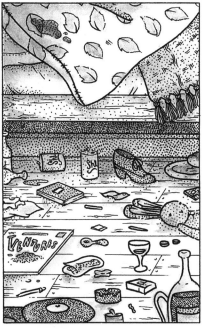

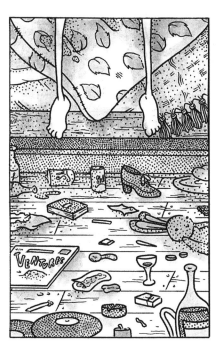

A shopgirl was the destiny prefigured for the newcomer. She would get in one of the great shops and do well enough until — well, until something happened.
KRSH-SHHH
Neither of them knew exactly what.
MARSHY!!! What are you doin' in here? Out!
BLAH!!
RUBBING ALCOHOL
They did not figure on promotion.
and ONE TWO THREE four...
They did not exactly count on marriage.
...and TWO TWO THREE FOUR...
Munch Munch Munch
Things would go on, though, in a dim kind of way...
...until the better thing would eventuate...
...and (she) would be rewarded for coming and toiling in the city.

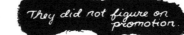

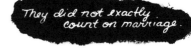

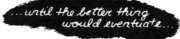

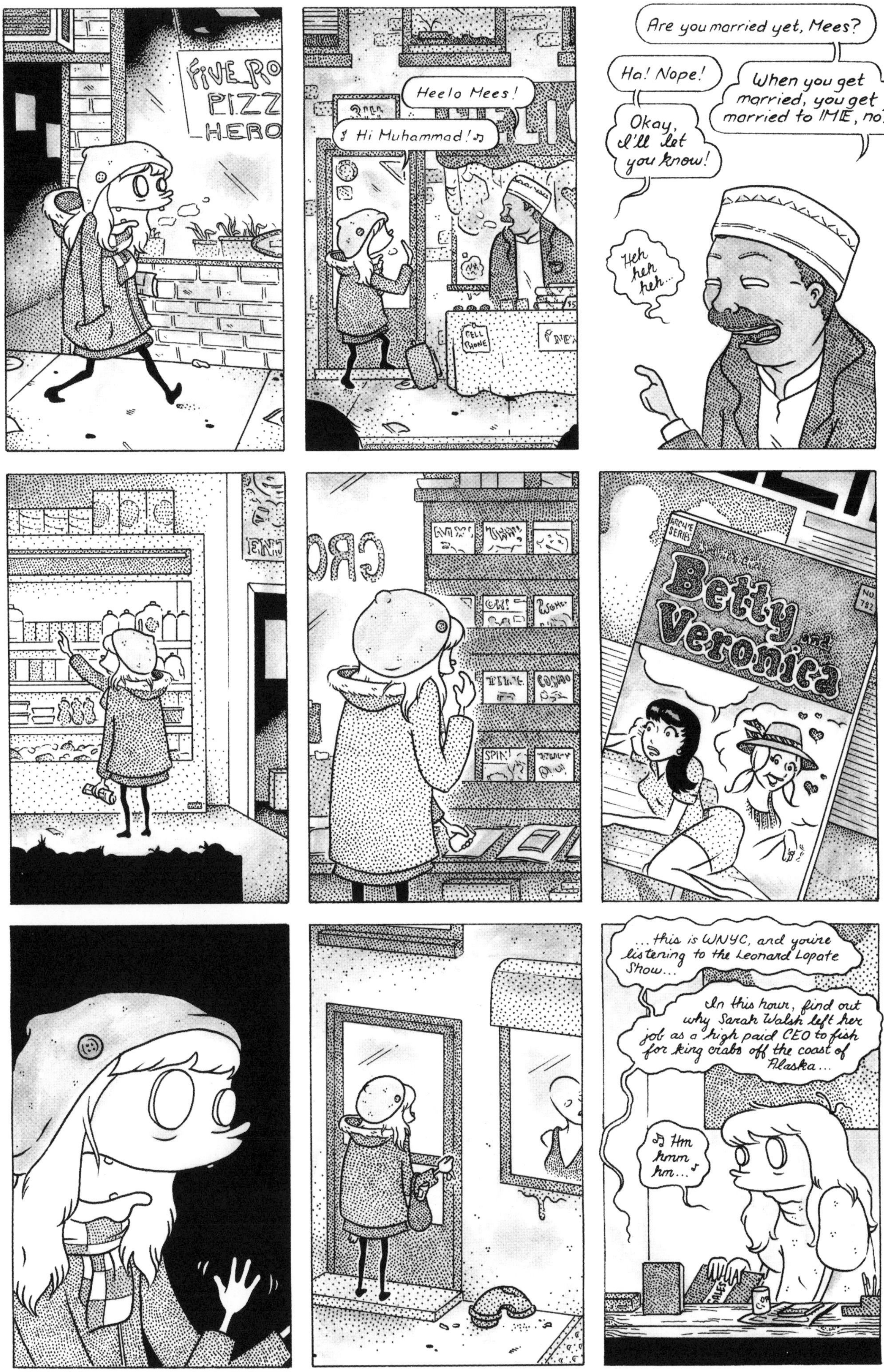
FIVE RO
PIZZ
HERO
Heelo Mees!
Hi Muhammad!
Are you married yet, Mees?
Ha! Nope!
When you get married, you get married to ME, no?
Okay, I'll let you know!
Heh heh heh...
Betty and Veronica
...this is WNYC, and you're listening to the Leonard Lopate Show...
In this hour, find out why Sarah Walsh left her job as a high paid CEO to fish for king crabs off the coast of Alaska...
Hm hmm hm...

Sales (February) cont.
Monday 3rd 0-
Tues 4th 0-
Wed 5th 56.00 (pencil skirt M.)
Thursday 6th 0-
Friday 7th 0-
Saturday 8th 182.00 (Nancy Dress Sm.)
Sunday 9th 60.00 (Blue Blouse L.)
Monday 10th 0-
Tuesday 11th 0-
click click click
Hi there!... Let me know if you need help with anything, okay?
Hello...
Can I try this on?
Sure! The dressing room is right in the back...
A woman should some day write the complete philosophy of clothes. No matter how young, it is one of the things she wholly comprehends.
Skrit!
Umm... I'm not exactly sure what's going on here...
There's no room for boobs... ...and... WAAAAY too much in the back...
Is it a sample size or something?
Mmm...
God, this fit is BIZZARRE!
...

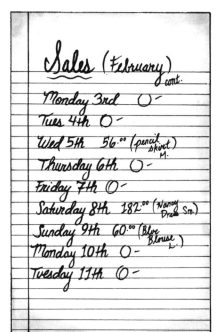

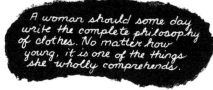

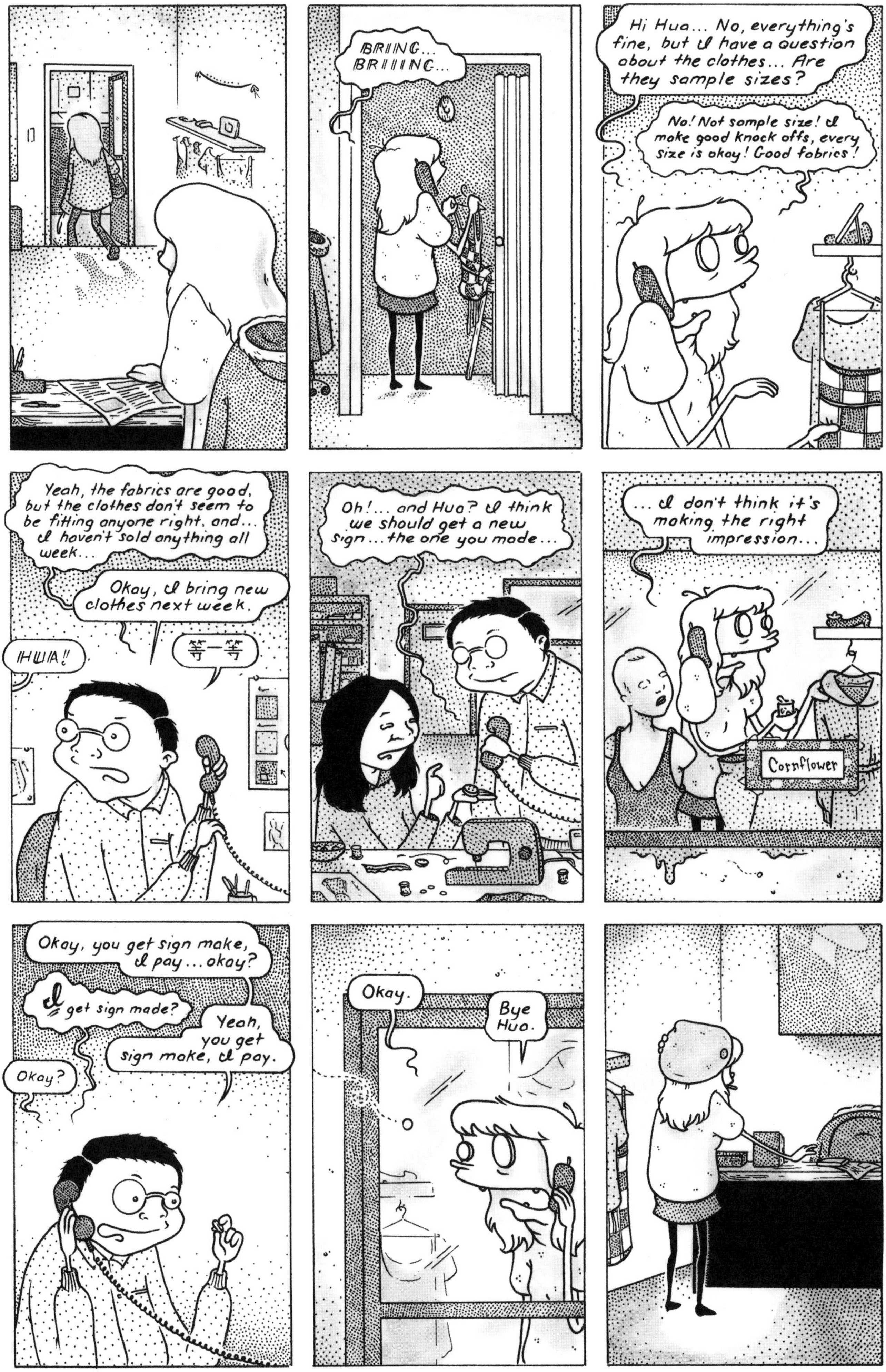
BRIING... BRIIIING...
Hi Hua... No, everything's fine, but I have a question about the clothes... Are they sample sizes?
No! Not sample size! I make good knock offs, every size is okay! Good fabrics!
Yeah, the fabrics are good, but the clothes don't seem to be fitting anyone right, and... I haven't sold anything all week...
Okay, I bring new clothes next week.
HUA!!
等一等
Oh!... and Hua? I think we should get a new sign... the one you made...
...I don't think it's making the right impression...
Cornflower
Okay, you get sign make, I pay... okay?
I get sign made?
Yeah, you get sign make, I pay.
Okay?
Okay.
Bye Hua.

(She) was not familiar with the appearance of her more fortunate sisters of the city.

Neither had she before known the nature and appearance of the shop girls with whom she now compared poorly.

They were pretty in the main, some even handsome, and with an air of independence and indifference that added... a certain piquancy.

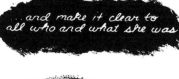

...wherever she encountered the eye of one it was only to recognise in it a keen analysis of her own position — her individual shortcomings of dress and that shadow of manner which she thought must hang about her...

...and make it clear to all who and what she was.

Seven o'clock!

YES!!

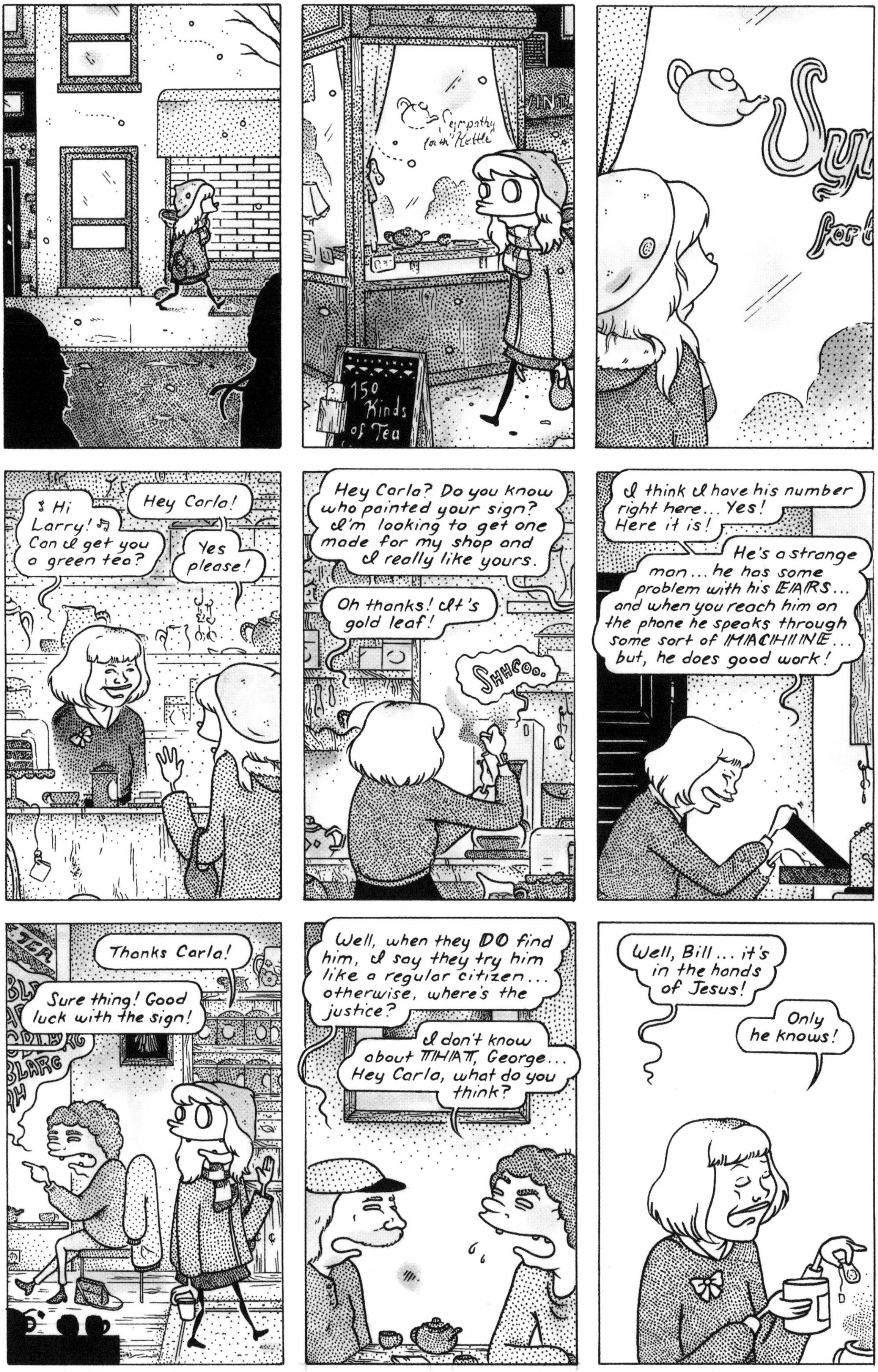

Sympathy for the Kettle
150 Kinds of Tea
Sym
for t
Hi Larry! Can I get you a green tea?
Hey Carla!
Yes please!
Hey Carla? Do you know who painted your sign? I'm looking to get one made for my shop and I really like yours.
Oh thanks! It's gold leaf!
SHHCOO.
I think I have his number right here... Yes! Here it is!
He's a strange man... he has some problem with his EARS... and when you reach him on the phone he speaks through some sort of MACHINE... but, he does good work!
Thanks Carla!
Sure thing! Good luck with the sign!
BLARG
BLARG
Well, when they DO find him, I say they try him like a regular citizen... otherwise, where's the justice?
I don't know about THAT, George... Hey Carla, what do you think?
Well, Bill... it's in the hands of Jesus!
Only he knows!

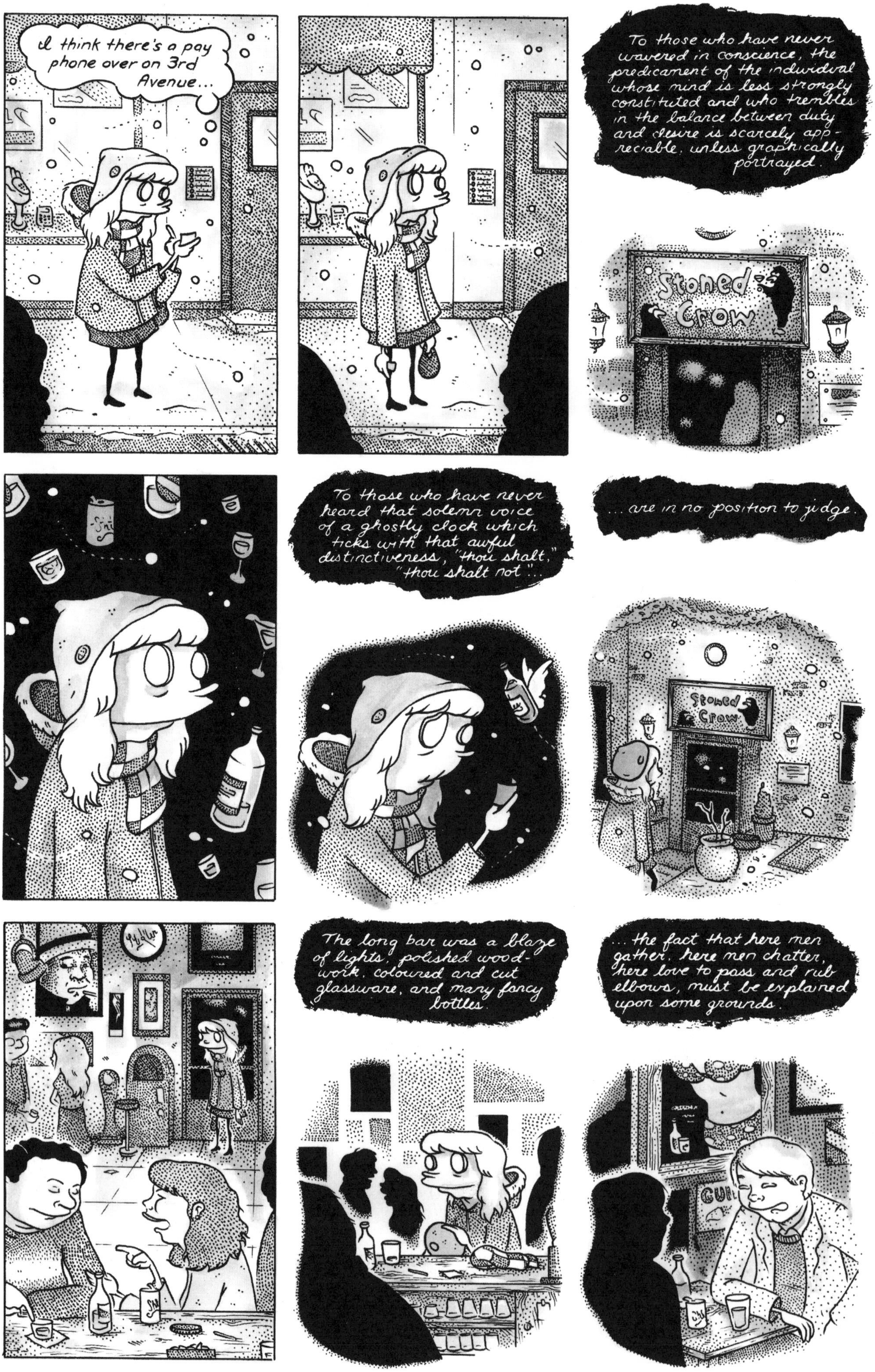

I think there's a pay phone over on 3rd Avenue...
To those who have never wavered in conscience, the predicament of the individual whose mind is less strongly constituted and who trembles in the balance between duty and desire is scarcely appreciable, unless graphically portrayed.
Stoned Crow
To those who have never heard that solemn voice of a ghostly clock which ticks with that awful distinctiveness, "thou shalt," "thou shalt not"...
...are in no position to judge.
Stoned Crow
The long bar was a blaze of lights, polished woodwork, coloured and cut glassware, and many fancy bottles.
...the fact that here men gather, here men chatter, here love to pass and rub elbows, must be explained upon some grounds.

It must be that a strange bundle of passions and vague desires give rise to such a curious social institution...

...or it would not be.

Can I get a Jameson neat and a half pint of Stella, please?

Our civilisation is still in a middle stage, scarcely beast, in that it is no longer wholly guided by instinct, scarcely human, in that it is not wholly guided by reason.

On the tiger no responsibility rests. We see him aligned by nature with the forces of life... without thought he is protected.

We see man far removed from the layers of the jungles... he is becoming too wise to hearken always to instincts and desires...

...too weak to always prevail against them.

He is even as a wisp in the wind, moved by every breath of passion, acting now by his free will and now by his instincts, erring with one, only to retrieve by the other, falling by one, only to rise by the other - a creature of incalculable variability.

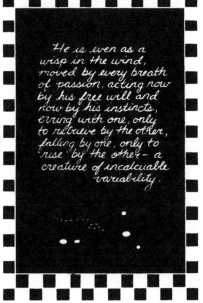

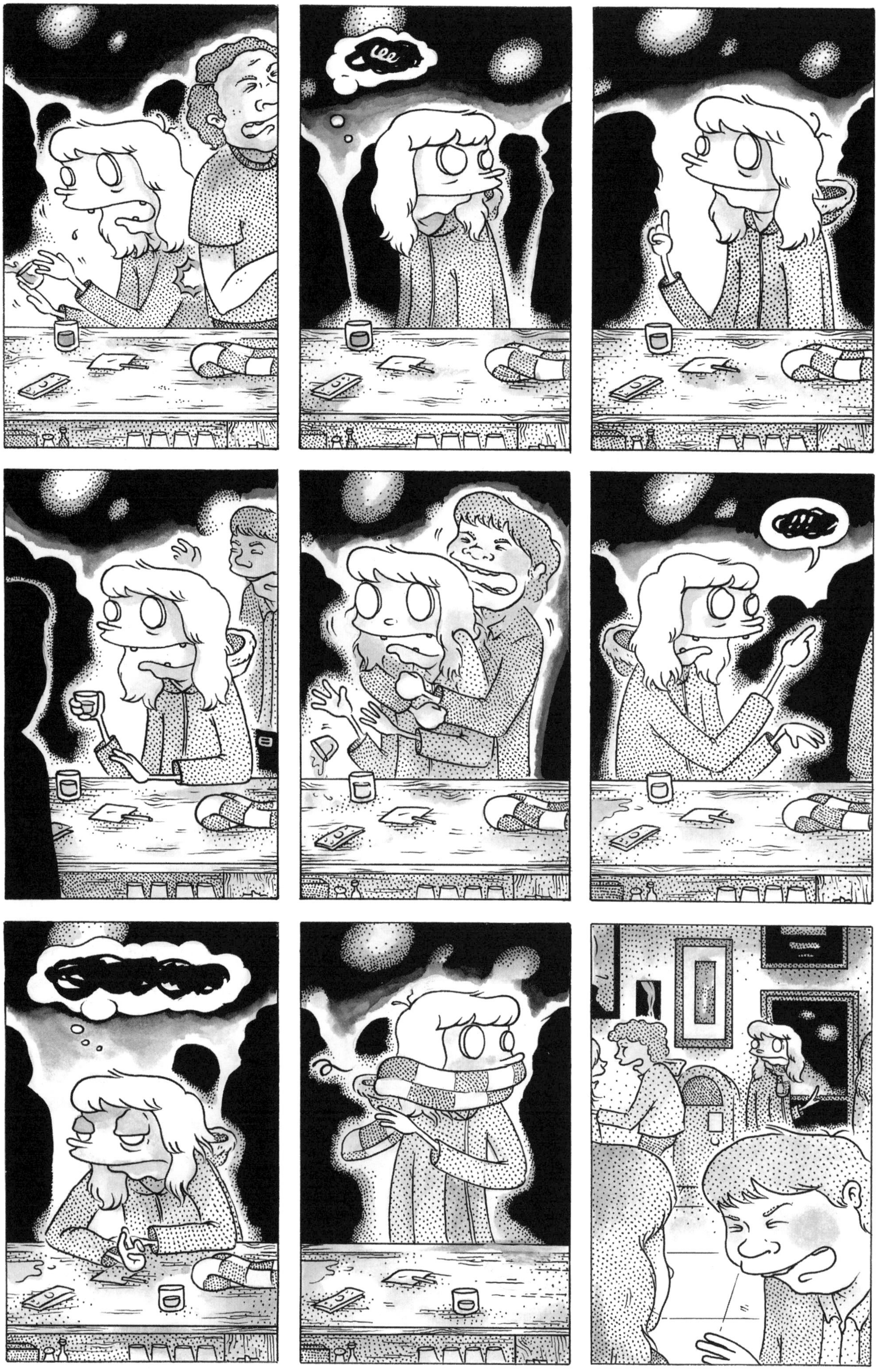

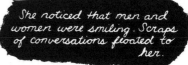
She walked out into a busy street and discovered a new atmosphere. Behold, the crowd was moving with a lightsome step.

She noticed that men and women were smiling. Scraps of conversations floated to her.

The air was light.

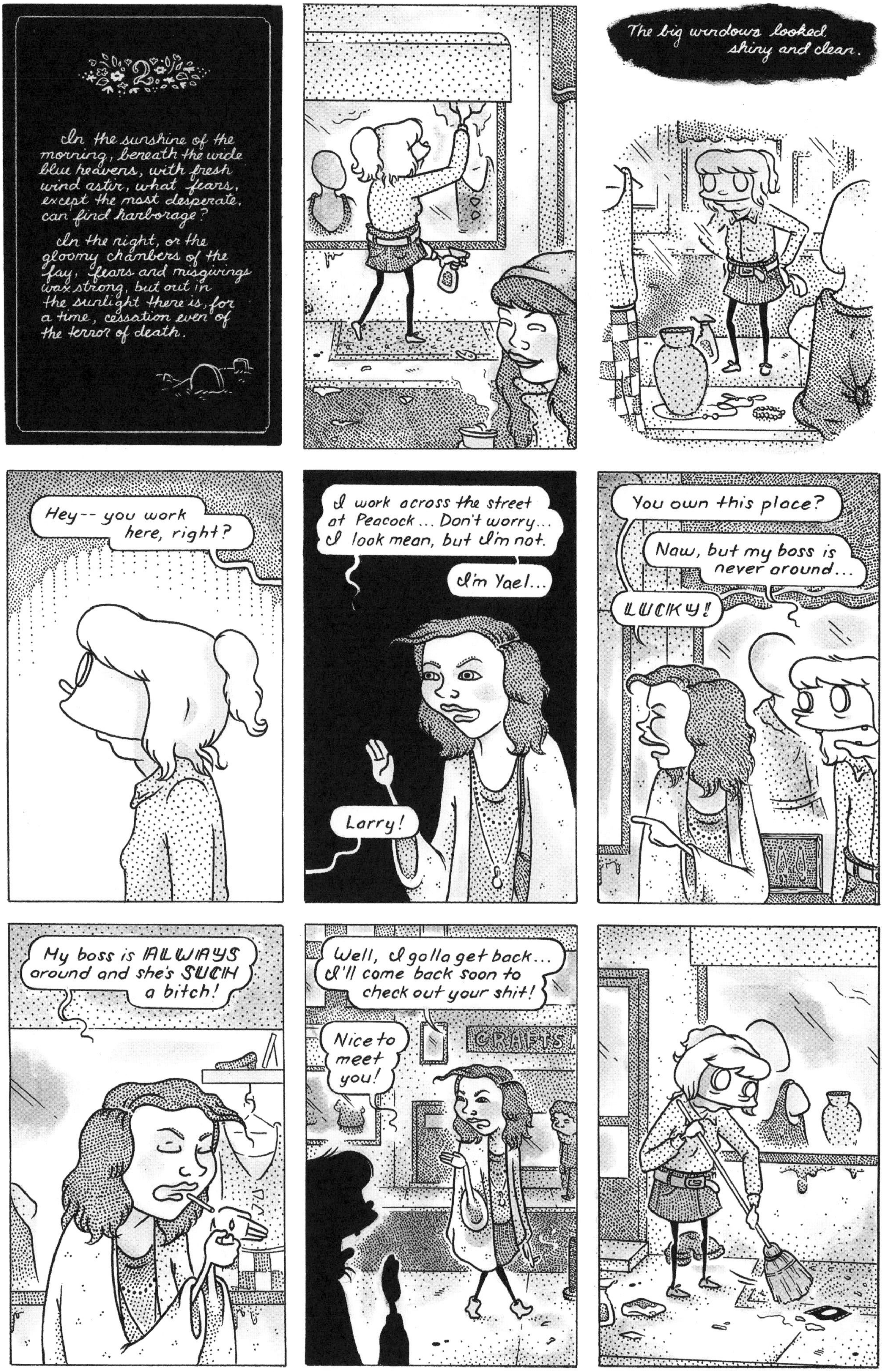
2
In the sunshine of the morning, beneath the wide blue heavens, with fresh wind astir, what fears, except the most desperate, can find harborage?
In the night, or the gloomy chambers of the fay, fears and misgivings wax strong, but out in the sunlight there is, for a time, cessation even of the terror of death.
The big windows looked shiny and clean.
Hey-- you work here, right?
I work across the street at Peacock... Don't worry... I look mean, but I'm not.
I'm Yael...
Larry!
You own this place?
Naw, but my boss is never around...
LUCKY!
My boss is ALWAYS around and she's SUCH a bitch!
Well, I gotta get back... I'll come back soon to check out your shit!
Nice to meet you!
CRAFTS

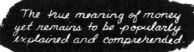
The true meaning of money yet remains to be popularly explained and comprehended.

When each individual realises for himself that this thing primarily stands for and should only be accepted as moral due —

— that it should be paid out as honestly stored energy, and not as usurped privilege —

— many of our social, religious, and political troubles will have permanently passed.

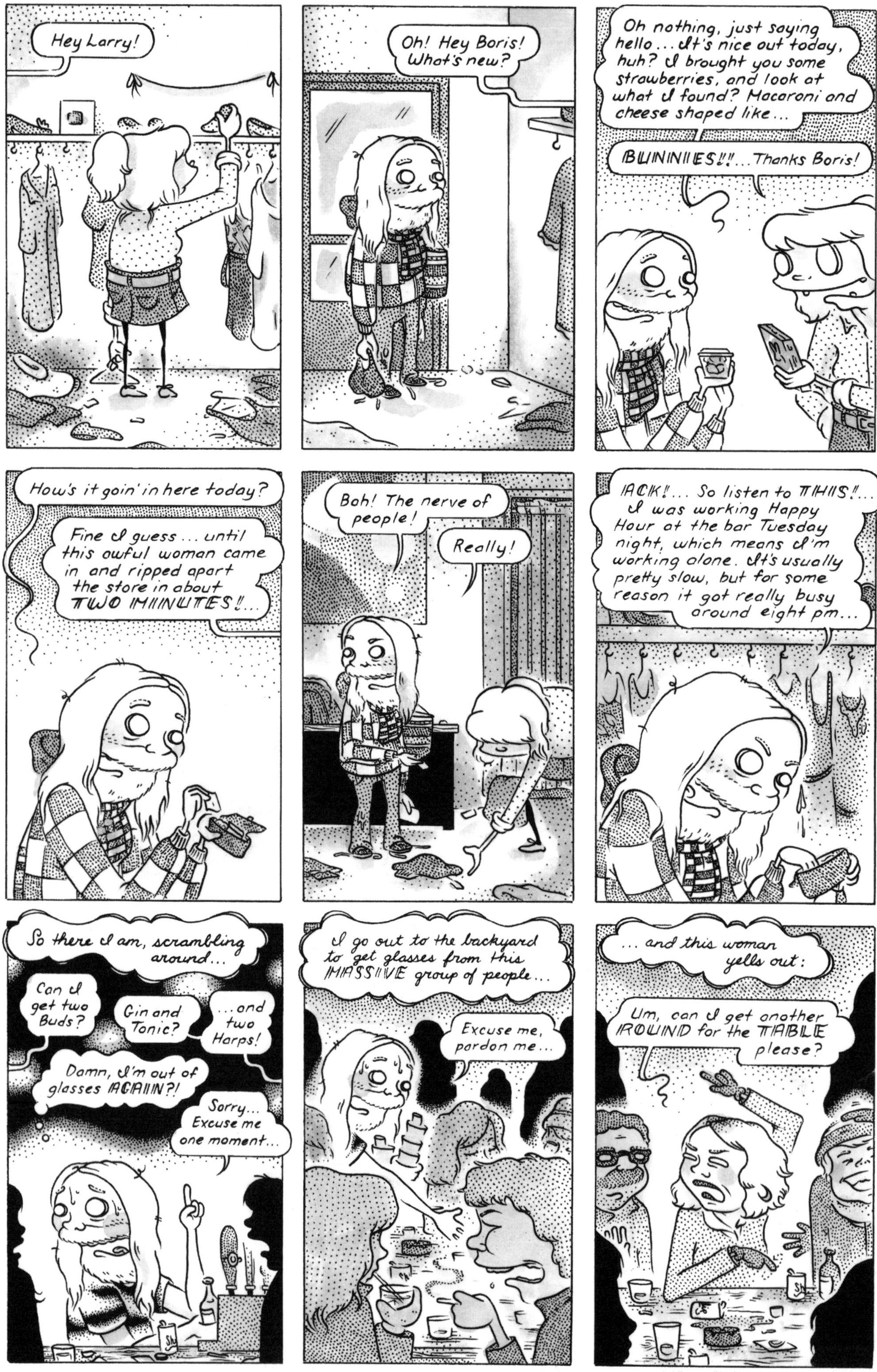

Hey Larry!
Oh! Hey Boris! What's new?
Oh nothing, just saying hello... It's nice out today, huh? I brought you some strawberries, and look at what I found? Macaroni and cheese shaped like...
BUNNIES!!!... Thanks Boris!
How's it goin' in here today?
Fine I guess... until this awful woman came in and ripped apart the store in about TWO MINUTES!!...
Bah! The nerve of people!
Really!
ACK!... So listen to THIS!!... I was working Happy Hour at the bar Tuesday night, which means I'm working alone. It's usually pretty slow, but for some reason it got really busy around eight pm...
So there I am, scrambling around...
Can I get two Buds?
Gin and Tonic?
...and two Harps!
Damn, I'm out of glasses AGAIN?!
Sorry... Excuse me one moment...
I go out to the backyard to get glasses from this MASSIVE group of people...
Excuse me, pardon me...
... and this woman yells out:
Um, can I get another ROUND for the TABLE please?

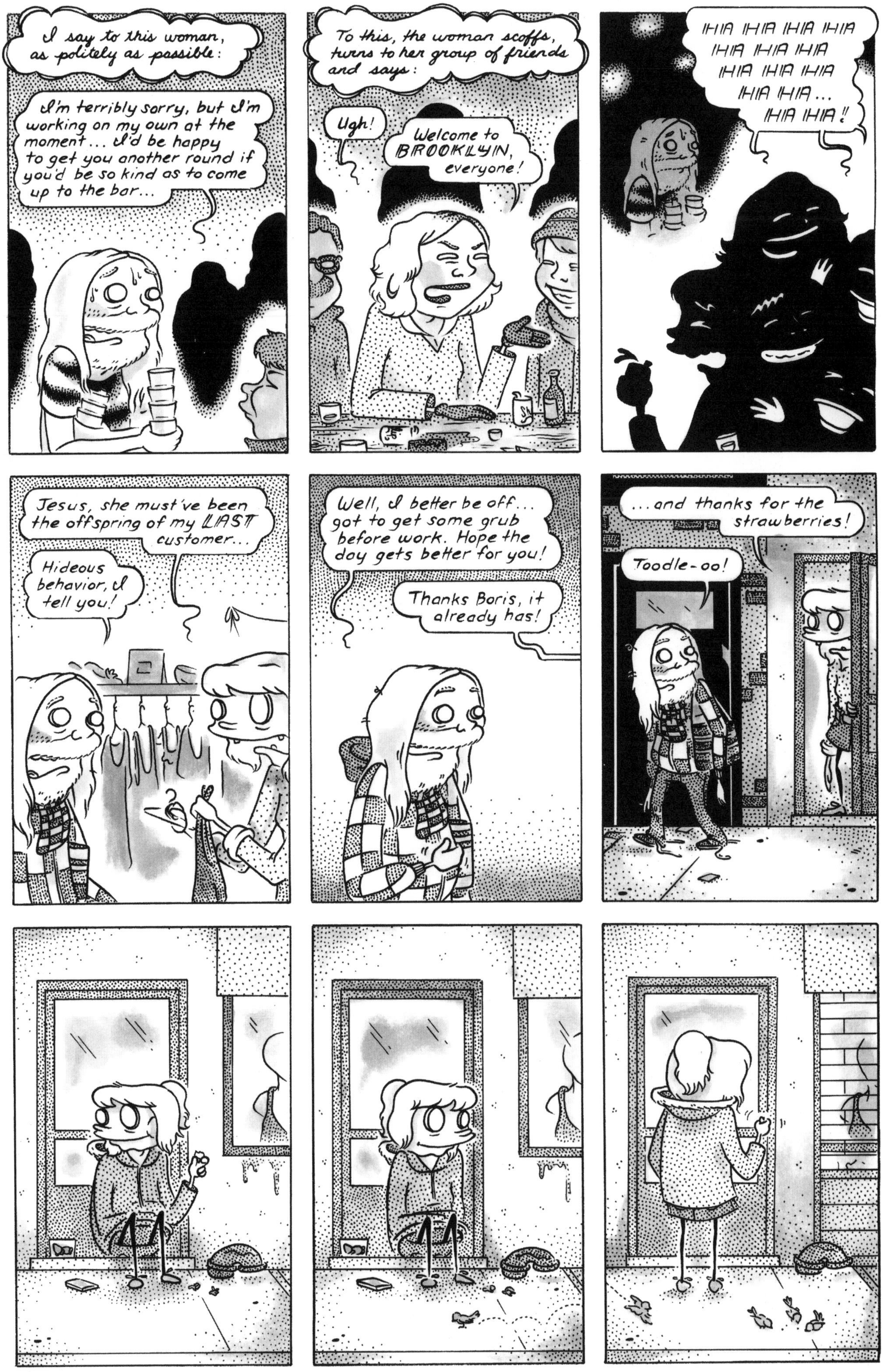
I say to this woman, as politely as possible:
I'm terribly sorry, but I'm working on my own at the moment... I'd be happy to get you another round if you'd be so kind as to come up to the bar...
To this, the woman scoffs, turns to her group of friends and says:
Ugh!
Welcome to BROOKLYN, everyone!
HA HA HA HA HA HA HA HA HA HA HA HA HA... HA HA!!
Jesus, she must've been the offspring of my LAST customer...
Hideous behavior, I tell you!
Well, I better be off... got to get some grub before work. Hope the day gets better for you!
Thanks Boris, it already has!
...and thanks for the strawberries!
Toodle-oo!

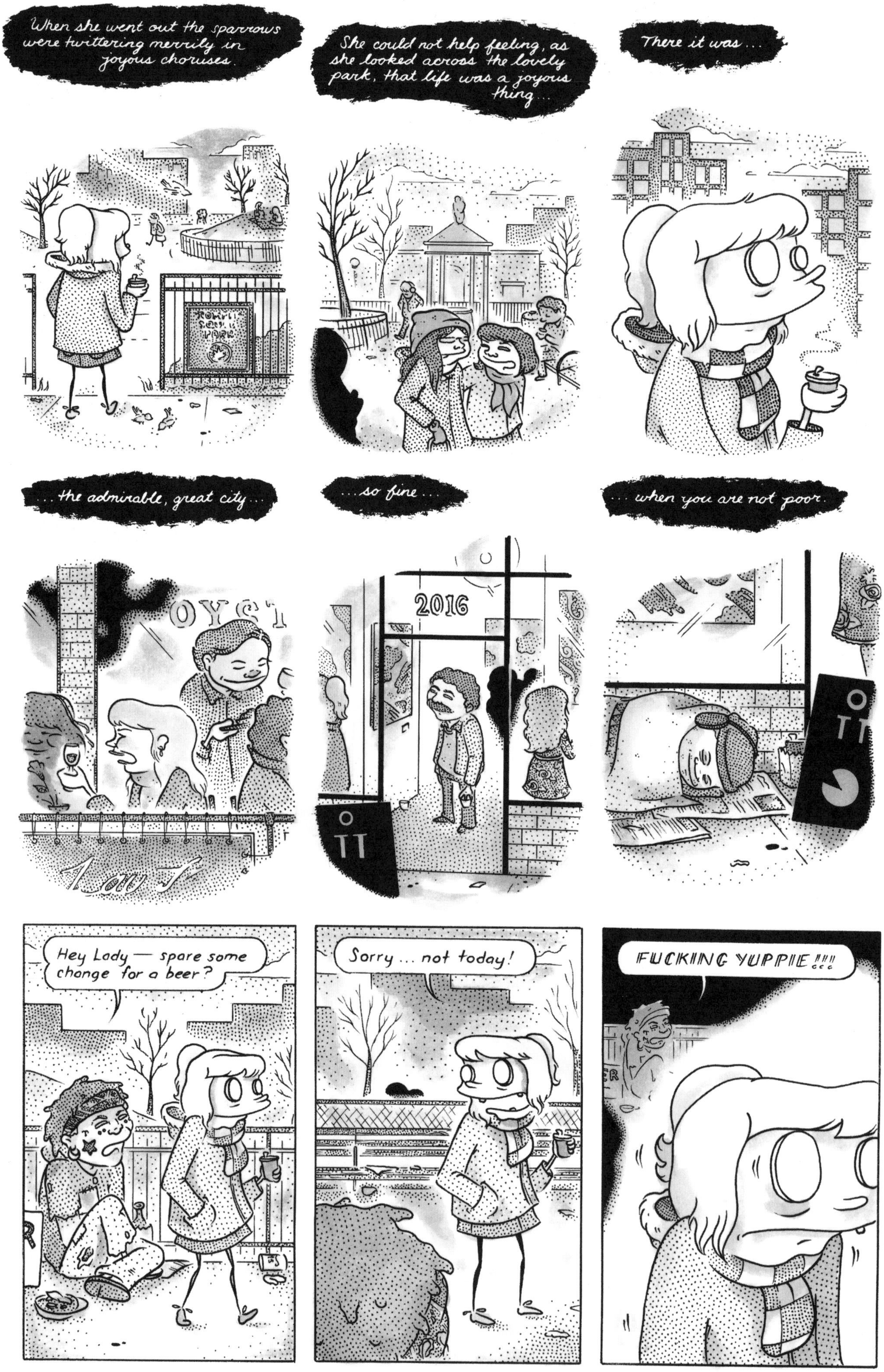
When she went out the sparrows were twittering merrily in joyous choruses.
She could not help feeling, as she looked across the lovely park, that life was a joyous thing...
There it was...
...the admirable, great city...
...so fine...
...when you are not poor.
Hey Lady — spare some change for a beer?
Sorry ... not today!
FUCKING YUPPIE!!!...

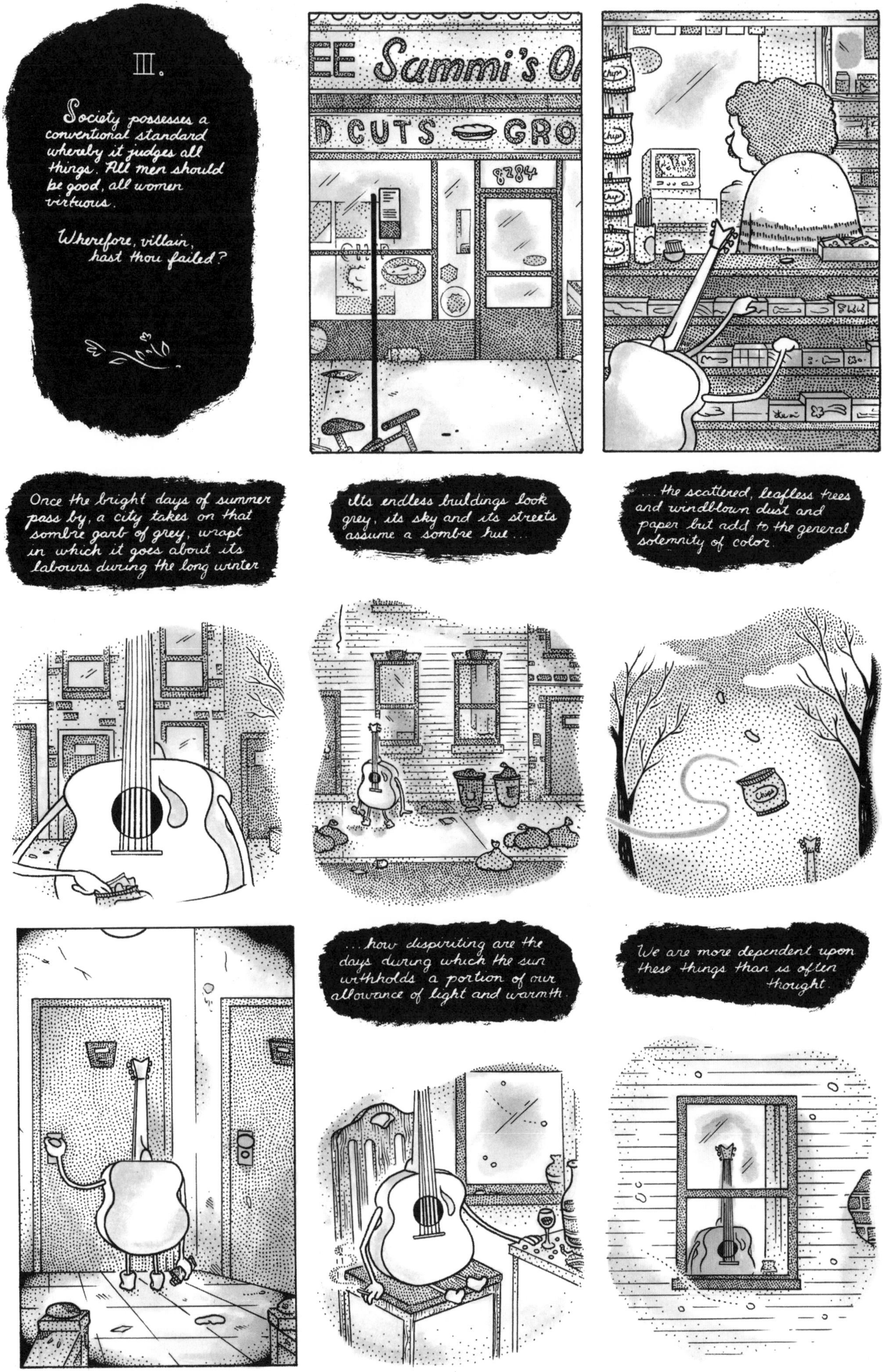
III.
Society possesses a conventional standard whereby it judges all things. All men should be good, all women virtuous.
Wherefore, villain, hast thou failed?
Summi's
CUTS
8284
Once the bright days of summer pass by, a city takes on that sombre garb of grey, wrapt in which it goes about its labours during the long winter
Its endless buildings look grey, its sky and its streets assume a sombre hue...
...the scattered, leafless trees and windblown dust and paper but add to the general solemnity of color.
...how dispiriting are the days during which the sun withholds a portion of our allowance of light and warmth.
We are more dependent upon these things than is often thought.

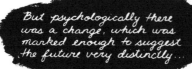
There was no apparent slope downward, and distinctly none upward, so far as the casual observer might have seen

But psychologically there was a change, which was marked enough to suggest the future very distinctly...

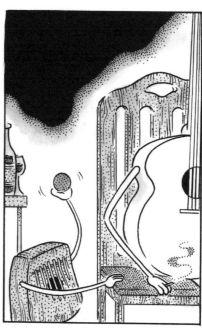

The mental difficulties of an individual reveal themselves whether he voluntarily confesses them or not. Trouble gets in the air and contributes gloom, which speaks for itself.

This often happens to the best regulated families. Little things brought out on such occasions need great love to obliterate them afterward.

Where that is not, both parties count two and two and make a problem after a while.

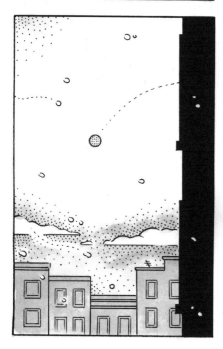

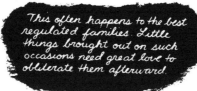

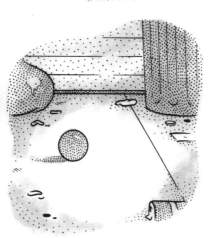

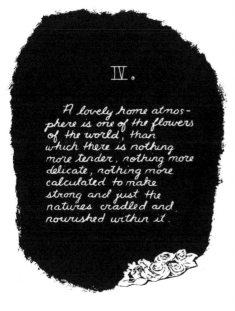

IV.

A lovely home atmosphere is one of the flowers of the world, than which there is nothing more tender, nothing more delicate, nothing more calculated to make strong and just the natures cradled and nourished within it.

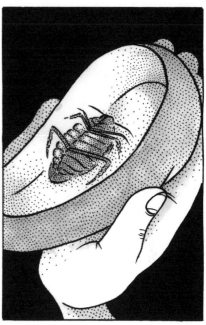

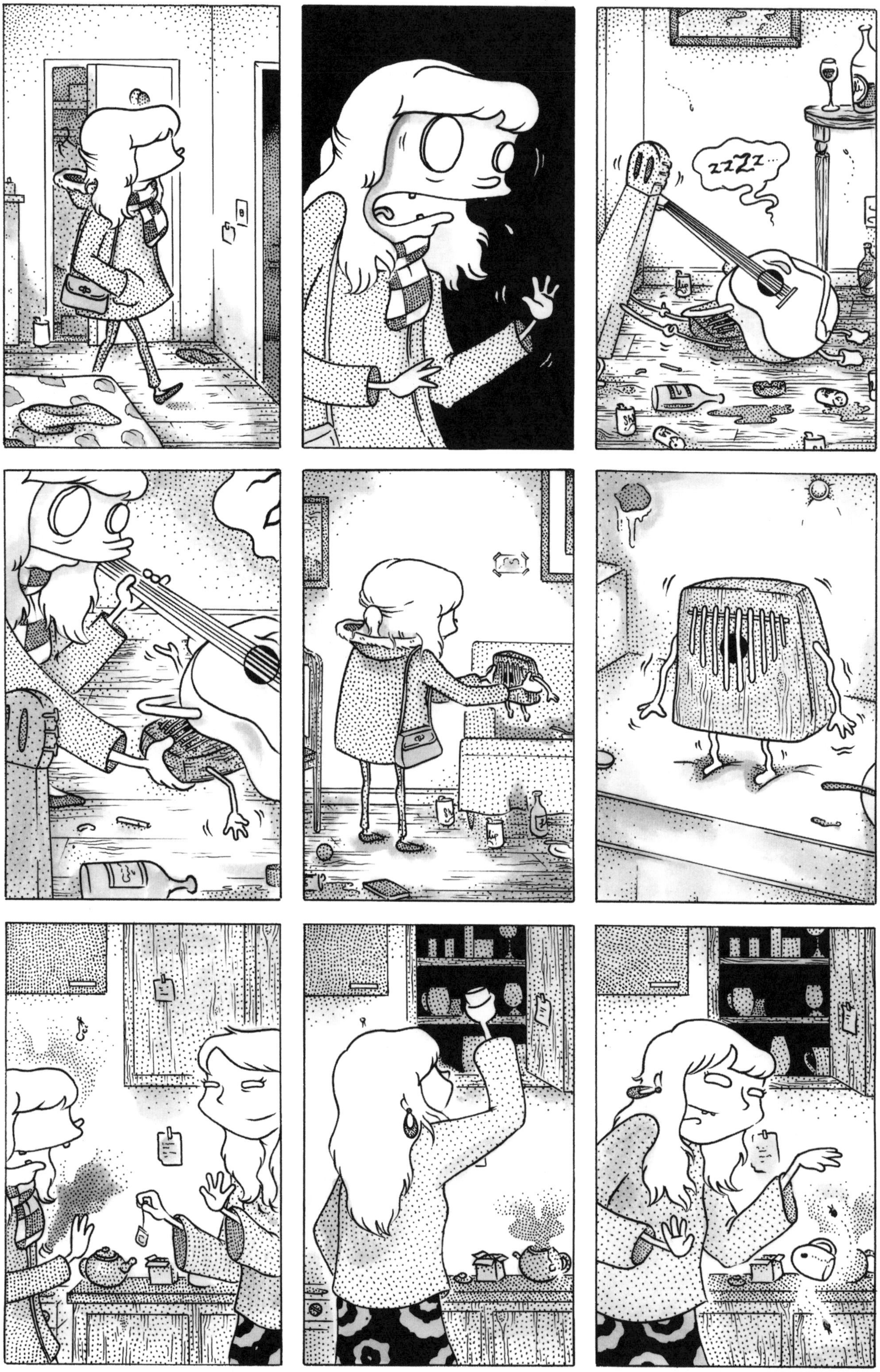
zzZz...

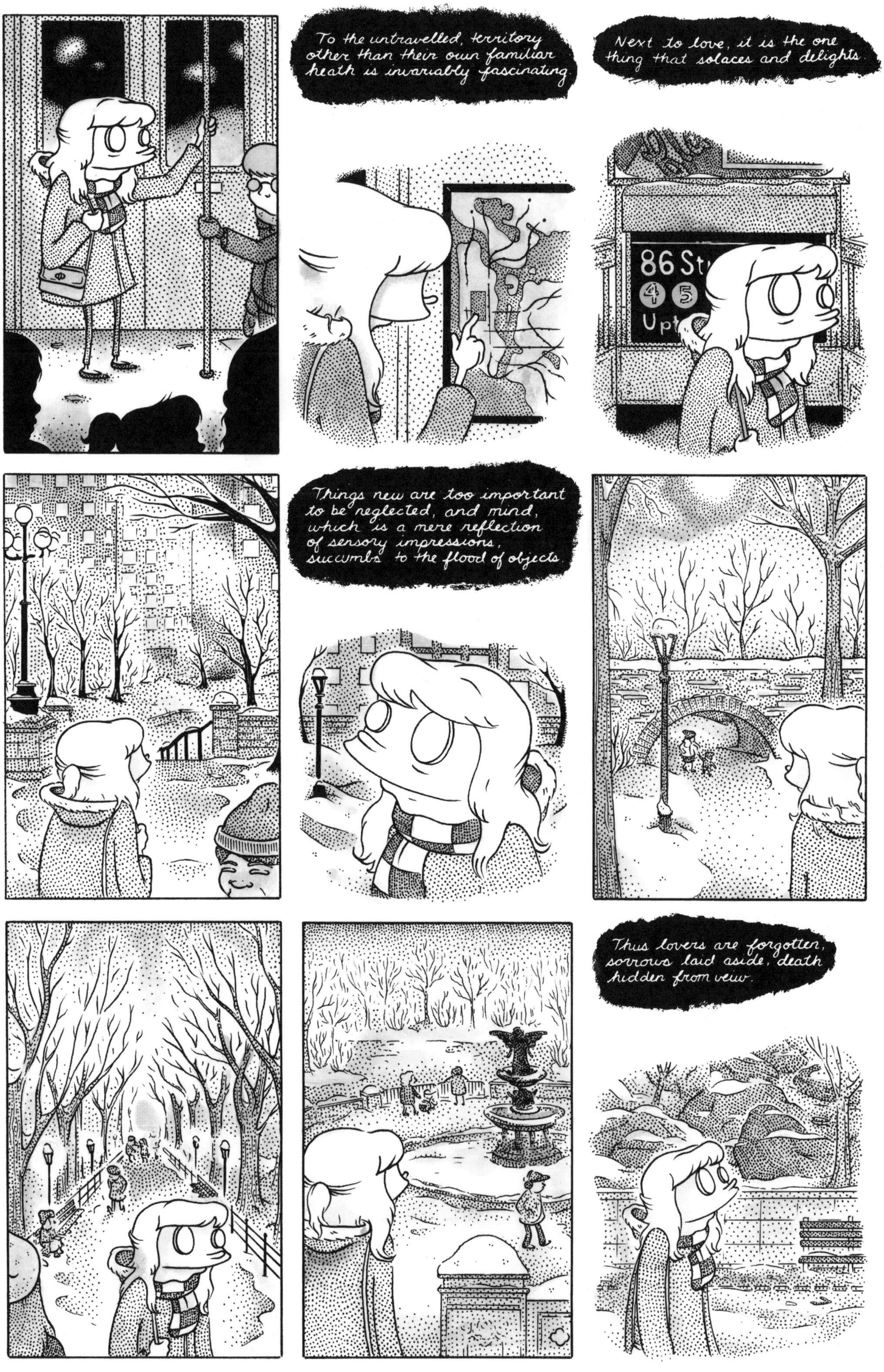
To the untravelled, territory other than their own familiar heath is invariably fascinating.
Next to love, it is the one thing that solaces and delights.
86 St
4
5
Upt
Things new are too important to be neglected, and mind, which is a mere reflection of sensory impressions, succumbs to the flood of objects.
Thus lovers are forgotten, sorrows laid aside, death hidden from veiw.

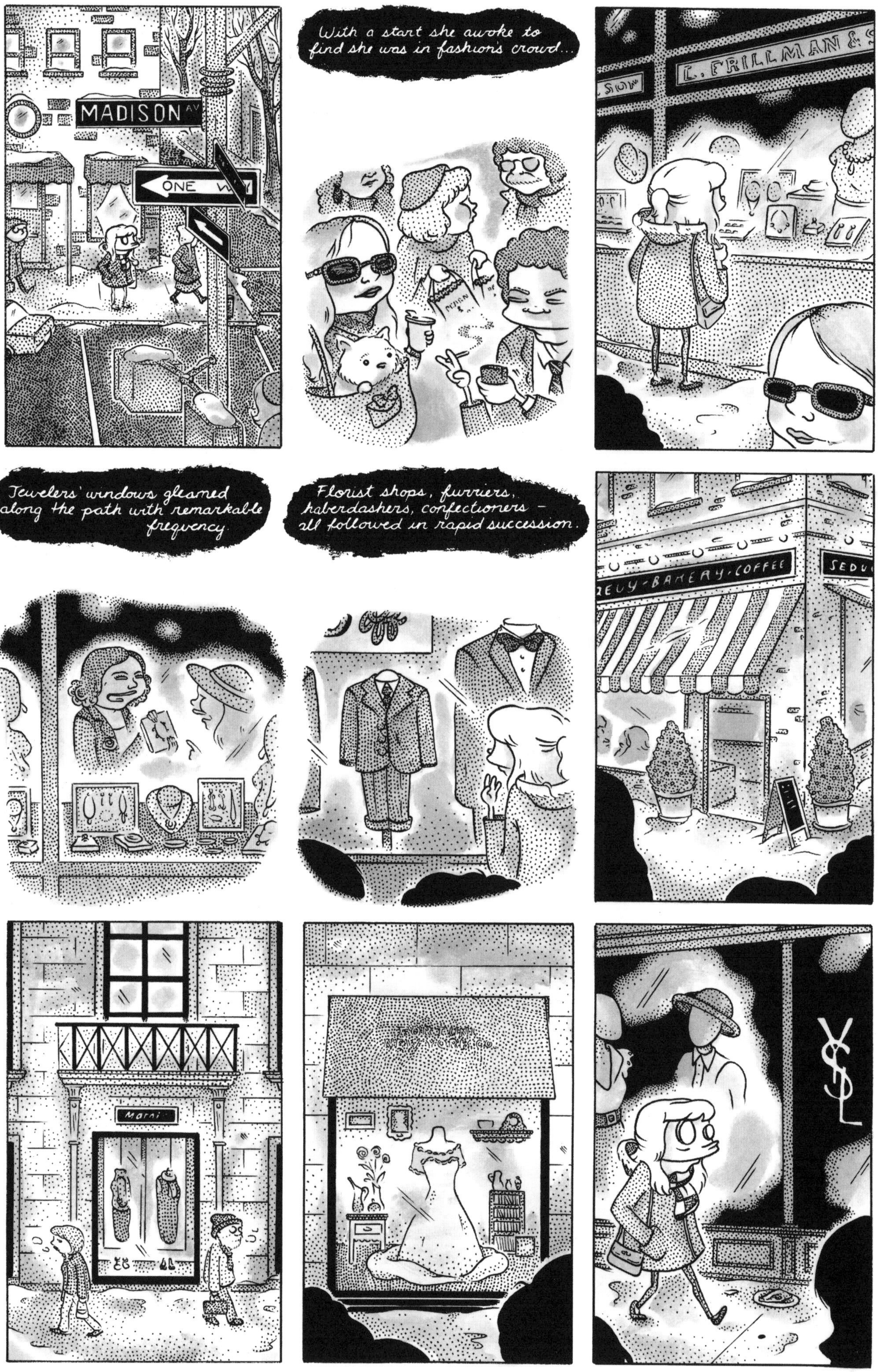

MADISON AV
ONE WAY
With a start she awoke to find she was in fashion's crowd...
L. FRILLMAN & S
Jewelers' windows gleamed along the path with remarkable frequency.
Florist shops, furriers, haberdashers, confectioners - all followed in rapid succession.
BAKERY · COFFEE
Marni
YSL

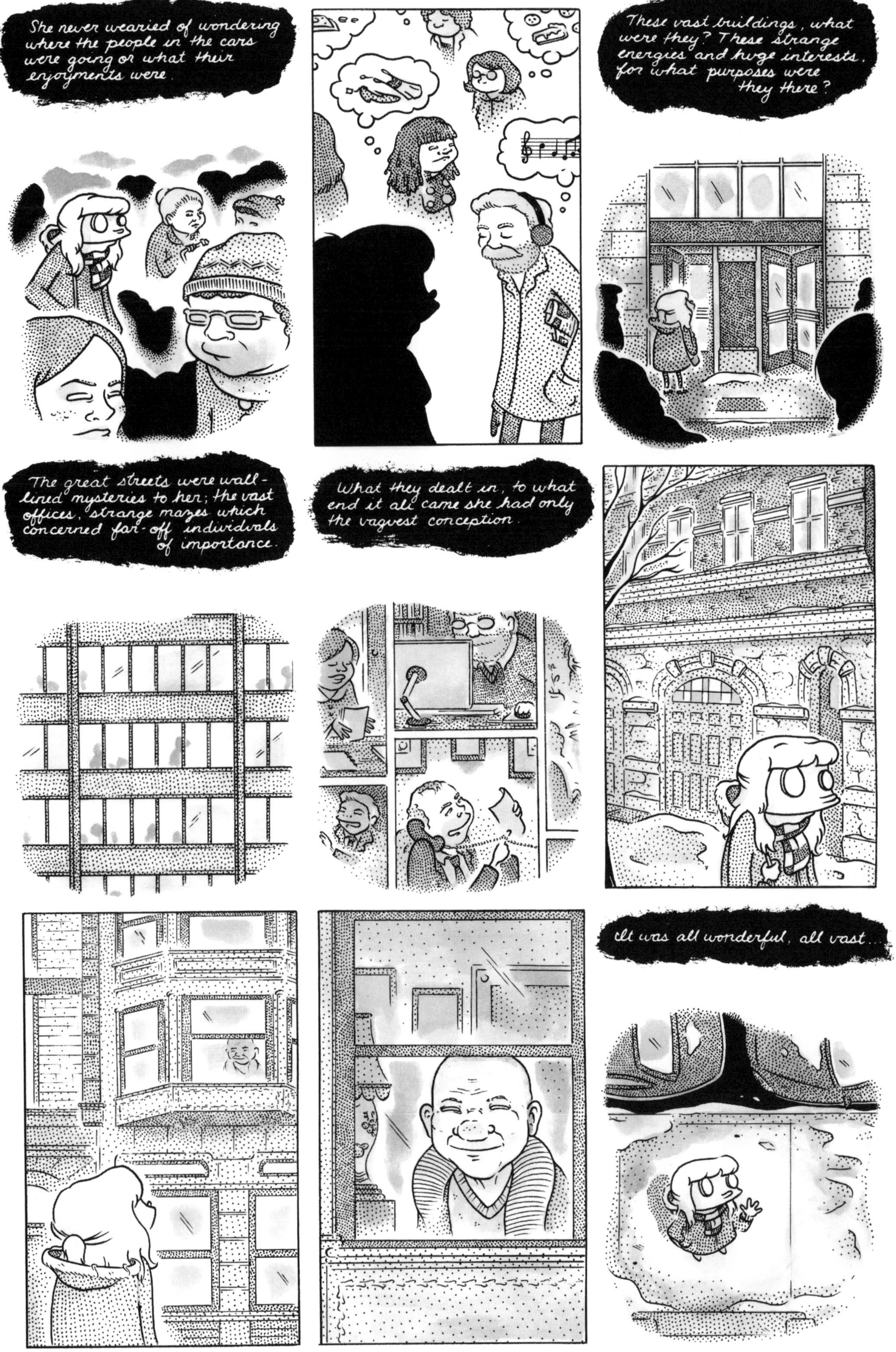
She never wearied of wondering where the people in the cars were going or what their enjoyments were.
These vast buildings, what were they? These strange energies and huge interests, for what purposes were they there?
The great streets were wall-lined mysteries to her; the vast offices, strange mazes which concerned far-off individuals of importance.
What they dealt in, to what end it all came she had only the vaguest conception.
It was all wonderful, all vast...

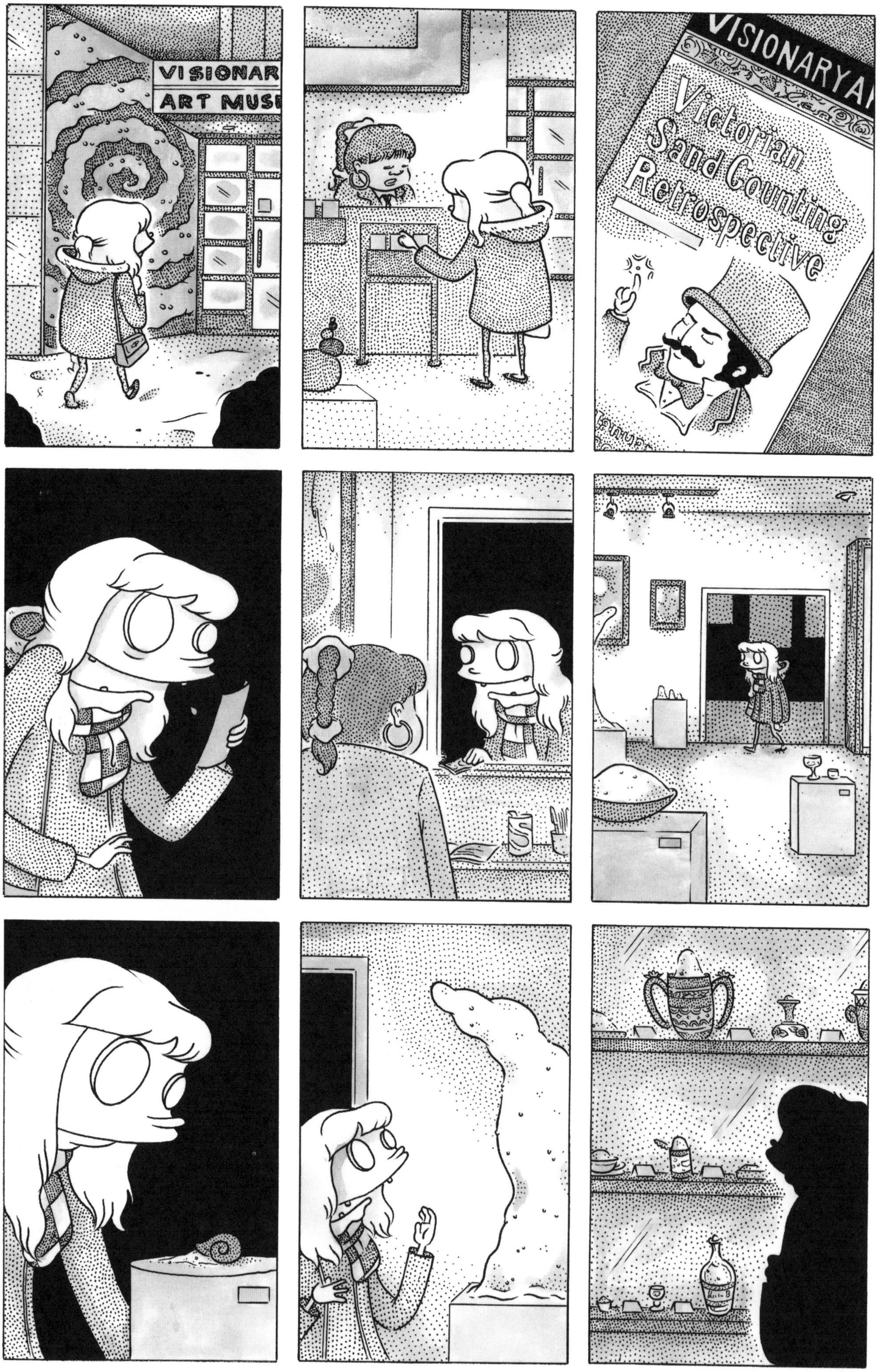
VISIONAR
ART MUS
VISIONARYA
Victorian Sand Counting Retrospective

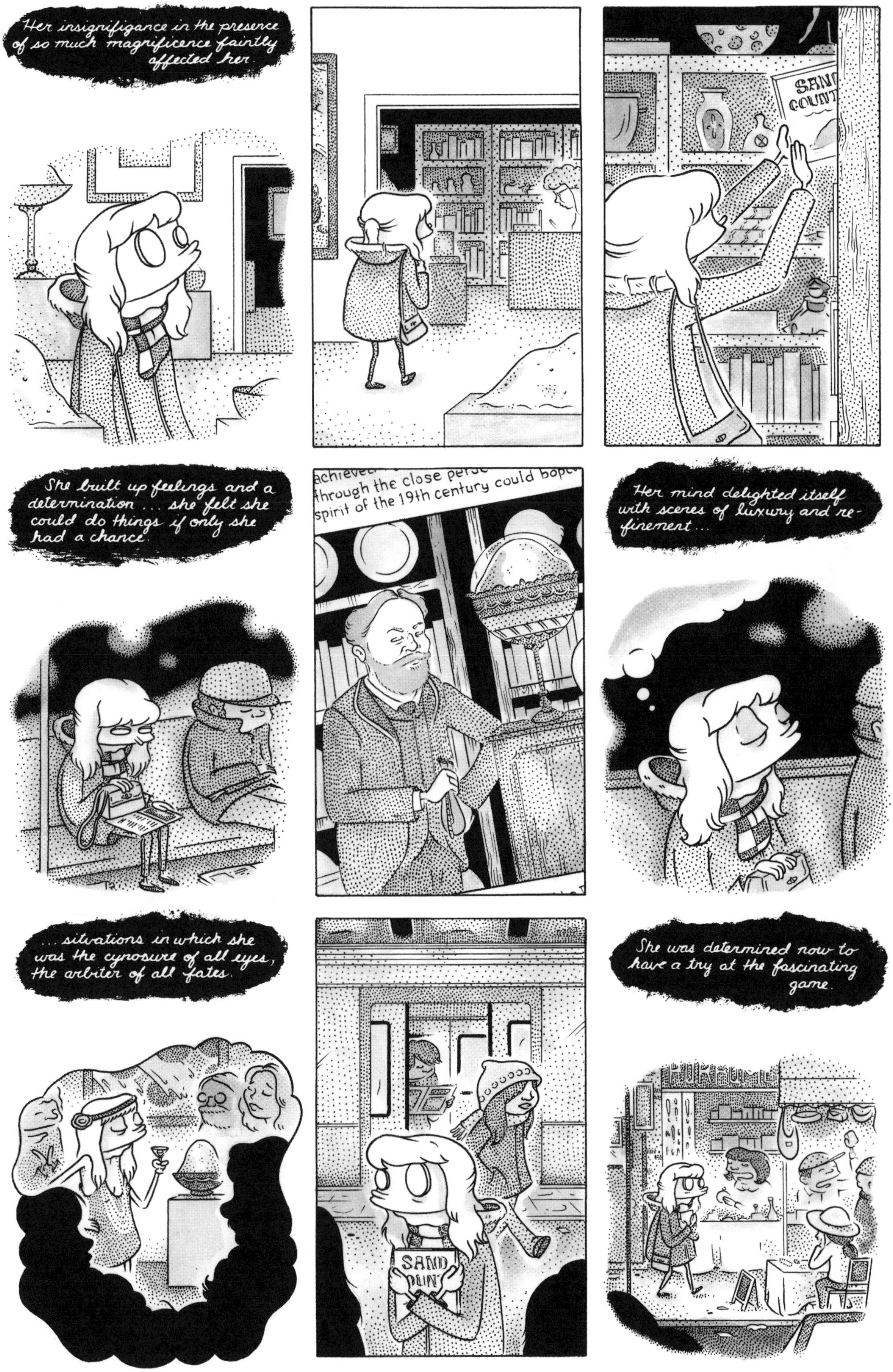
Her insignifigance in the presence of so much magnificence faintly affected her.
SAND COUNT
She built up feelings and a determination ... she felt she could do things if only she had a chance.
through the close perso
spirit of the 19th century could hope
Her mind delighted itself with scenes of luxury and refinement ...
... situations in which she was the cynosure of all eyes, the arbiter of all fates.
SAND DUN
She was determined now to have a try at the fascinating game.

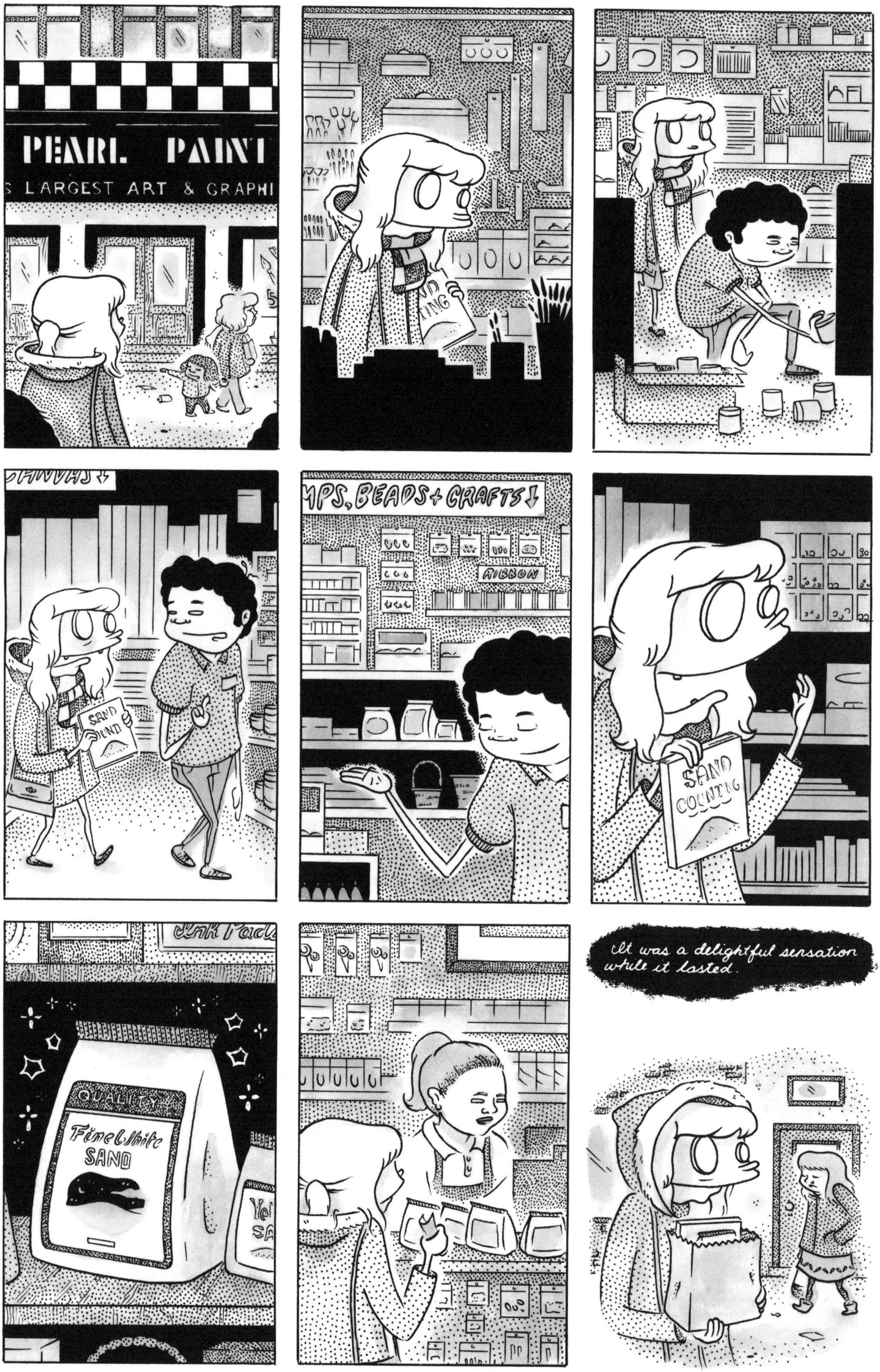
PEARL PAINT
S LARGEST ART & GRAPHI
SAND COUNTING
MPS, BEADS + CRAFTS
RIBBON
QUALITY
Fine White SAND
It was a delightful sensation while it lasted.

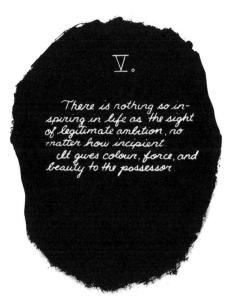

V.

There is nothing so in-spiring in life as the sight of legitimate ambition, no matter how incipient.
It gives colour, force, and beauty to the possessor.

...and here's your receipt! Thanks again!

BRIIIIIING!...

Hello?... Oh hi, thanks for getting back to me! Let's see, the sign would be about four or five feet wide by one foot high... how much would that cost?

I just have to check with my boss but I think that'll be okay... Monday? Yeah, sounds great, see you then!

click

Sigh...

It is curious to note how quickly a profession absorbs one.

Let's see... I have one pile of 126 grains, and one pile of 201...

Maybe tonight I'll try for 300! That's a nice number!

Already she was enlivened and suffused with a glow.

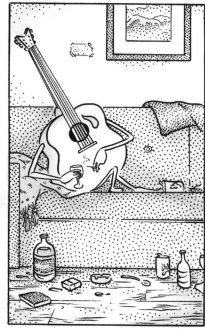

He was given to thinking, thinking, thinking...

Bad thoughts had put a shade into his eyes that did not impress others favourably.

...it told upon his temper.

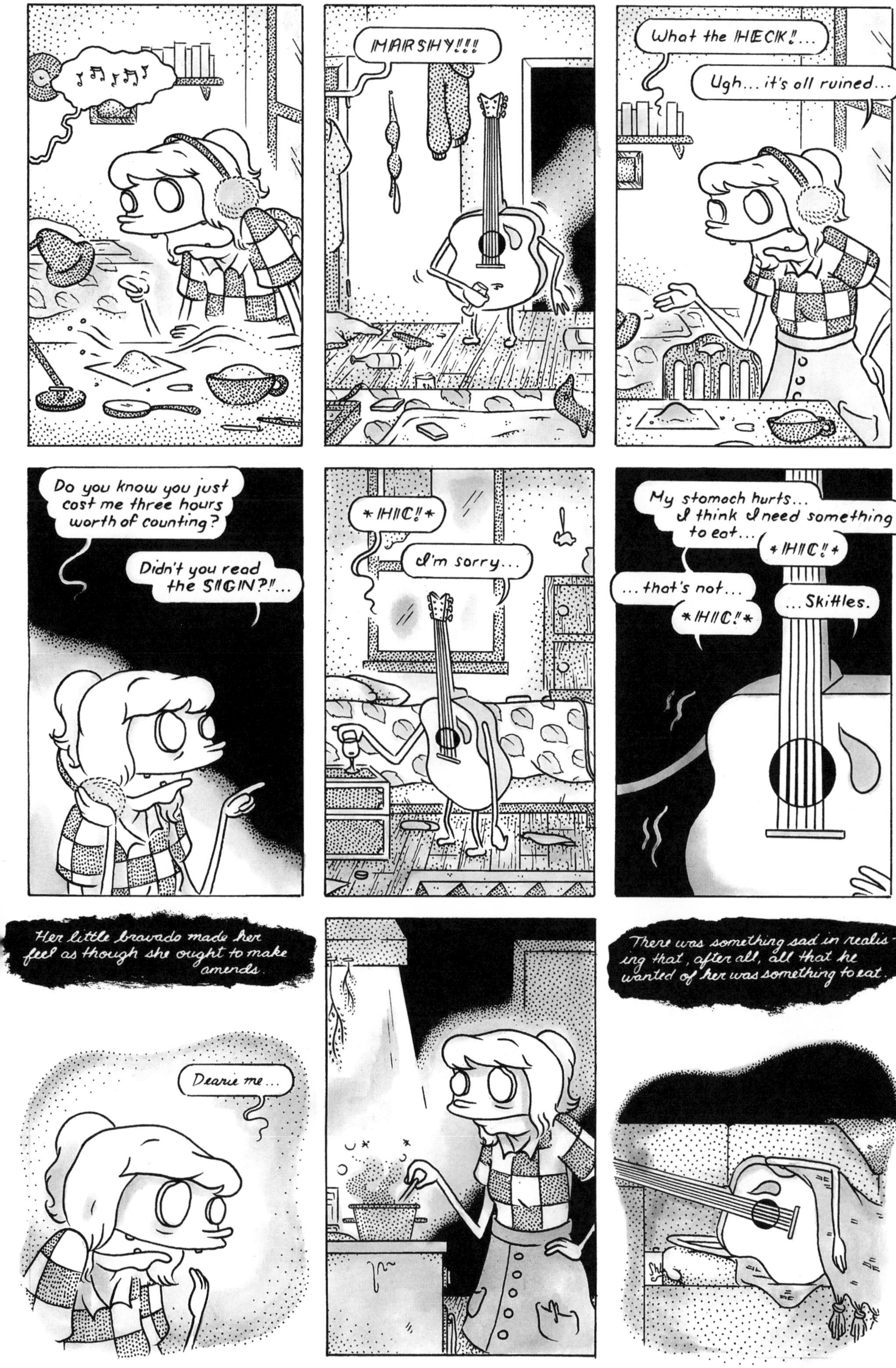
MARSHY!!!
What the HECK!...
Ugh... it's all ruined...
Do you know you just cost me three hours worth of counting?
Didn't you read the SIGN?!...
HIC!
I'm sorry...
My stomach hurts... I think I need something to eat...
HIC!
... that's not...
HIC!
... Skittles.
Her little bravado made her feel as though she ought to make amends.
Dearie me...
There was something sad in realising that, after all, all that he wanted of her was something to eat.

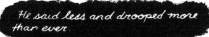

Here you go...

It's macaroni and cheese...

...shaped like bunnies...

He said less and drooped more than ever.

Thanks.

Hey Marshy... are you okay? You don't seem so good lately...

...there was something pathetic...

plop!

I know it's boring to be stuck in the house all the time now that we're in the city... but try to remember that it's not permanent...

Hey! When's the last time you played the xylophone? That always made you happy!

Life had always seemed a precious thing, but now a constant want and weakened vitality had made the charms of earth rather dull and inconspicuous.

feh.

I know! You and Ping and Himolette should start a BAND!! You can play xylophone, I'll buy Mim some drums to bounce on, and Ping... let's see, what could he play?...

"What's the use?" he said, weakly, as he stretched himself out to rest.

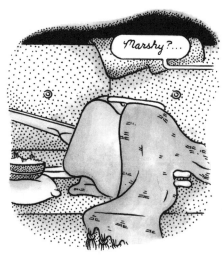

Marshy?...

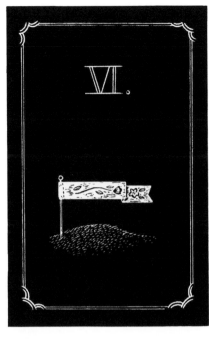

VI.

...my FAVORITE sand counter was Maxwell Meriwether CHEESLEY... ...not much was written about him 'cus he ended up in a psychiatric institution... but in my view, he was the BEST.

Ah, those Victorians!... Have you ever heard of the way they went about SWIMMIING?...

They rode a CARRIIAGE out to sea, then got out into the water when they were chest deep! ... A modest bunch!

Hey, you Larry?

That's me! You must be Gerry.

That I am.

Well, I ought to be going, Larry. Good luck with the sign!

Thanks, Boris! See you later!

Cheerio!

Well, let's see what we're working with here...

So I was thinking that the sign would be in cursive... in an arc, right over where the mannequin is, you see?

Hmpf! That ain't gonna work.

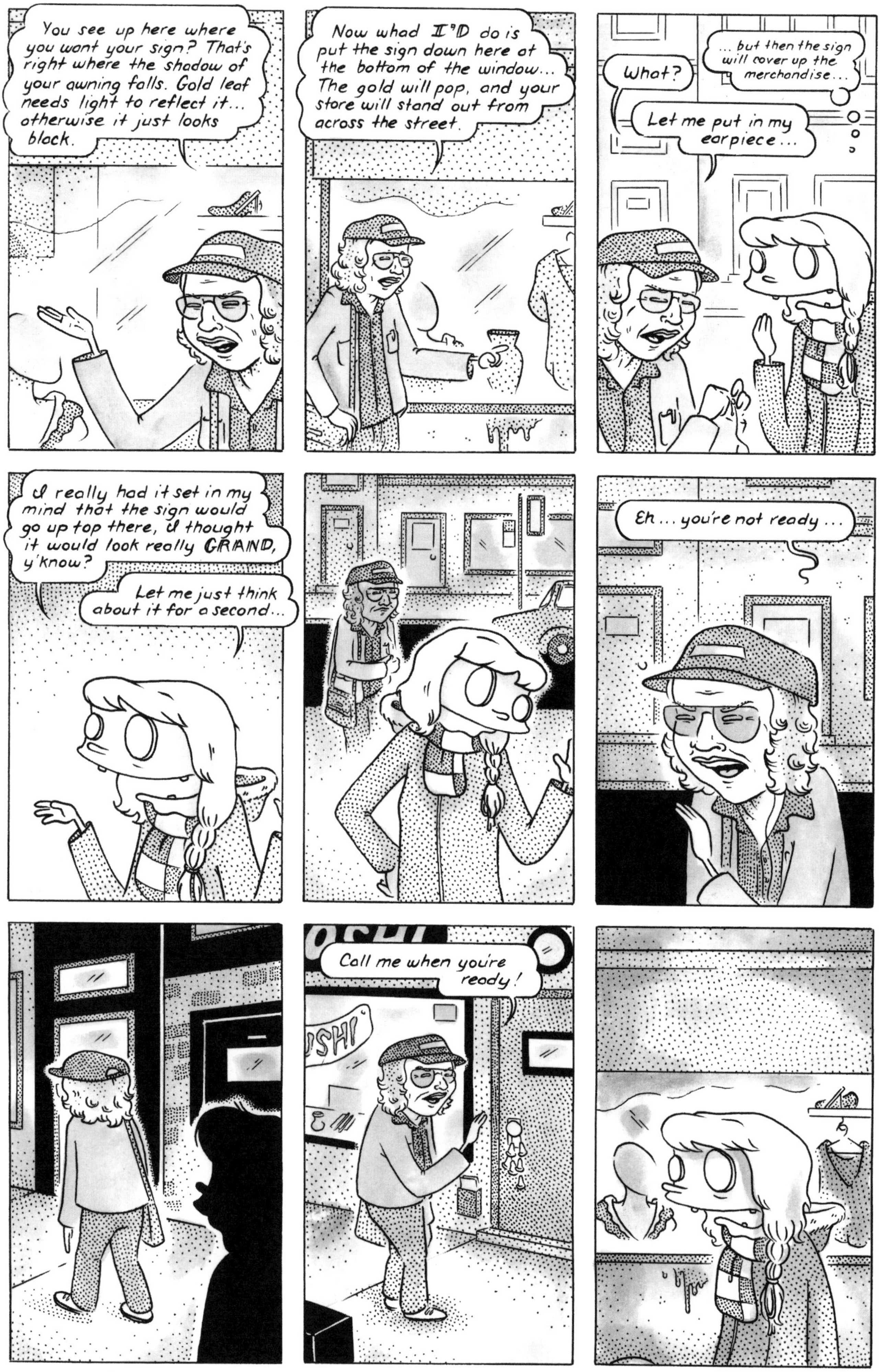
You see up here where you want your sign? That's right where the shadow of your awning falls. Gold leaf needs light to reflect it... otherwise it just looks black.
Now whad I'D do is put the sign down here at the bottom of the window... The gold will pop, and your store will stand out from across the street.
What?
... but then the sign will cover up the merchandise...
Let me put in my earpiece...
I really had it set in my mind that the sign would go up top there, I thought it would look really GRAND, y'know?
Let me just think about it for a second...
Eh... you're not ready...
SHI
Call me when you're ready!

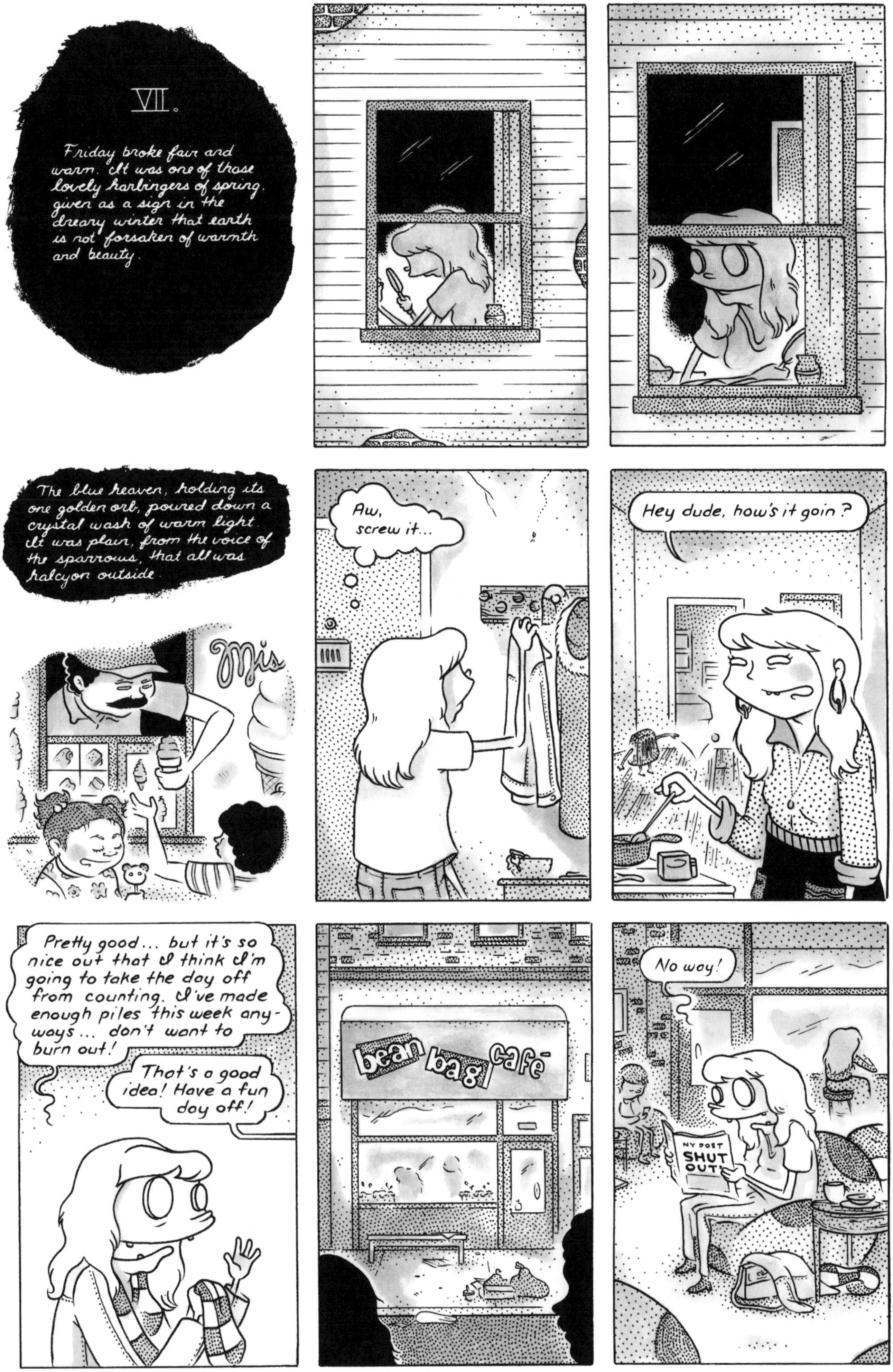
VII.
Friday broke fair and warm. It was one of those lovely harbingers of spring, given as a sign in the dreary winter that earth is not forsaken of warmth and beauty.
The blue heaven, holding its one golden orb, poured down a crystal wash of warm light. It was plain, from the voice of the sparrows, that all was halcyon outside.
Aw, screw it...
Hey dude, how's it goin?
Pretty good... but it's so nice out that I think I'm going to take the day off from counting. I've made enough piles this week anyways... don't want to burn out!
That's a good idea! Have a fun day off!
bean bag café
No way!
NY POST
SHUT OUT

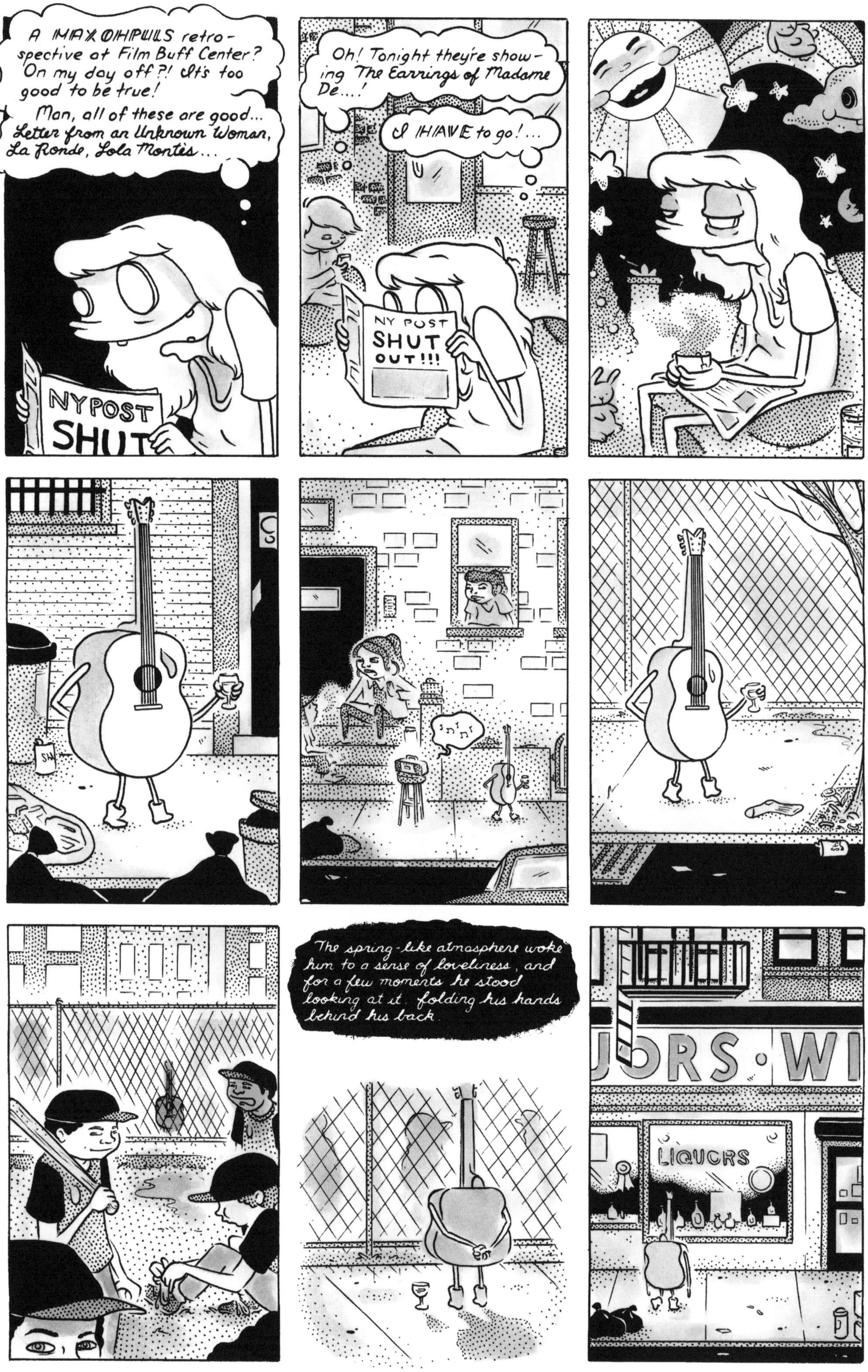
A MAX OHPULS retrospective at Film Buff Center? On my day off?! It's too good to be true!
Man, all of these are good... Letter from an Unknown Woman, La Ronde, Lola Montès...
NY POST SHUT
Oh! Tonight they're showing The Earrings of Madame De...!
I HAVE to go!...
NY POST SHUT OUT!!!
LIQUORS
The spring-like atmosphere woke him to a sense of loveliness, and for a few moments he stood looking at it, folding his hands behind his back.
ORS · WI
LIQUORS

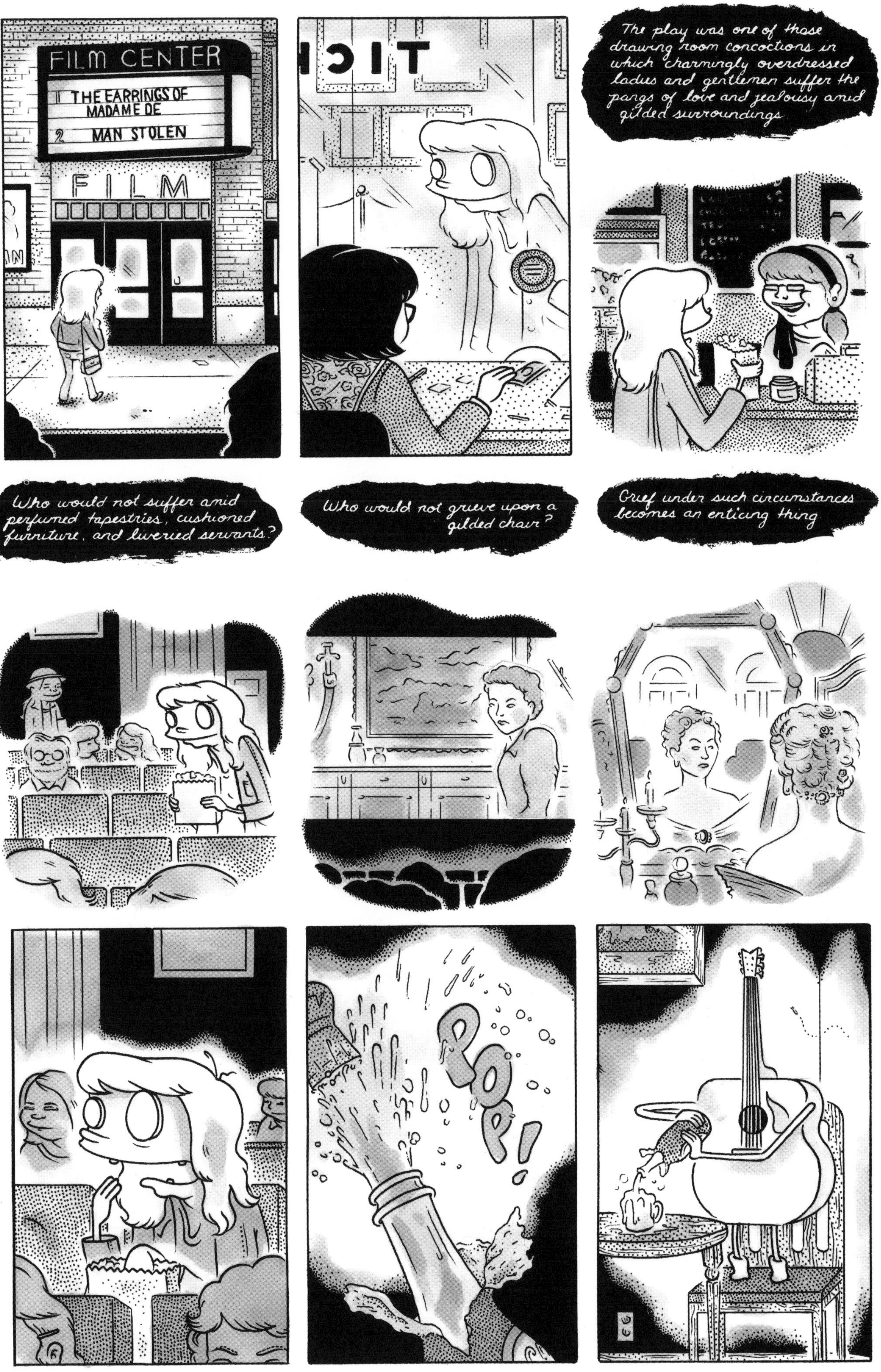
FILM CENTER
1 THE EARRINGS OF MADAME DE
2 MAN STOLEN
FILM
The play was one of those drawing room concoctions in which charmingly overdressed ladies and gentlemen suffer the pangs of love and jealousy amid gilded surroundings
Who would not suffer amid perfumed tapestries, cushioned furniture, and liveried servants?
Who would not grieve upon a gilded chair?
Grief under such circumstances becomes an enticing thing
POP!

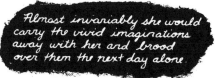

Some scenes made her long to be a part of them – to give expression to the feelings which she, in place of the character represented, would feel.

Almost invariably she would carry the vivid imaginations away with her and brood over them the next day alone.

She lived in these things as in the realities which made up her daily life.

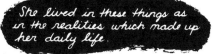

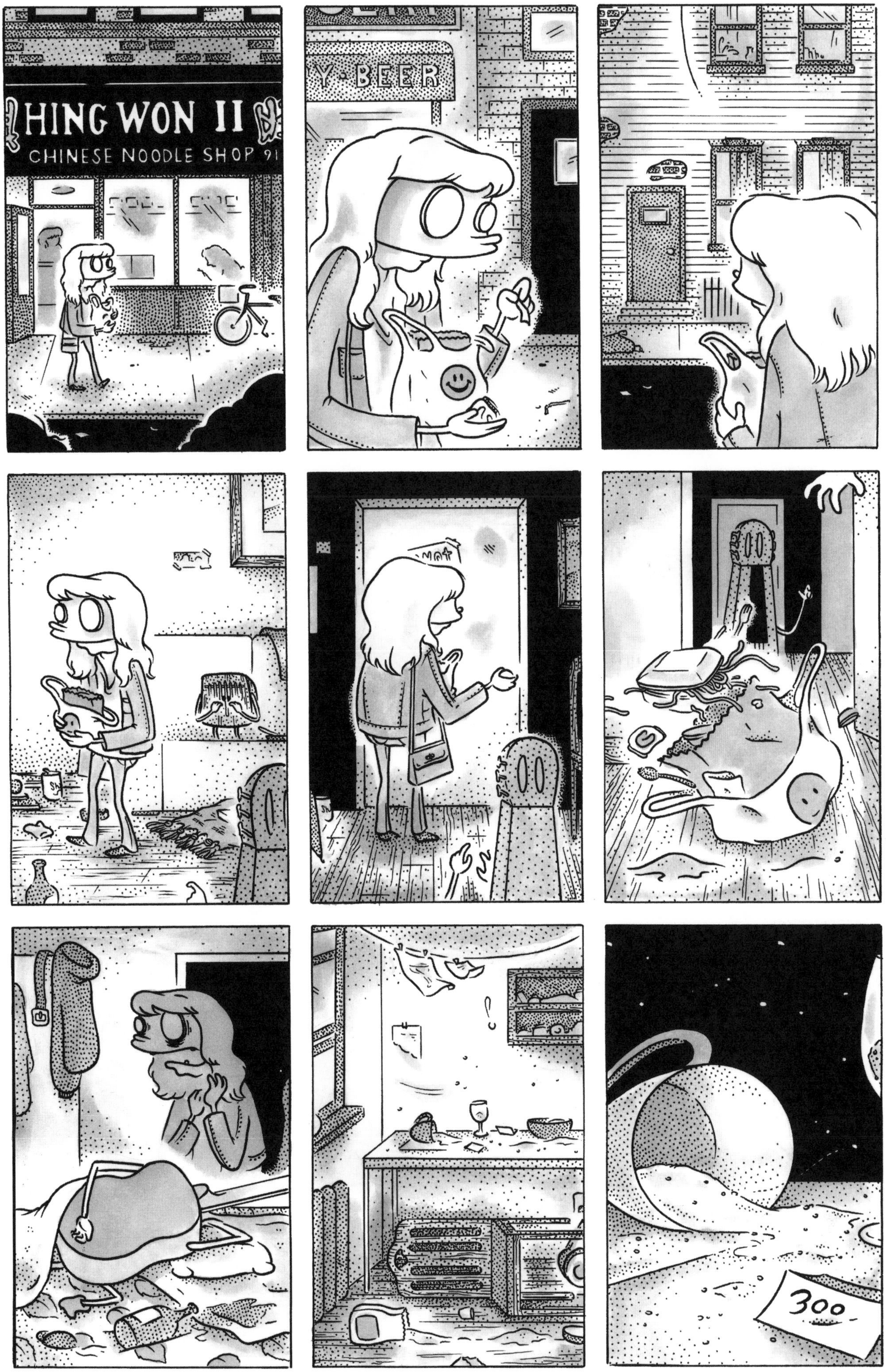
HING WON II
CHINESE NOODLE SHOP 91
Y·BEER
300-

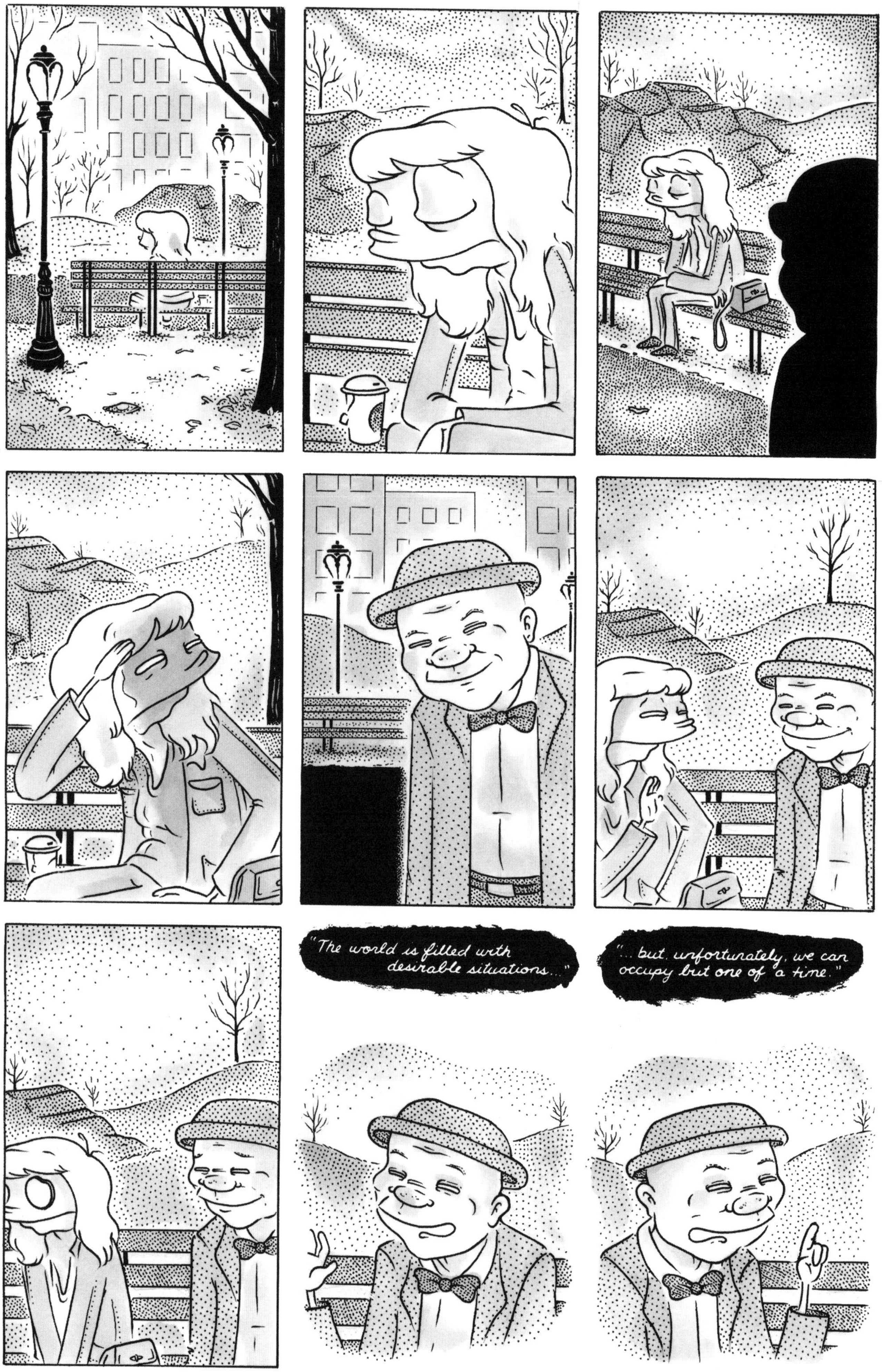
"The world is filled with desirable situations..."
"...but, unfortunately, we can occupy but one at a time."

"It doesn't do us any good to wring our hands over the far-off things."

"The world is always struggling to express itself..."

"Most people are not capable of voicing their feelings."

"They depend on others."

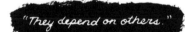

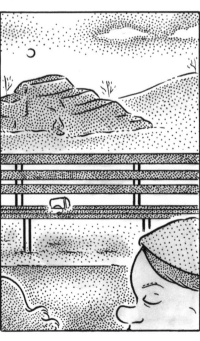

Sitting alone...

...she was now an illustration of the devious ways by which one who feels, rather than reasons...

...may be led in the pursuit of beauty.

Though often disillusioned...

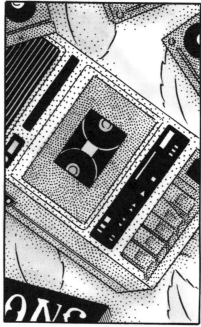

...she was still waiting for that halycon day...

...when she would be led forth...

...among dreams become real.

Thus in life...

...there is ever the intellectual and the emotional nature...

...the mind that reasons, and the mind that feels

Of one come the men of action — generals and statesmen...

...of the other, poets and dreamers — artists all.

As harps in the wind, the latter respond to every breath of fancy, voicing in their moods all the ebb and flow of the ideal.

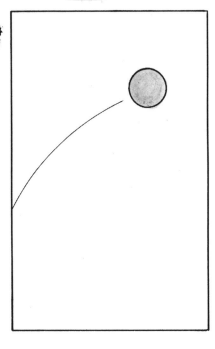

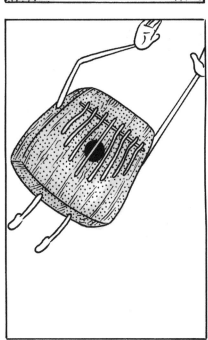

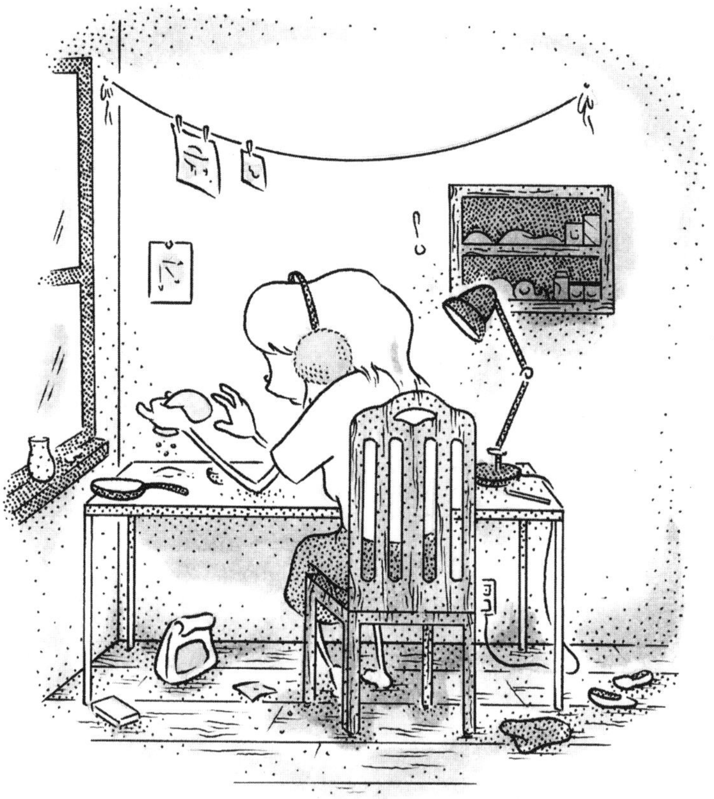

In your rocking-chair,
by your window dreaming, shall
you long, alone. In your rocking-
chair, by your window, shall
you dream such happiness
as you may never feel.
— Theodore Dreiser

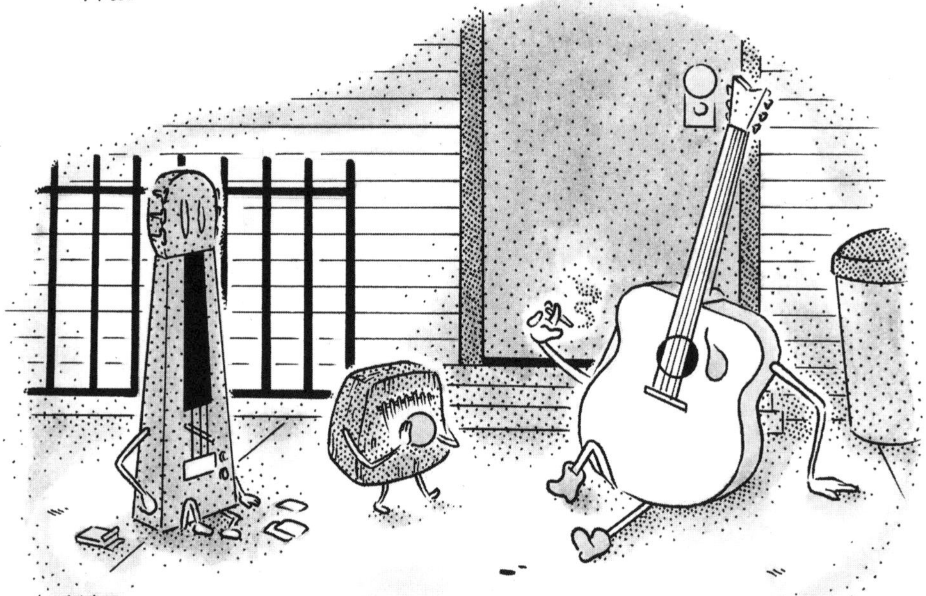
LAMS

6

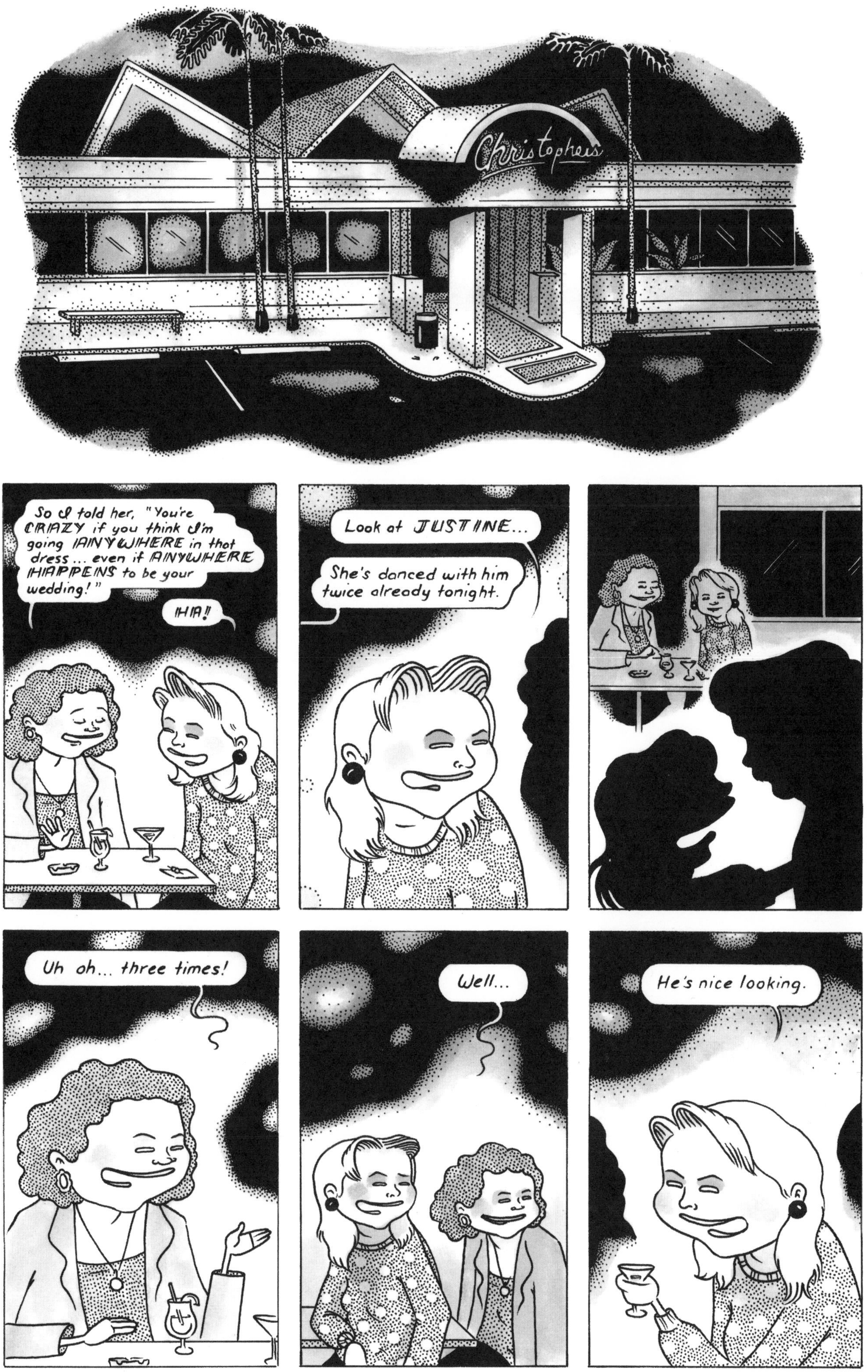
Christopher's
So I told her, "You're CRAZY if you think I'm going ANYWHERE in that dress ... even if ANYWHERE HAPPENS to be your wedding!"
HA!!
Look at JUSTINE...
She's danced with him twice already tonight.
Uh oh... three times!
Well...
He's nice looking.

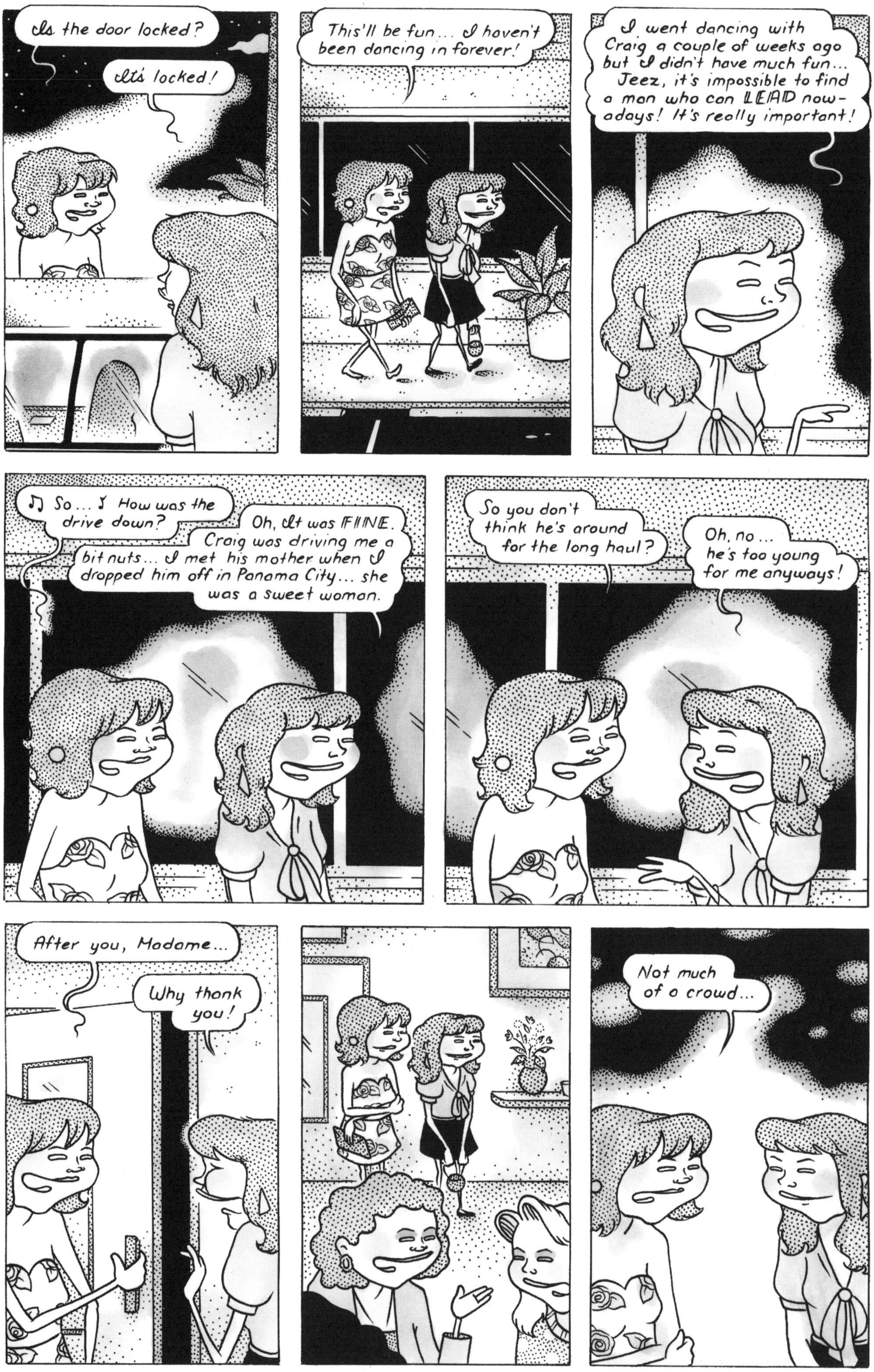
Is the door locked?
It's locked!
This'll be fun... I haven't been dancing in forever!
I went dancing with Craig a couple of weeks ago but I didn't have much fun... Jeez, it's impossible to find a man who can LEAD nowadays! It's really important!
♫ So... ♪ How was the drive down?
Oh, It was FINE. Craig was driving me a bit nuts... I met his mother when I dropped him off in Panama City... she was a sweet woman.
So you don't think he's around for the long haul?
Oh, no... he's too young for me anyways!
After you, Madame...
Why thank you!
Not much of a crowd...

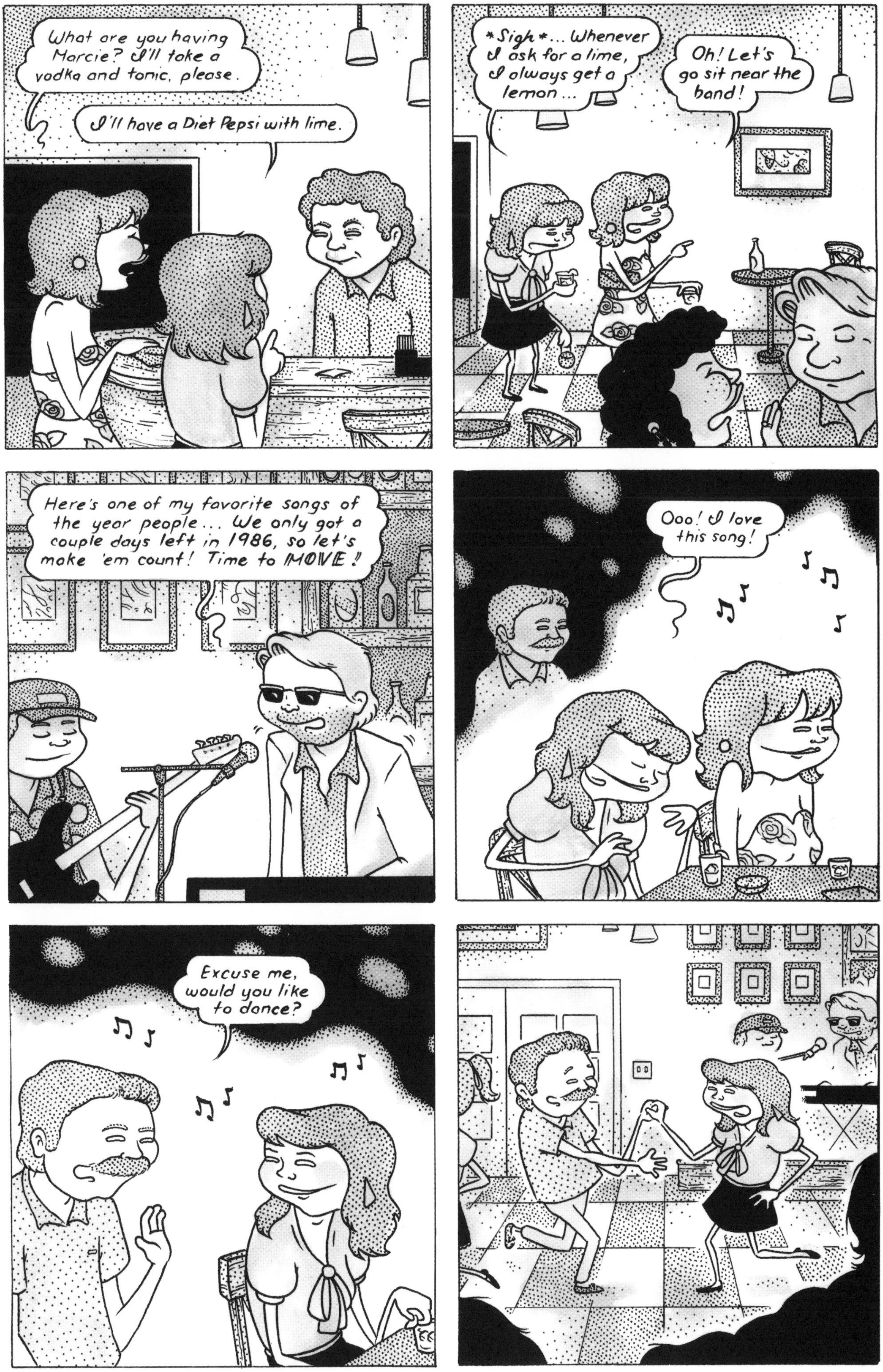
What are you having Marcie? I'll take a vodka and tonic, please.
I'll have a Diet Pepsi with lime.
Sigh... Whenever I ask for a lime, I always get a lemon...
Oh! Let's go sit near the band!
Here's one of my favorite songs of the year people... We only got a couple days left in 1986, so let's make 'em count! Time to MOVE!
Ooo! I love this song!
Excuse me, would you like to dance?

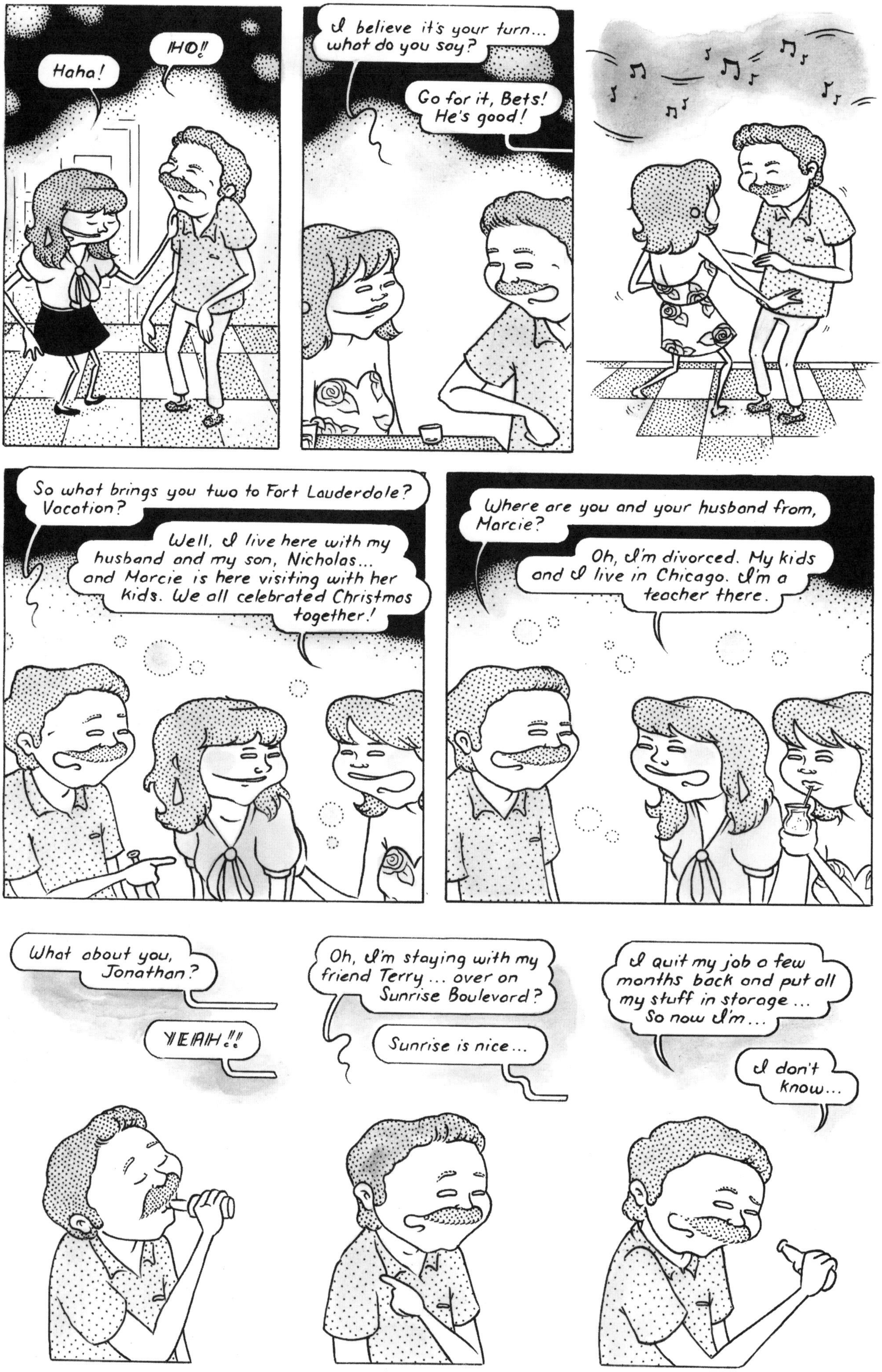
Haha!
HO!!
I believe it's your turn... what do you say?
Go for it, Bets! He's good!
So what brings you two to Fort Lauderdale? Vacation?
Well, I live here with my husband and my son, Nicholas... and Marcie is here visiting with her kids. We all celebrated Christmas together!
Where are you and your husband from, Marcie?
Oh, I'm divorced. My kids and I live in Chicago. I'm a teacher there.
What about you, Jonathan?
YEAH!!
Oh, I'm staying with my friend Terry ... over on Sunrise Boulevard?
Sunrise is nice...
I quit my job a few months back and put all my stuff in storage ... So now I'm...
I don't know...

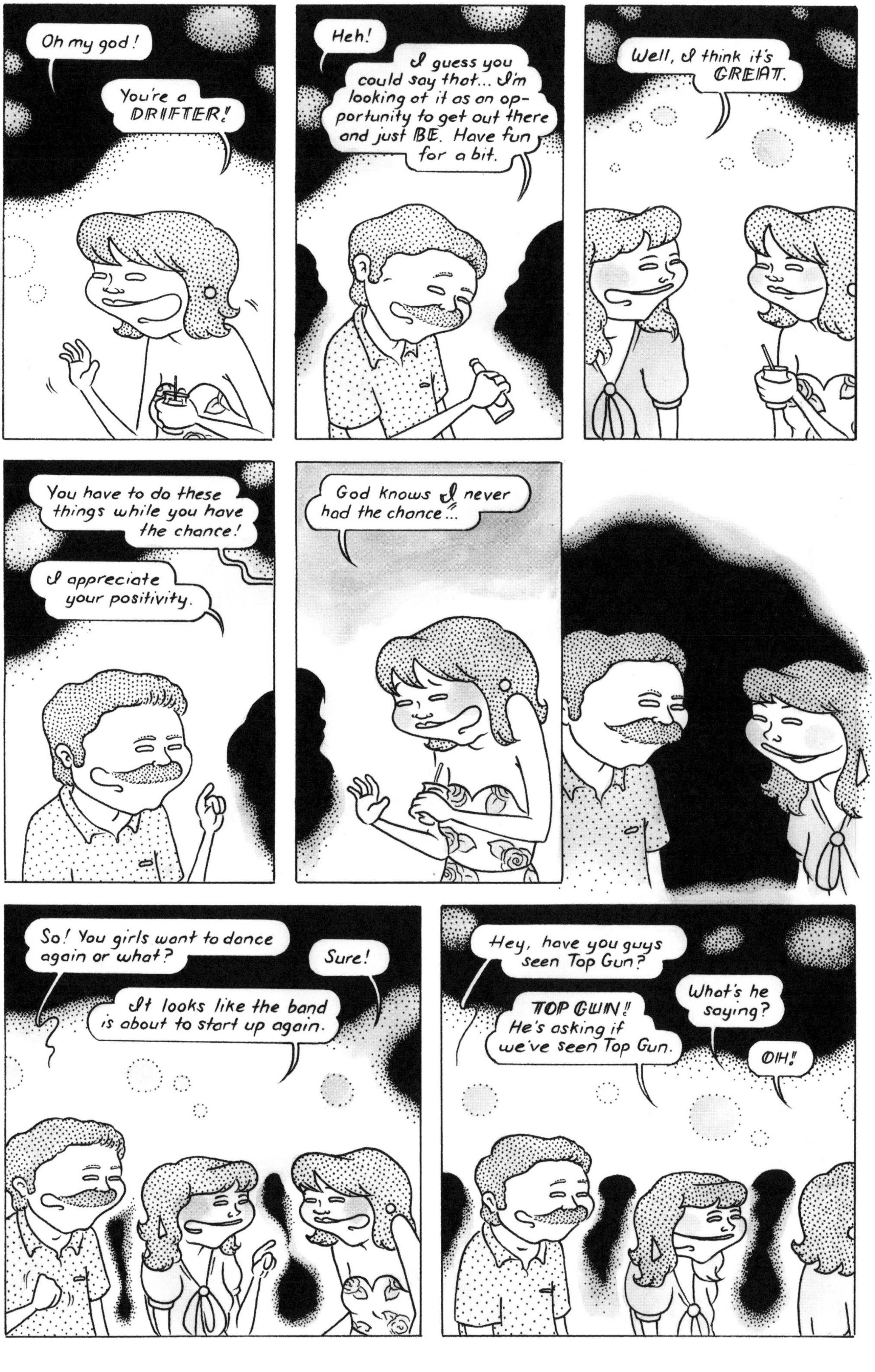
Oh my god!
You're a DRIFTER!
Heh!
I guess you could say that... I'm looking at it as an opportunity to get out there and just BE. Have fun for a bit.
Well, I think it's GREAT.
You have to do these things while you have the chance!
I appreciate your positivity.
God knows I never had the chance...
So! You girls want to dance again or what?
Sure!
It looks like the band is about to start up again.
Hey, have you guys seen Top Gun?
TOP GUN!! He's asking if we've seen Top Gun.
What's he saying?
OH!!

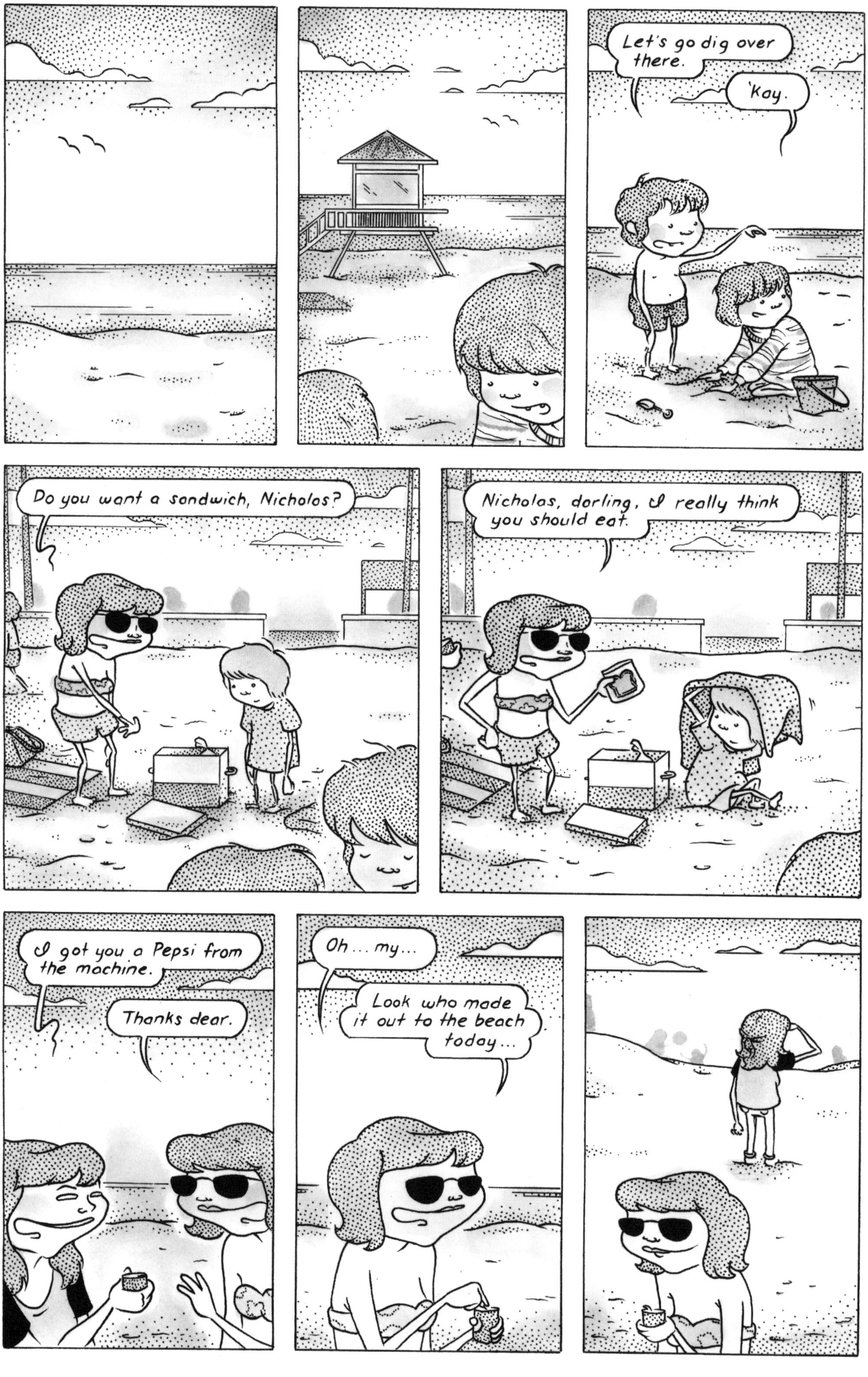

Let's go dig over there.
'Kay.
Do you want a sandwich, Nicholas?
Nicholas, darling, I really think you should eat.
I got you a Pepsi from the machine.
Thanks dear.
Oh ... my...
Look who made it out to the beach today...

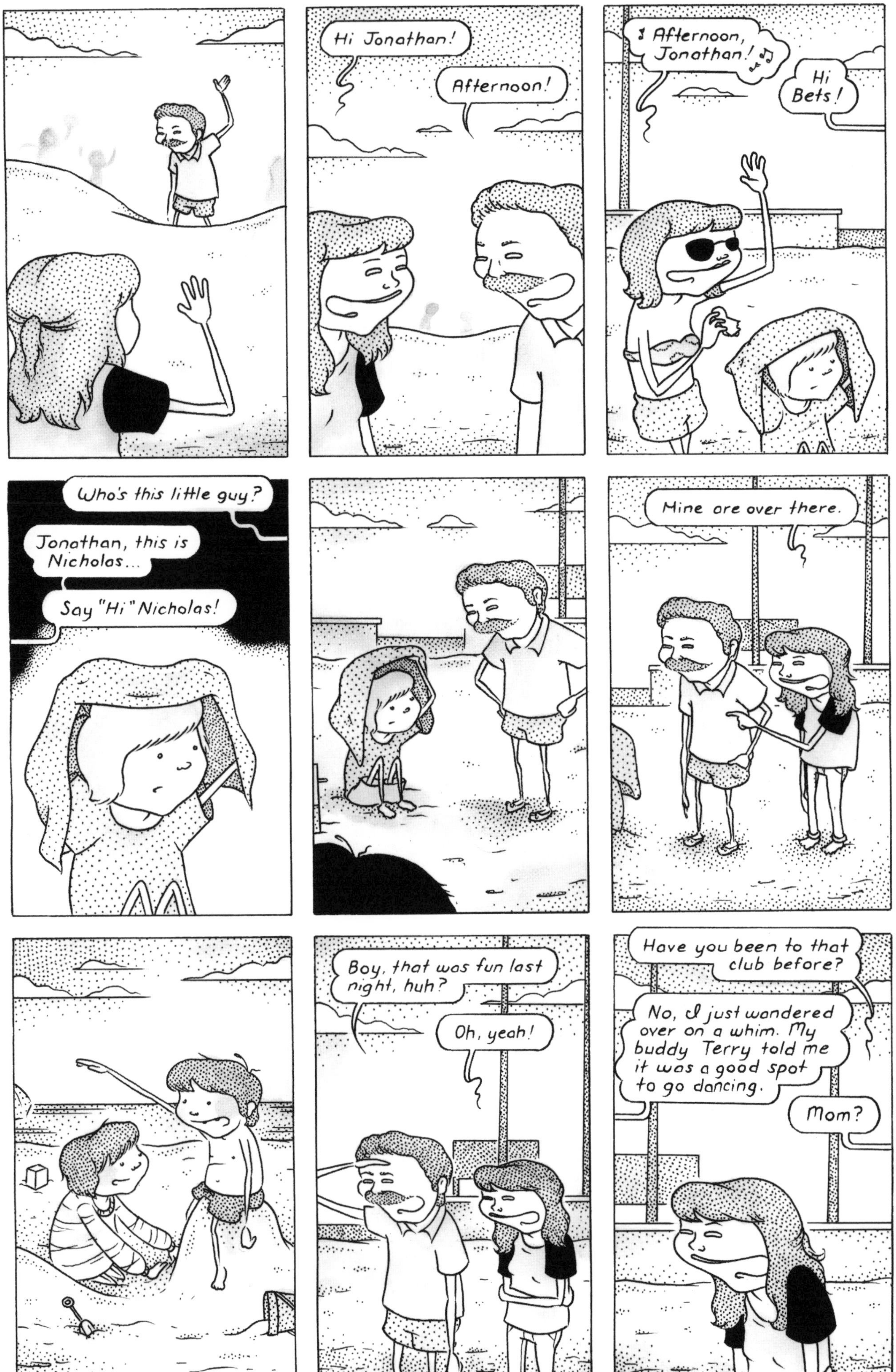

Hi Jonathan!
Afternoon!
Afternoon, Jonathan!
Hi Bets!
Who's this little guy?
Jonathan, this is Nicholas...
Say "Hi" Nicholas!
Mine are over there.
Boy, that was fun last night, huh?
Oh, yeah!
Have you been to that club before?
No, I just wandered over on a whim. My buddy Terry told me it was a good spot to go dancing.
Mom?

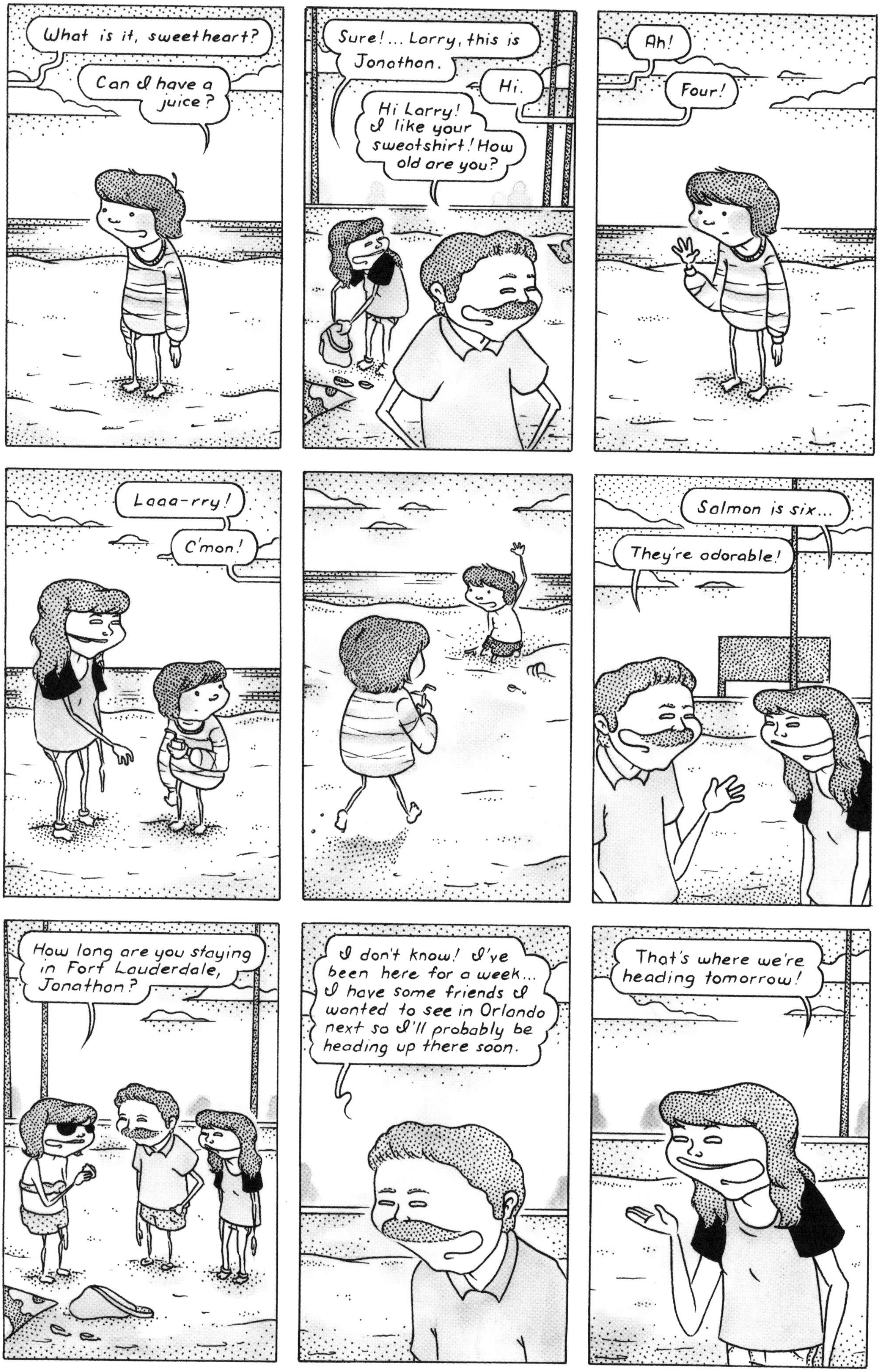
What is it, sweetheart?
Can I have a juice?
Sure! ... Larry, this is Jonathan.
Hi.
Hi Larry! I like your sweatshirt! How old are you?
Ah!
Four!
Laaa-rry!
C'mon!
Salmon is six...
They're adorable!
How long are you staying in Fort Lauderdale, Jonathan?
I don't know! I've been here for a week... I have some friends I wanted to see in Orlando next so I'll probably be heading up there soon.
That's where we're heading tomorrow!

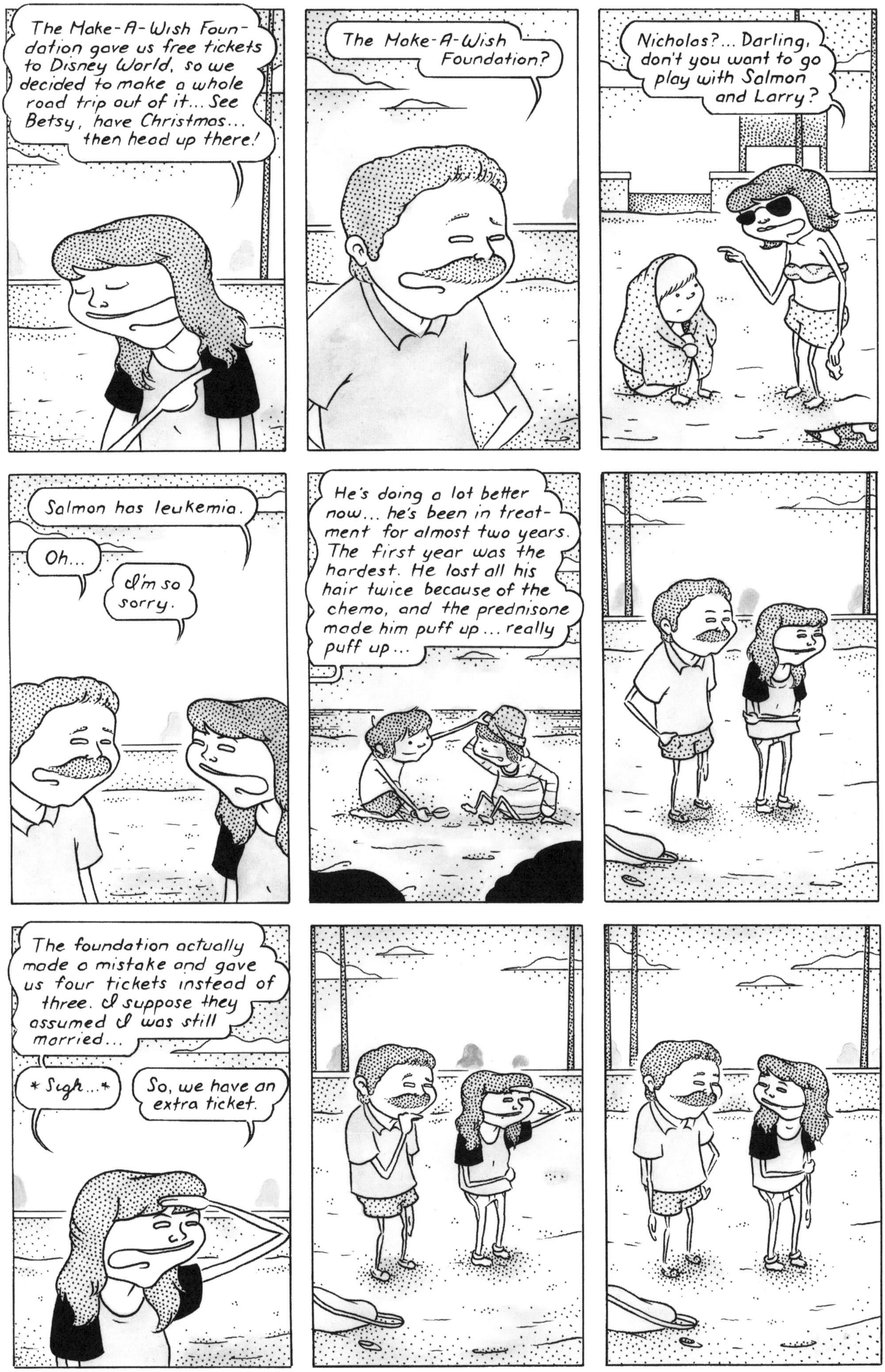
The Make-A-Wish Foundation gave us free tickets to Disney World, so we decided to make a whole road trip out of it... See Betsy, have Christmas... then head up there!
The Make-A-Wish Foundation?
Nicholas?... Darling, don't you want to go play with Salmon and Larry?
Salmon has leukemia.
Oh...
I'm so sorry.
He's doing a lot better now... he's been in treatment for almost two years. The first year was the hardest. He lost all his hair twice because of the chemo, and the prednisone made him puff up... really puff up...
The foundation actually made a mistake and gave us four tickets instead of three. I suppose they assumed I was still married...
Sigh...
So, we have an extra ticket.

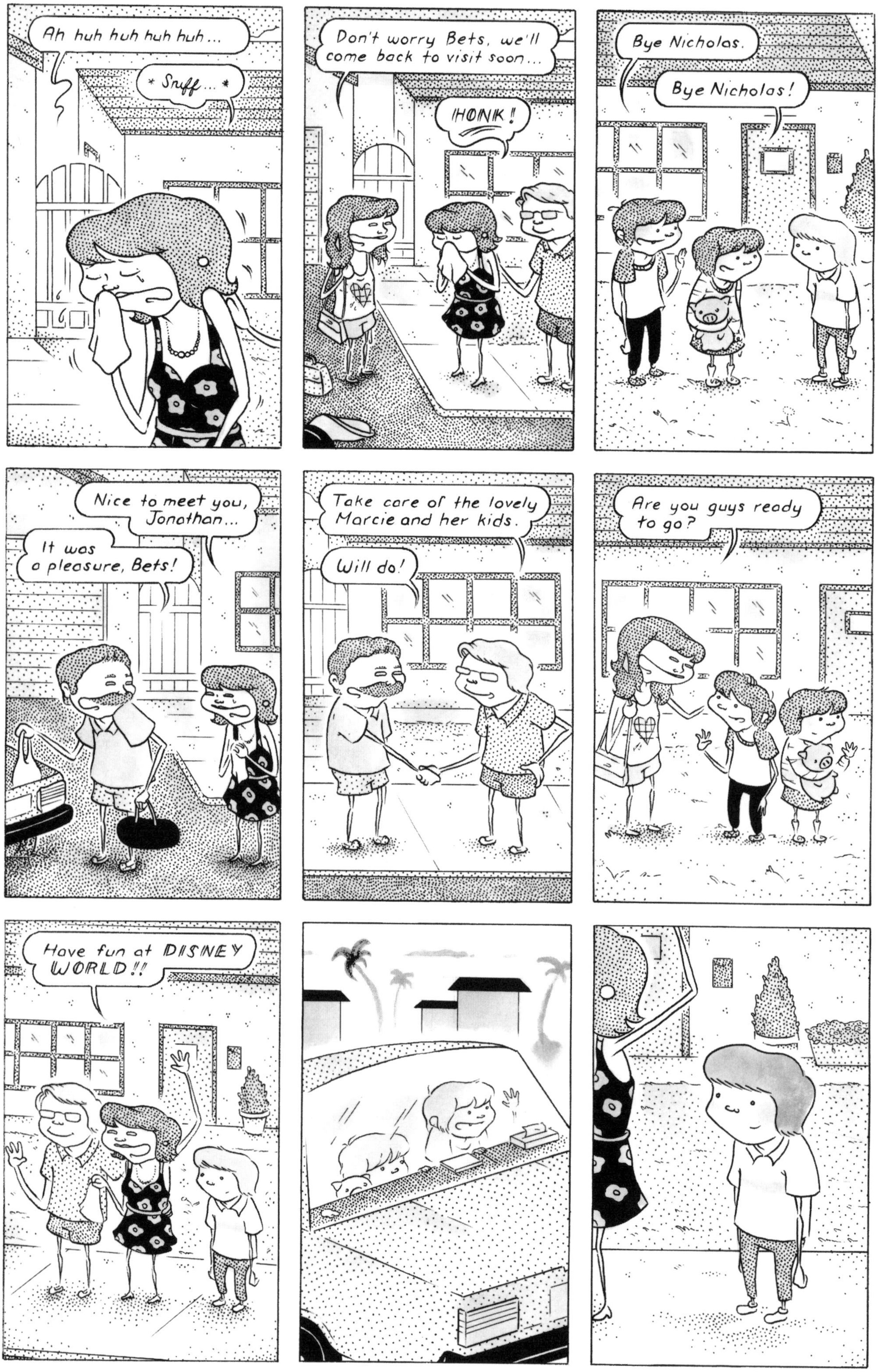
Ah huh huh huh huh...
* Snff... *
Don't worry Bets, we'll come back to visit soon...
HONK!
Bye Nicholas.
Bye Nicholas!
Nice to meet you, Jonathan...
It was a pleasure, Bets!
Take care of the lovely Marcie and her kids.
Will do!
Are you guys ready to go?
Have fun at DISNEY WORLD!!

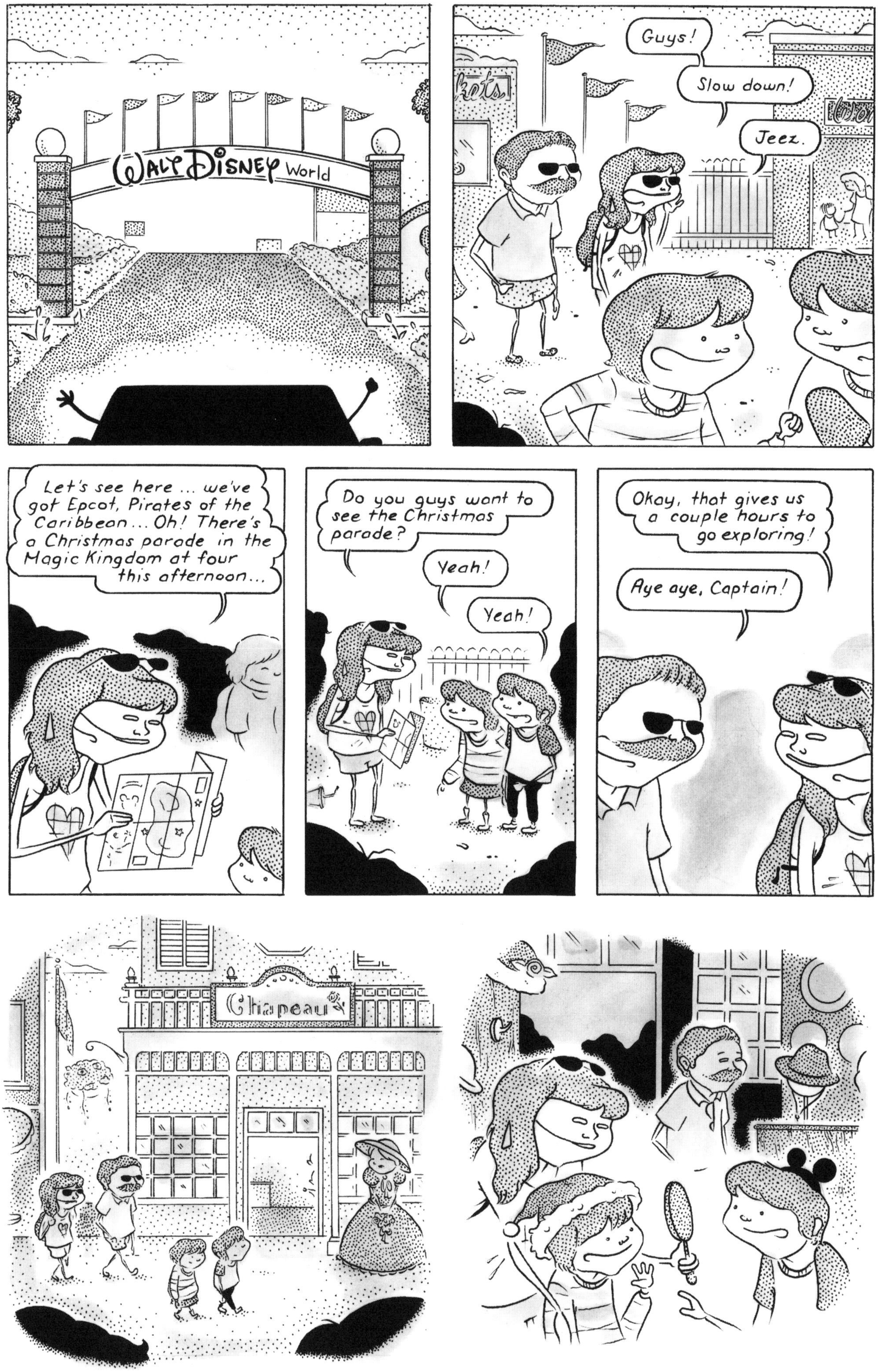
WALT DISNEY World
Guys!
Slow down!
Jeez.
Let's see here ... we've got Epcot, Pirates of the Caribbean ... Oh! There's a Christmas parade in the Magic Kingdom at four this afternoon ...
Do you guys want to see the Christmas parade?
Yeah!
Yeah!
Okay, that gives us a couple hours to go exploring!
Aye aye, Captain!
Chapeau

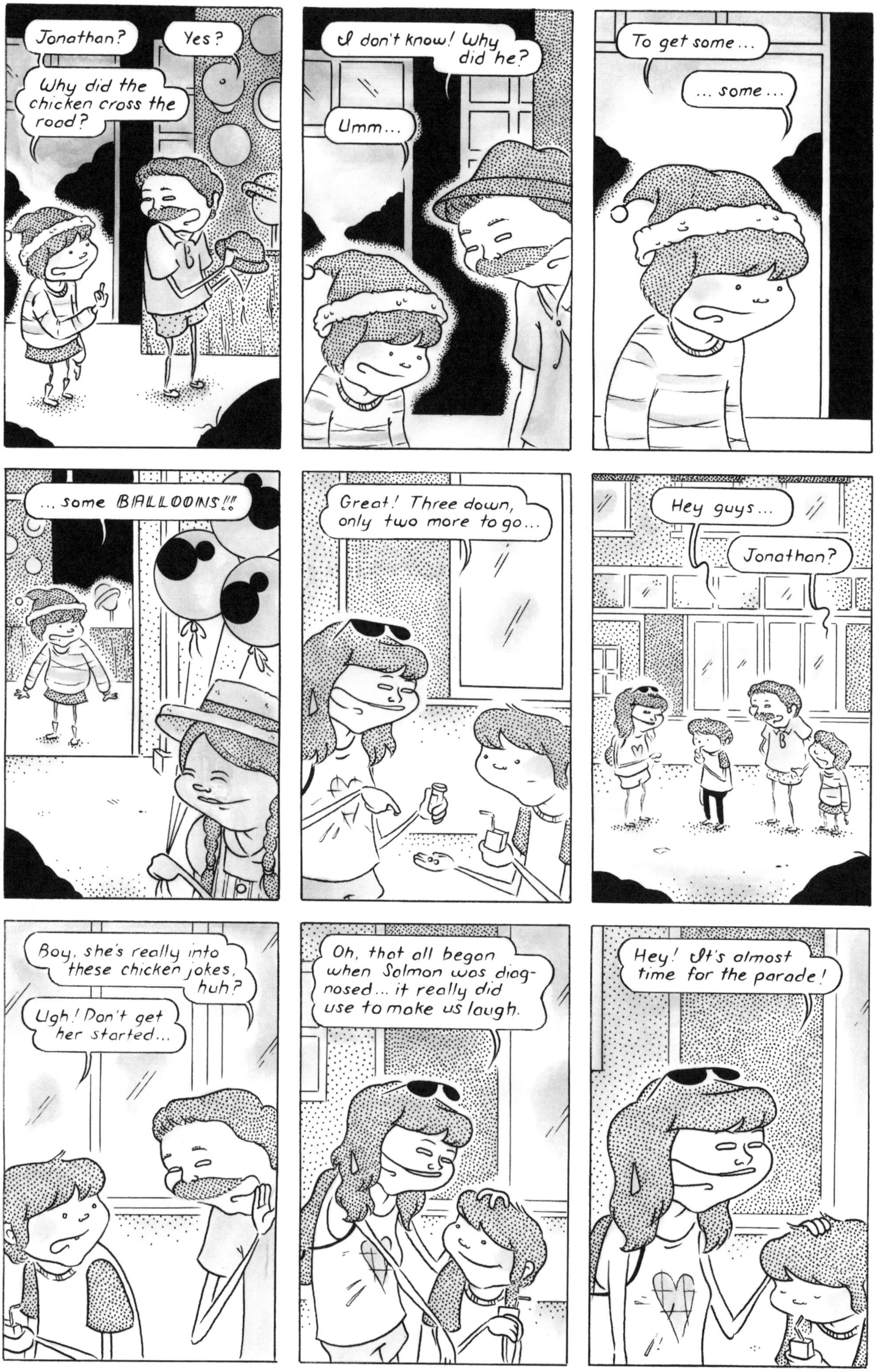
Jonathan?
Yes?
Why did the chicken cross the road?
I don't know! Why did he?
Umm...
To get some...
... some...
... some BALLOONS!!!
Great! Three down, only two more to go...
Hey guys...
Jonathan?
Boy, she's really into these chicken jokes, huh?
Ugh! Don't get her started...
Oh, that all began when Salmon was diagnosed... it really did use to make us laugh.
Hey! It's almost time for the parade!

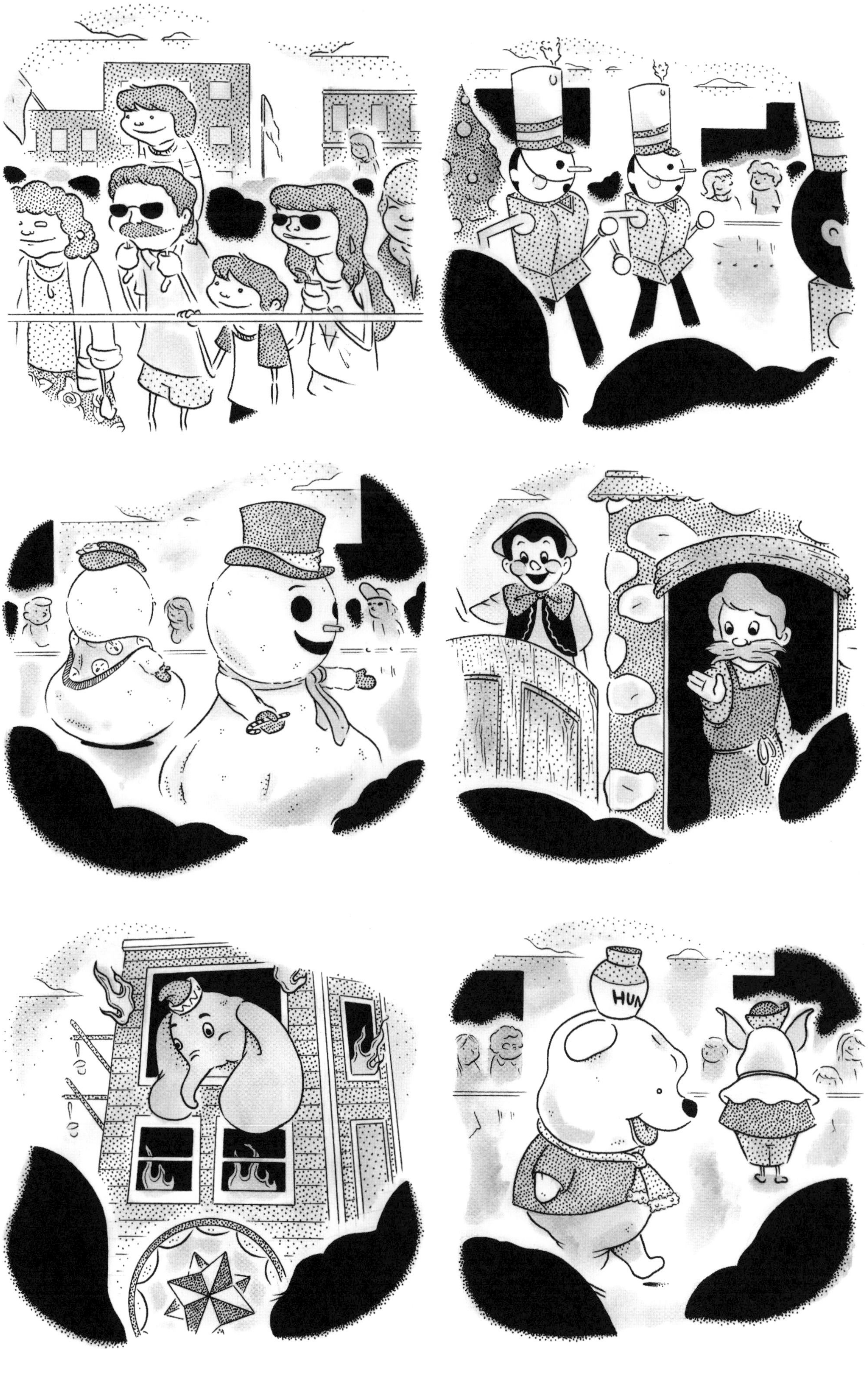
HUN

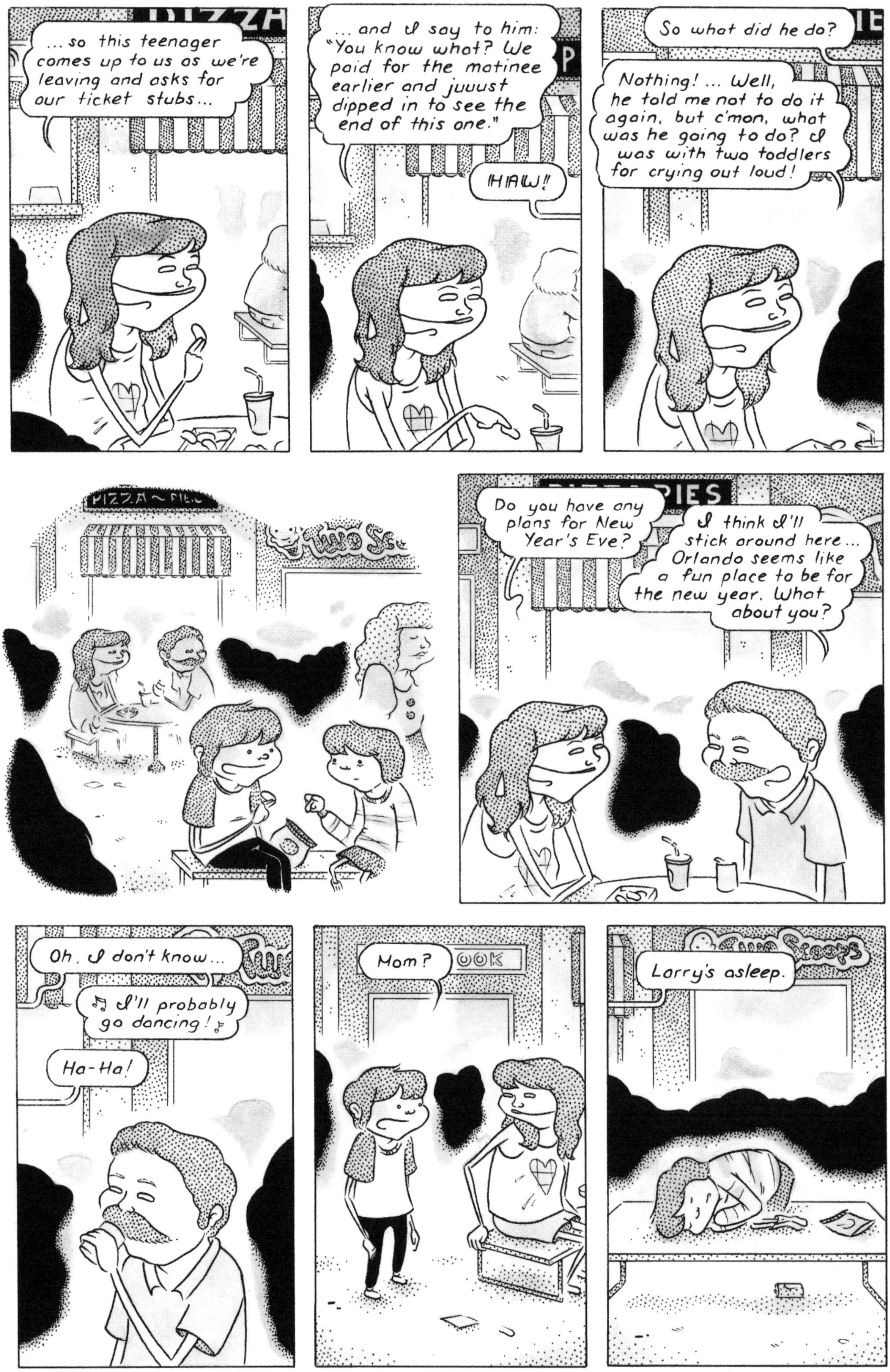
... so this teenager comes up to us as we're leaving and asks for our ticket stubs...
... and I say to him: "You know what? We paid for the matinee earlier and juuust dipped in to see the end of this one."
HAW!!
So what did he do?
Nothing! ... Well, he told me not to do it again, but c'mon, what was he going to do? I was with two toddlers for crying out loud!
PIZZA
Do you have any plans for New Year's Eve?
I think I'll stick around here... Orlando seems like a fun place to be for the new year. What about you?
Oh, I don't know...
♫ I'll probably go dancing! ♪
Ha-Ha!
Mom?
Larry's asleep.

Salmon, time for PJ's!

Okay...

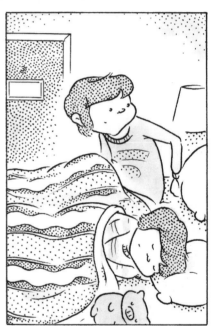

Goodnight, sweetie.

Goodnight champ!

Goodnight.

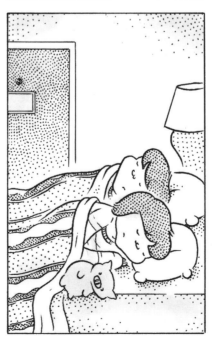

Click.

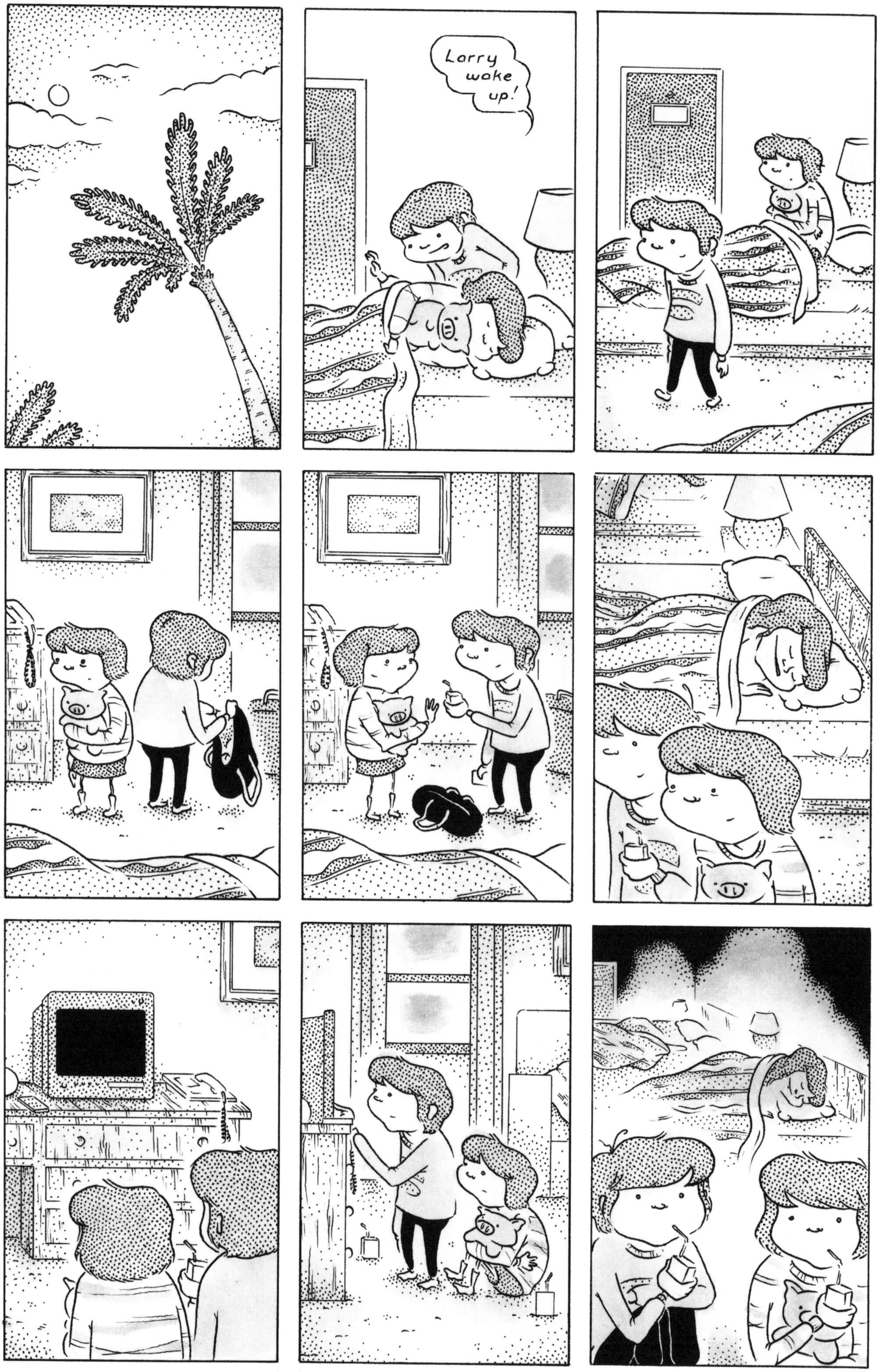
Larry wake up!

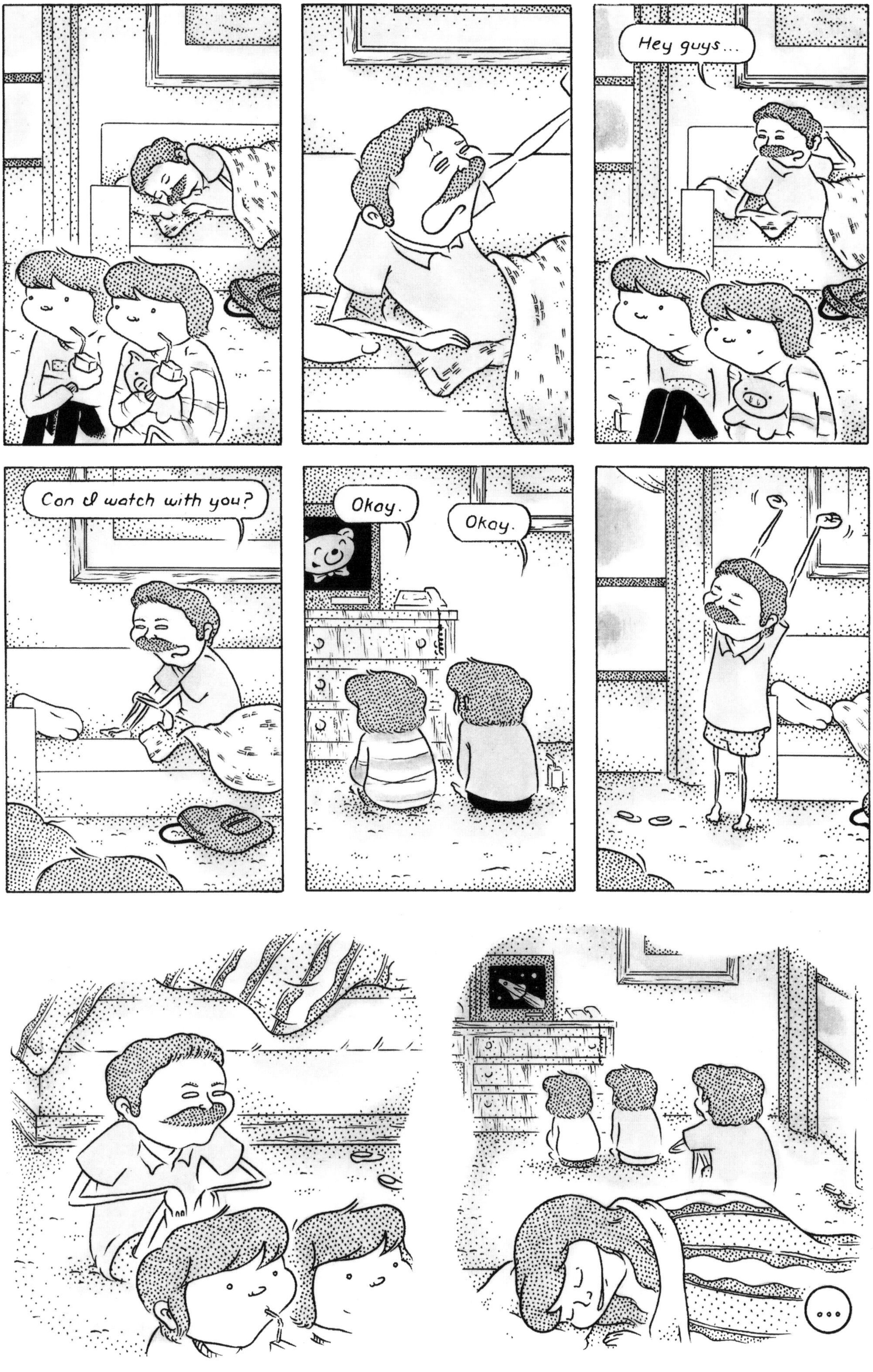
Hey guys...
Can I watch with you?
Okay.
Okay.
...

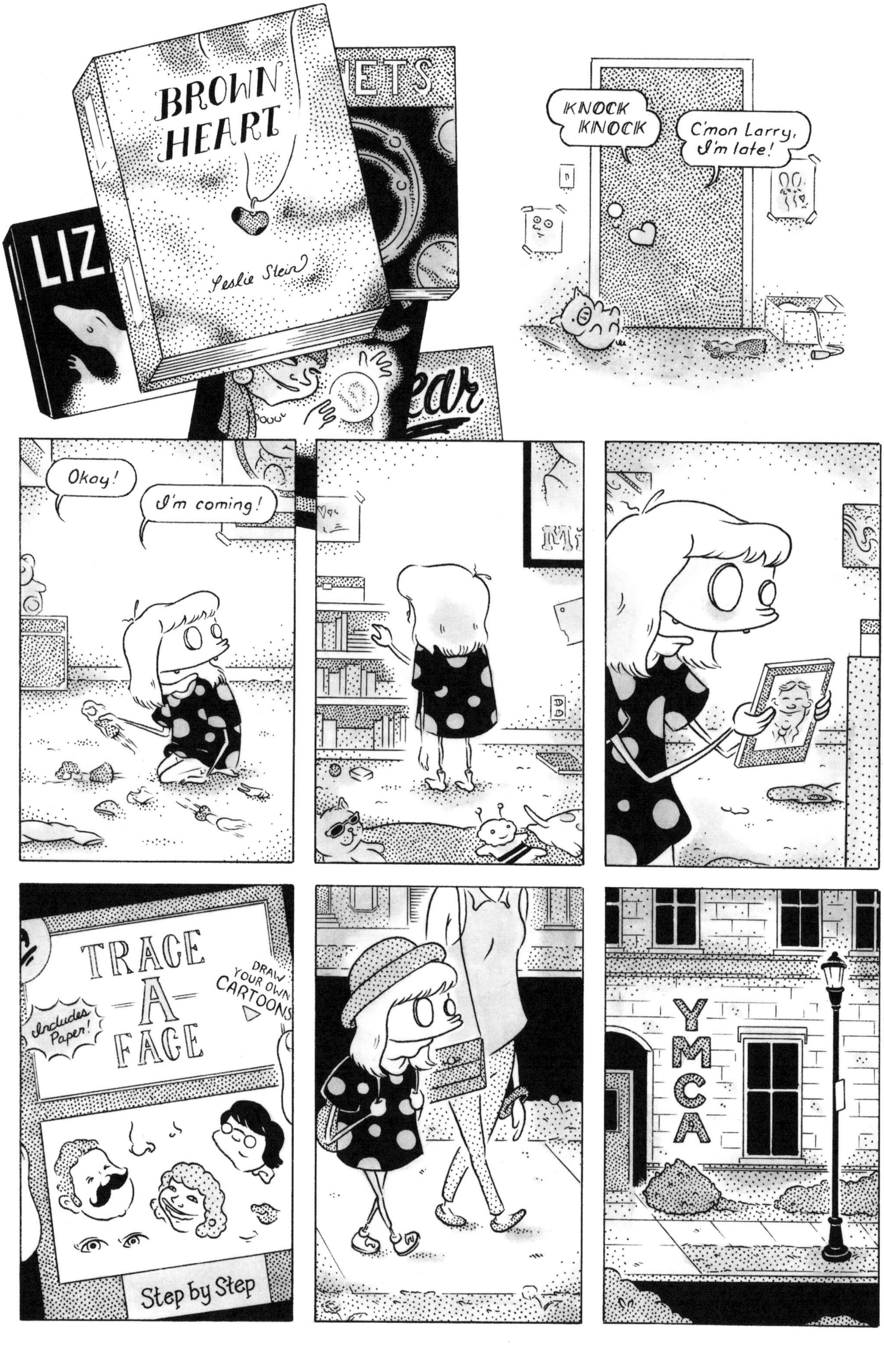
BROWN HEART
Leslie Stein
KNOCK KNOCK
C'mon Larry, I'm late!
Okay!
I'm coming!
TRACE A FACE
Includes Paper!
DRAW YOUR OWN CARTOONS
Step by Step
YMCA

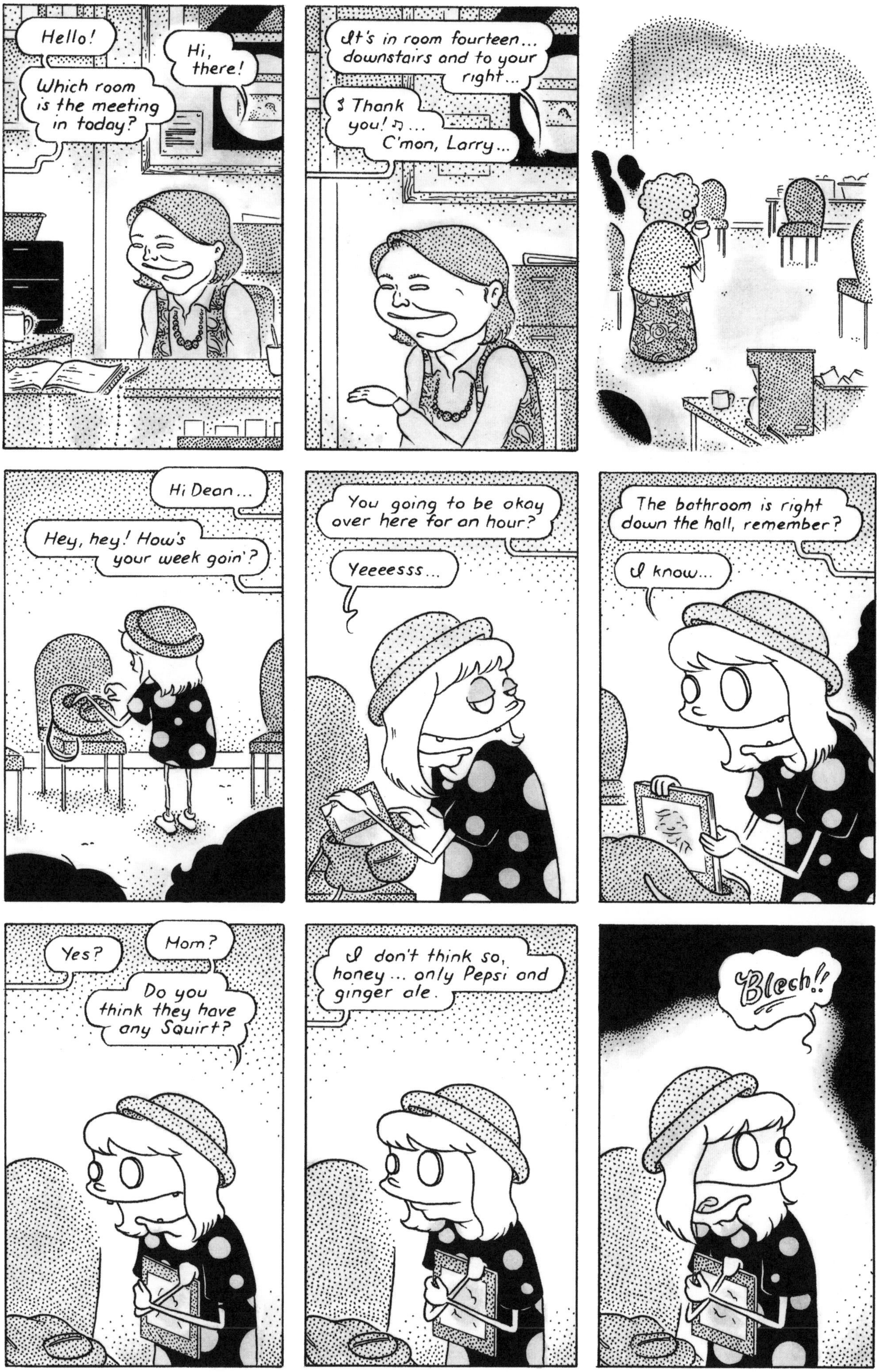
Hello!
Hi, there!
Which room is the meeting in today?
It's in room fourteen... downstairs and to your right...
Thank you!... C'mon, Larry...
Hi Dean...
Hey, hey! How's your week goin'?
You going to be okay over here for an hour?
Yeeeesss...
The bathroom is right down the hall, remember?
I know...
Mom?
Yes?
Do you think they have any Squirt?
I don't think so, honey... only Pepsi and ginger ale.
Blech!!

Okay, so everyone take a seat, we're ready to begin...

Cough

SCOOT

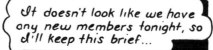

It doesn't look like we have any new members tonight, so I'll keep this brief...

Welcome everyone! We're so glad you could be here with us today, healthy and full of hope. Remember, we are not here to JUDGE, but to listen and support! So with that, let's begin...

Does anyone have anything they'd like to share with the group?

Ahem...

I'll go...

Hi my name is Bill, and I'm an alchoholic and a narcotics abuser.

HI BILL!

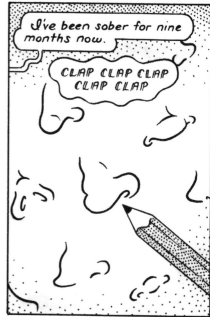

I've been sober for nine months now.

CLAP CLAP CLAP CLAP CLAP

Well... *sigh*... I had a rough time this past weekend. I almost relapsed at a party I went to on Saturday.

I got together with a buncha guys I used to play football with on the weekends. I hadn't seen most of them since I'd gotten sober. We were all hanging out at a pals house and everyone was drinking tons of beer...

Sigh I dunno why I thought it would be okay... They are tough guys, y'know? They think getting sober... Well, they were all giving me a hard time about it...

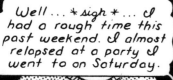

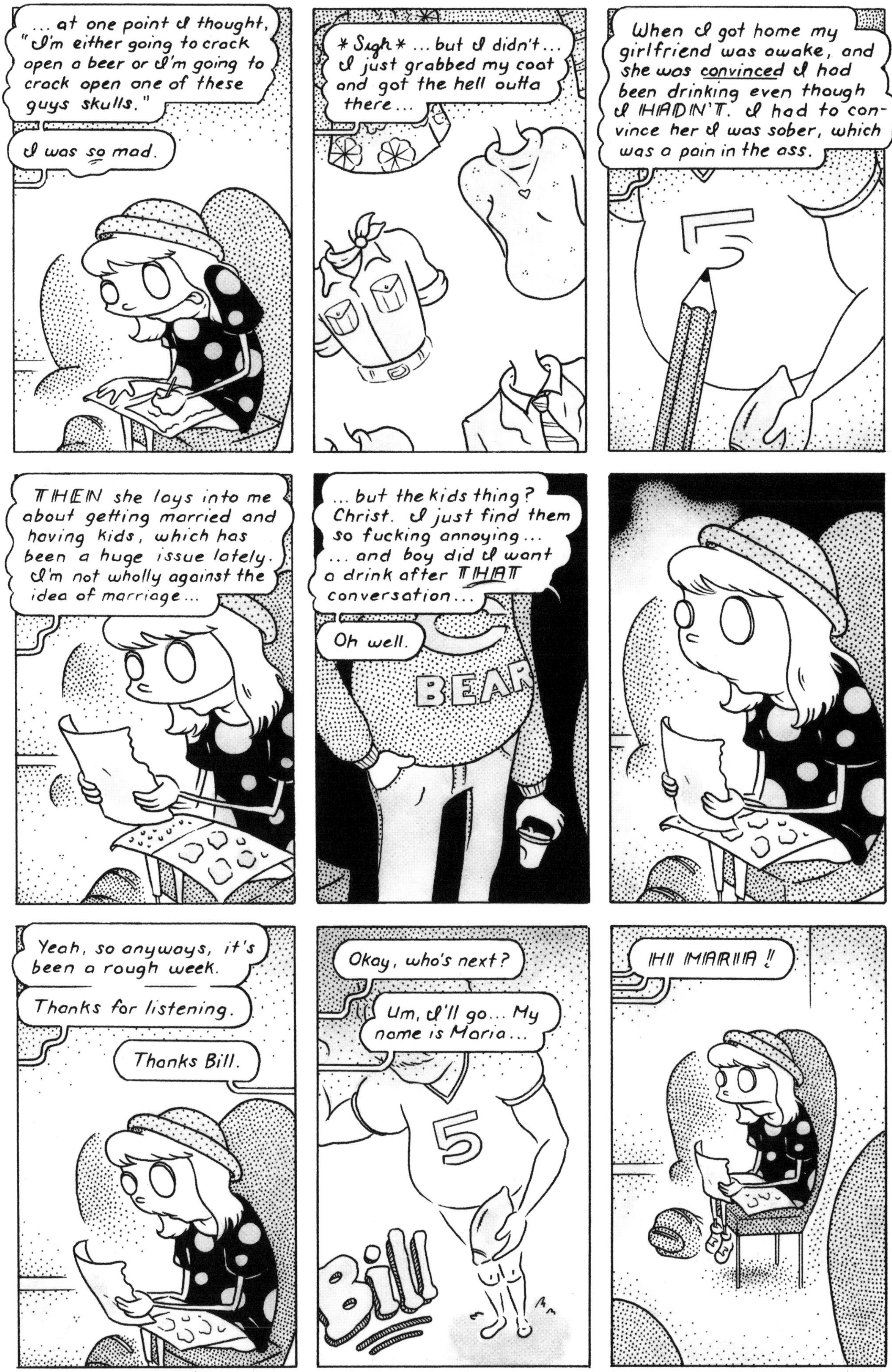
... at one point I thought, "I'm either going to crack open a beer or I'm going to crack open one of these guys skulls."
I was so mad.
Sigh ... but I didn't... I just grabbed my coat and got the hell outta there...
When I got home my girlfriend was awake, and she was convinced I had been drinking even though I HADN'T. I had to convince her I was sober, which was a pain in the ass.
THEN she lays into me about getting married and having kids, which has been a huge issue lately. I'm not wholly against the idea of marriage...
... but the kids thing? Christ. I just find them so fucking annoying...
... and boy did I want a drink after THAT conversation...
Oh well.
BEAR
Yeah, so anyways, it's been a rough week.
Thanks for listening.
Thanks Bill.
Okay, who's next?
Um, I'll go... My name is Maria...
5
Bill
HI MARIA!!

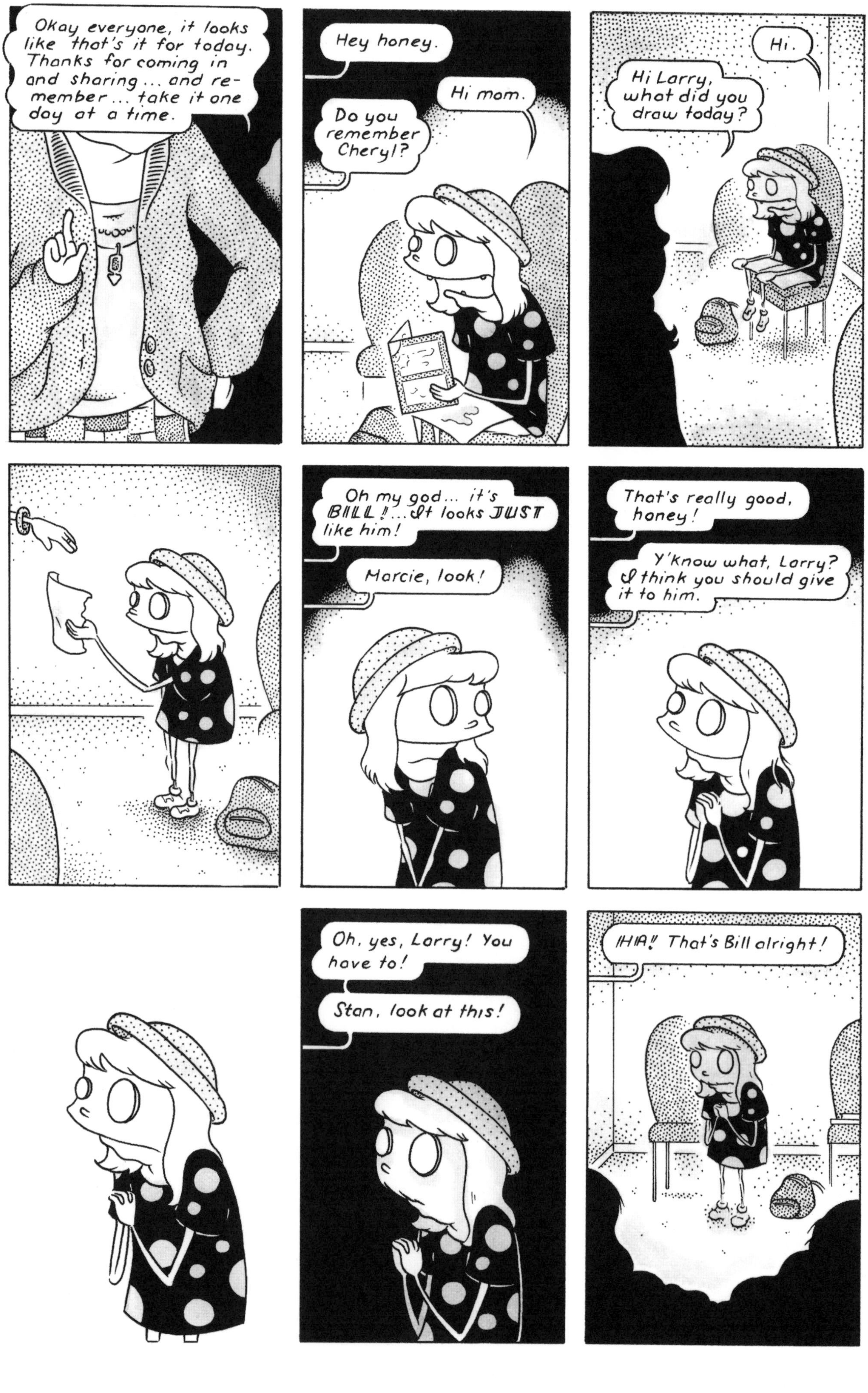
Okay everyone, it looks like that's it for today. Thanks for coming in and sharing... and remember... take it one day at a time.
Hey honey.
Hi mom.
Do you remember Cheryl?
Hi.
Hi Larry, what did you draw today?
Oh my god... it's BILL!... It looks JUST like him!
Marcie, look!
That's really good, honey!
Y'know what, Larry? I think you should give it to him.
Oh, yes, Larry! You have to!
Stan, look at this!
!HA! That's Bill alright!

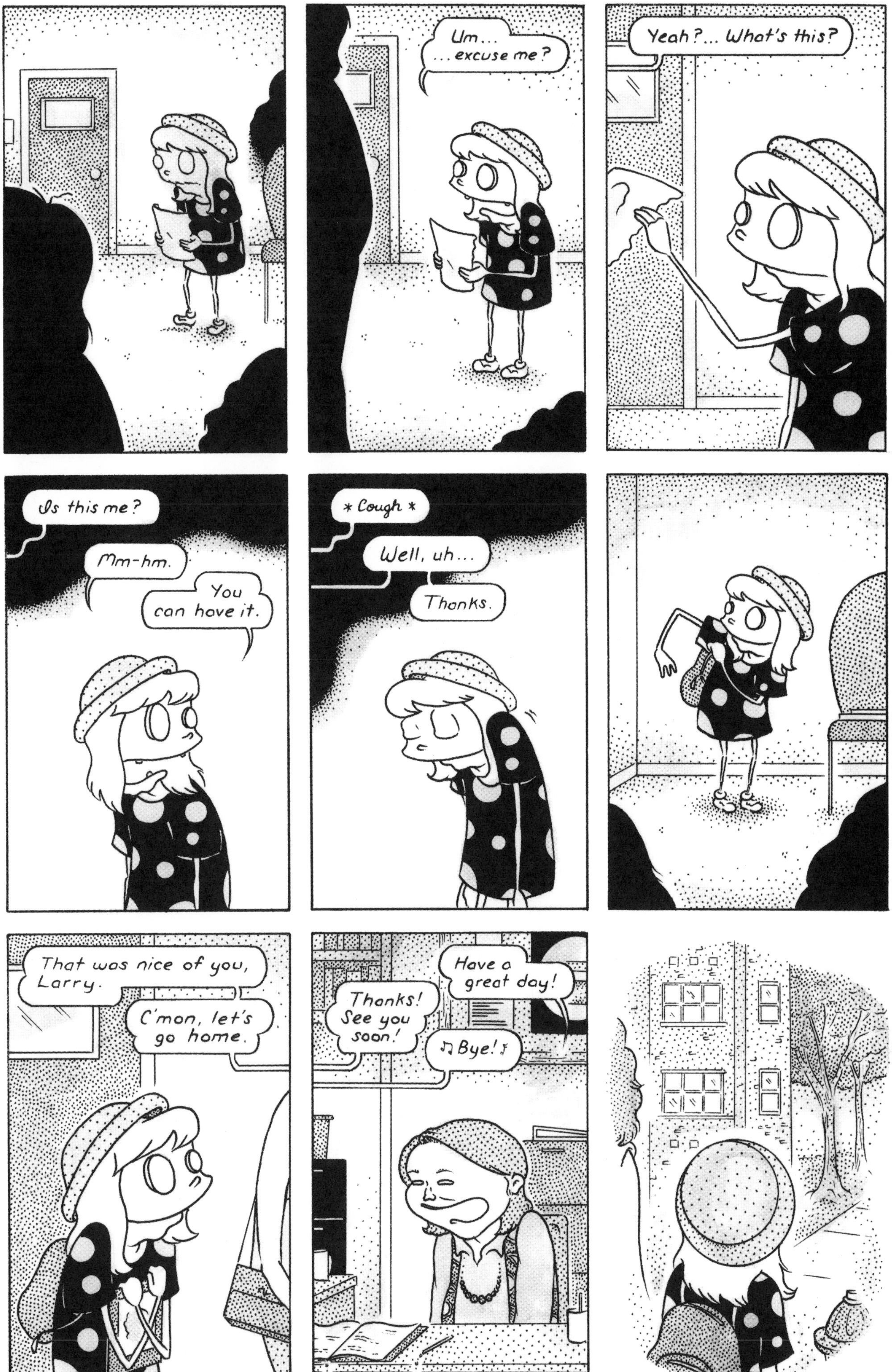
Um...
...excuse me?
Yeah?... What's this?
Is this me?
Mm-hm.
You can have it.
* Cough *
Well, uh...
Thanks.
That was nice of you, Larry.
C'mon, let's go home.
Have a great day!
Thanks! See you soon!
♫ Bye! ♫

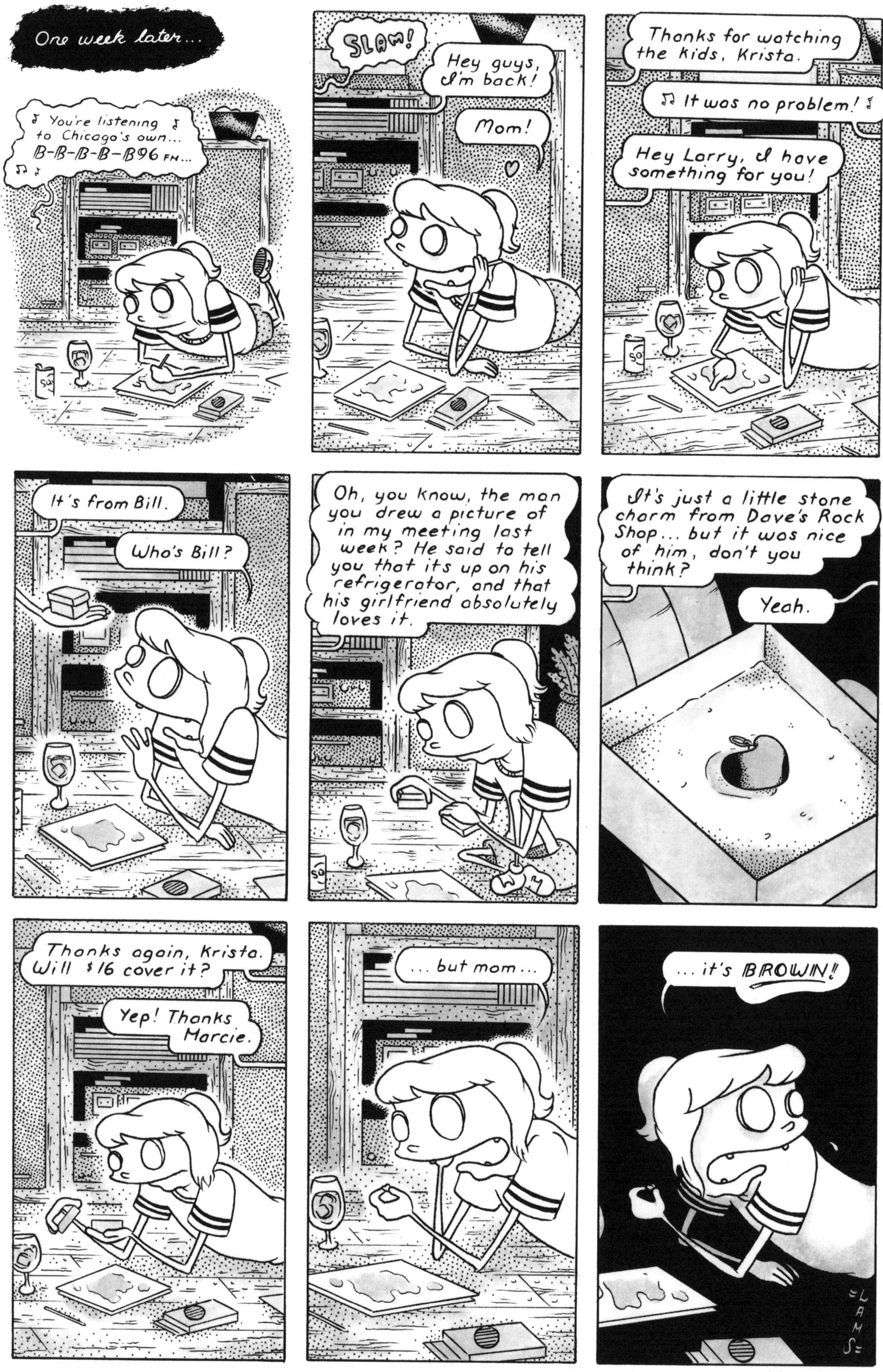
One week later...
♪ You're listening to Chicago's own... B-B-B-B-B96 FM... ♫ ♪
SLAM!
Hey guys, I'm back!
Mom!
Thanks for watching the kids, Krista.
♫ It was no problem! ♪
Hey Larry, I have something for you!
It's from Bill.
Who's Bill?
Oh, you know, the man you drew a picture of in my meeting last week? He said to tell you that its up on his refrigerator, and that his girlfriend absolutely loves it.
It's just a little stone charm from Dave's Rock Shop... but it was nice of him, don't you think?
Yeah.
Thanks again, Krista. Will $16 cover it?
Yep! Thanks Marcie.
... but mom...
... it's BROWN!!
LAMS

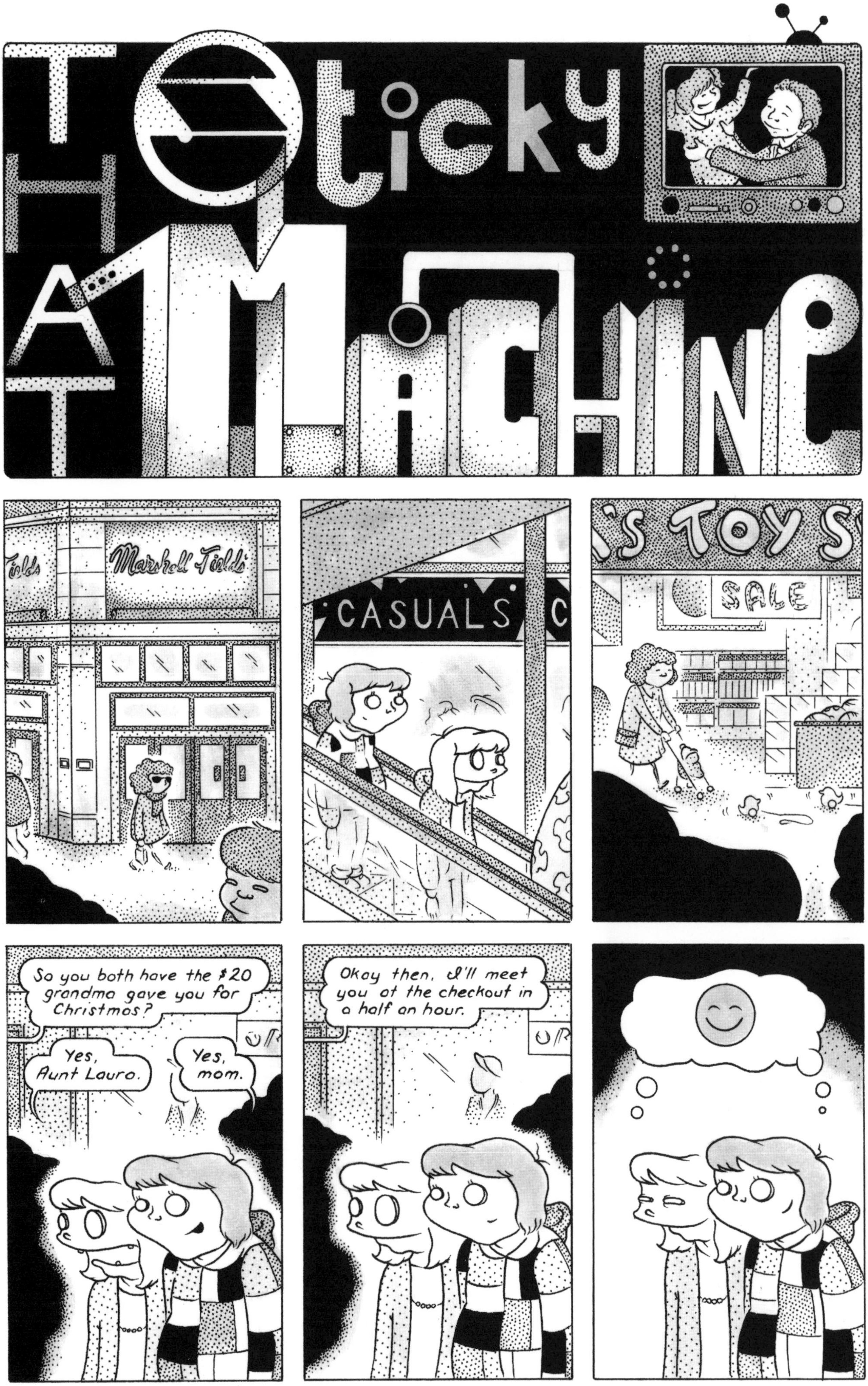
That Sticky Machine
Marshall Field's
CASUALS
'S TOYS
SALE
So you both have the $20 grandma gave you for Christmas?
Yes, Aunt Laura.
Yes, mom.
Okay then, I'll meet you at the checkout in a half an hour.

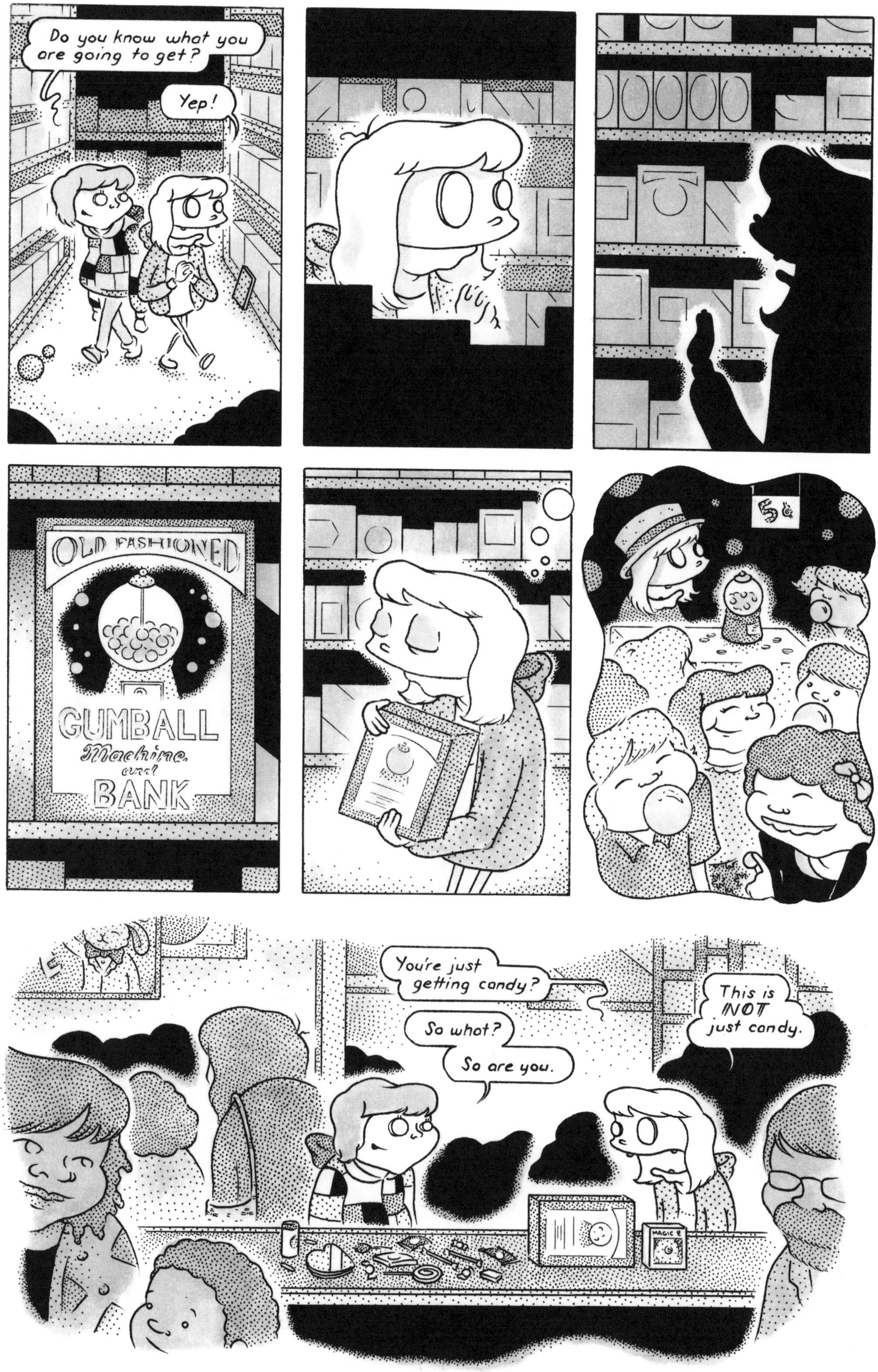

Do you know what you are going to get?
Yep!
OLD FASHIONED
GUMBALL
Machine
and
BANK
You're just getting candy?
So what?
So are you.
This is NOT just candy.

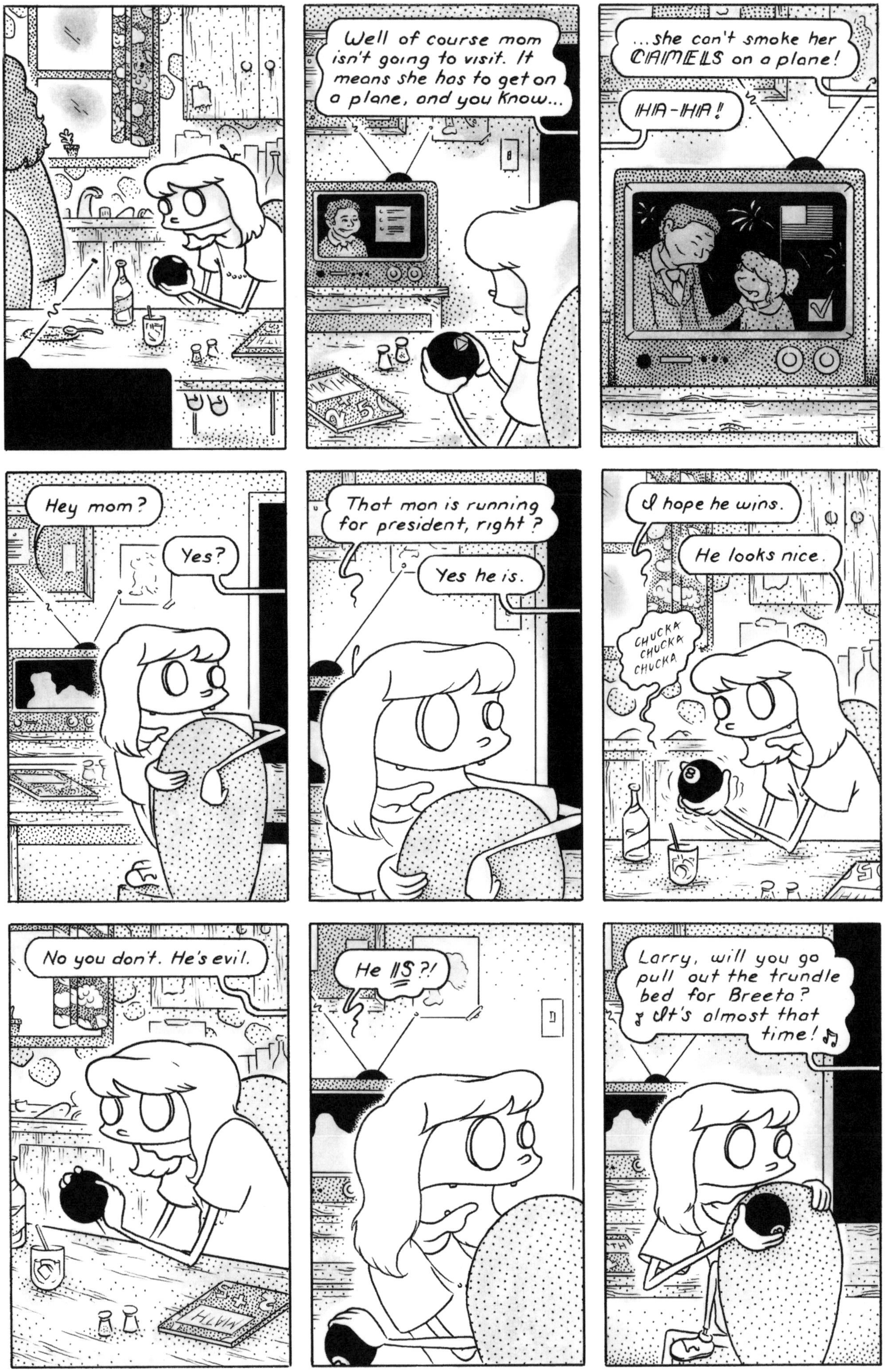
Well of course mom isn't going to visit. It means she has to get on a plane, and you know...
...she can't smoke her CAMELS on a plane!
HA-HA!
Hey mom?
Yes?
That man is running for president, right?
Yes he is.
I hope he wins.
He looks nice.
CHUCKA CHUCKA CHUCKA
No you don't. He's evil.
He IS?!
Larry, will you go pull out the trundle bed for Breeta? It's almost that time!

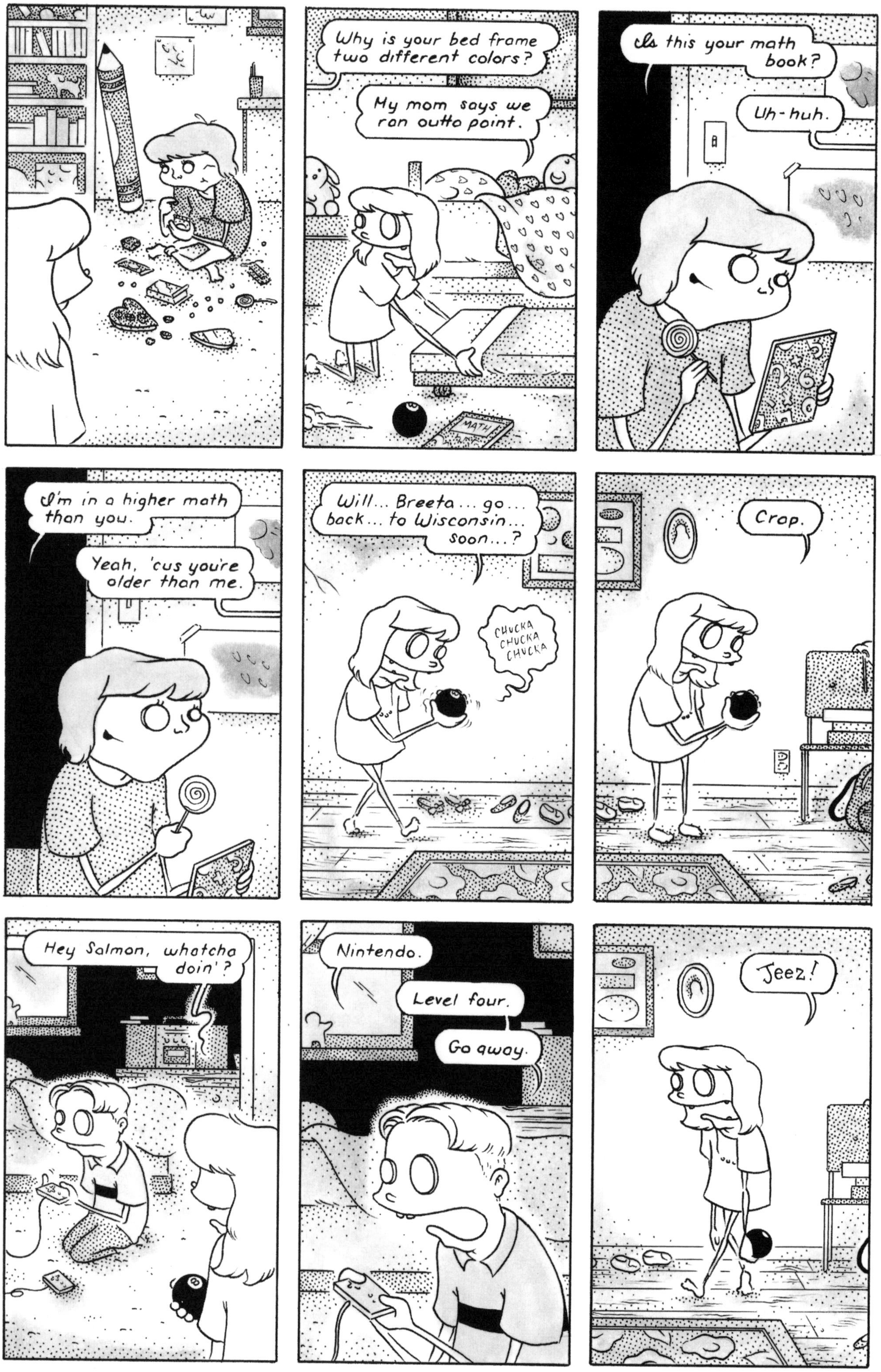
Why is your bed frame two different colors?
My mom says we ran outta point.
Is this your math book?
Uh-huh.
MATH
I'm in a higher math than you.
Yeah, 'cus you're older than me.
Will... Breeta... go... back... to Wisconsin... soon...?
CHUCKA CHUCKA CHUCKA
Crap.
Hey Salmon, whatcha doin'?
Nintendo.
Level four.
Go away.
Jeez!

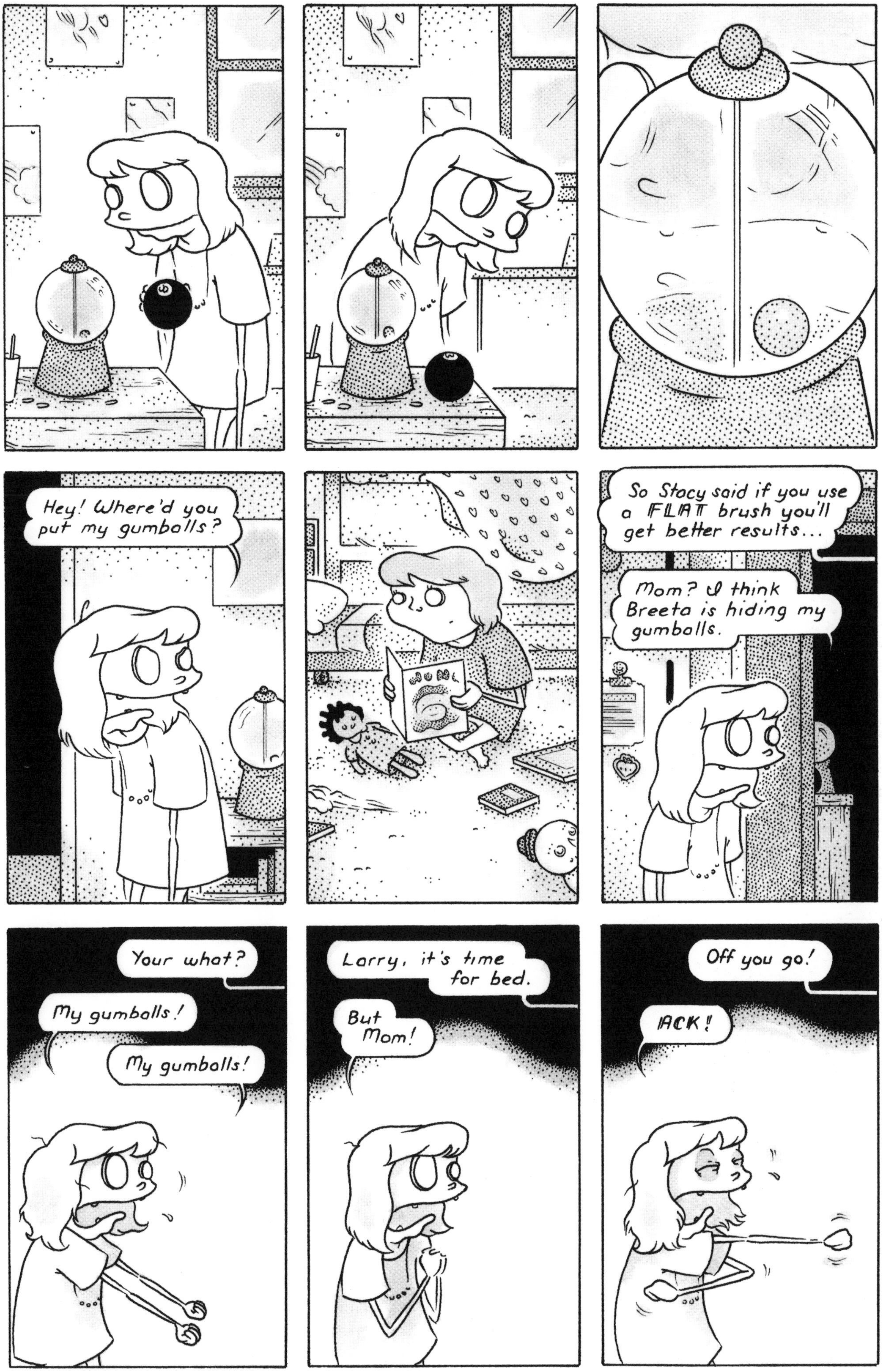
Hey! Where'd you put my gumballs?
So Stacy said if you use a FLAT brush you'll get better results...
Mom? I think Breeta is hiding my gumballs.
Your what?
My gumballs!
My gumballs!
Larry, it's time for bed.
But Mom!
Off you go!
ACK!

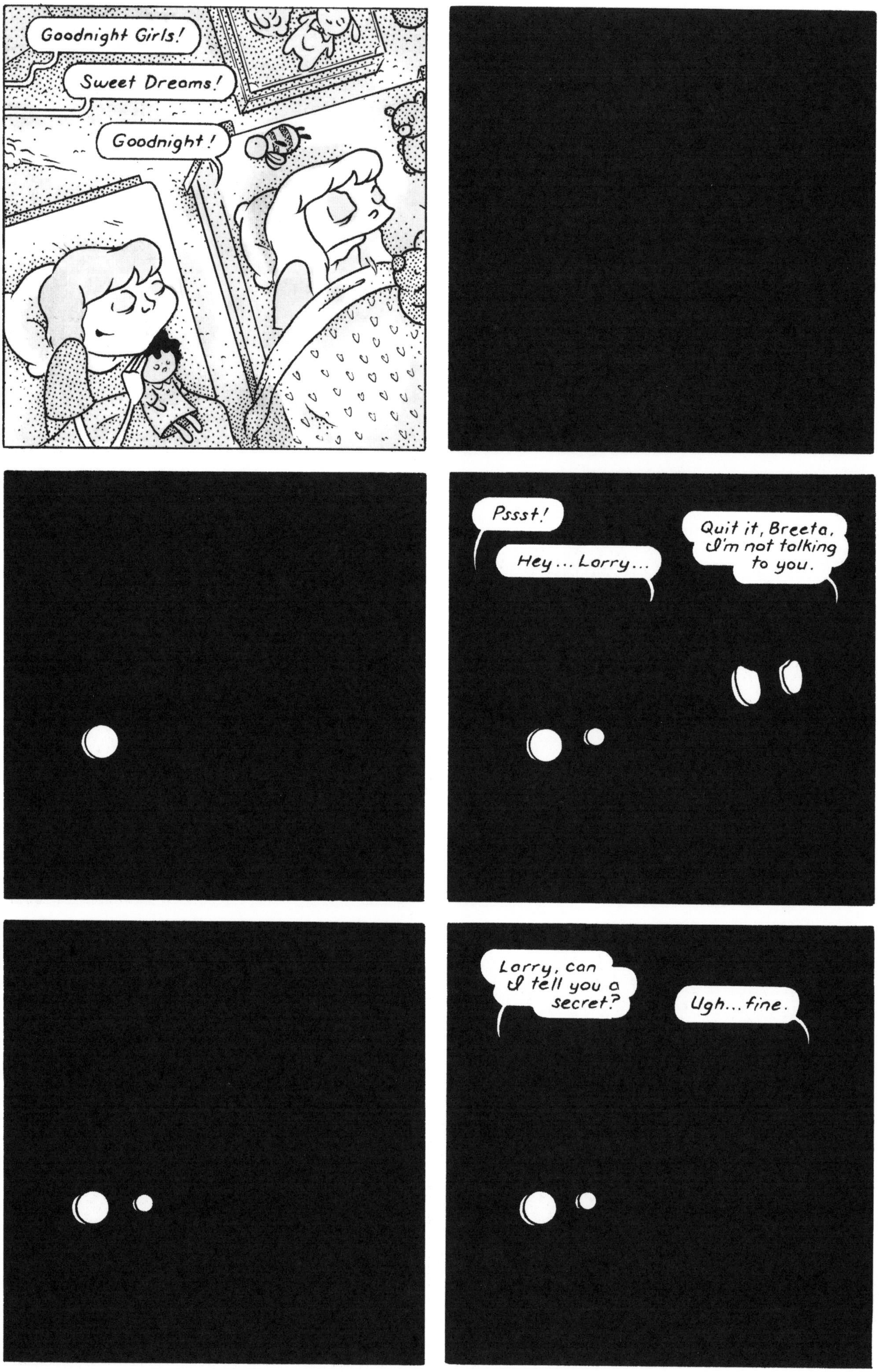
Goodnight Girls!
Sweet Dreams!
Goodnight!
Pssst!
Hey... Larry...
Quit it, Breeta, I'm not talking to you.
Larry, can I tell you a secret?
Ugh... fine.

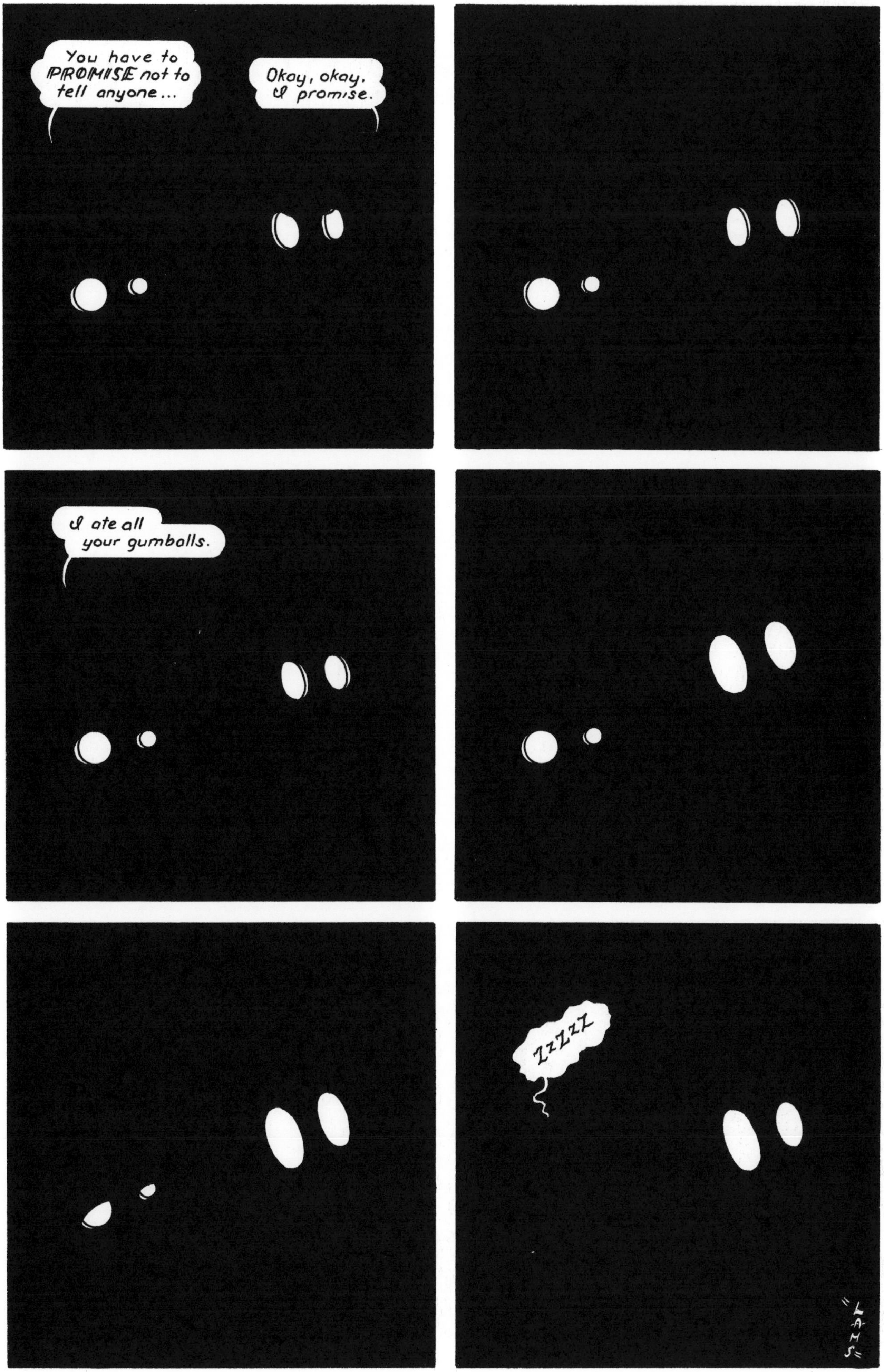

You have to PROMISE not to tell anyone...
Okay, okay. I promise.
I ate all your gumballs.
ZZZZZ
LAMS

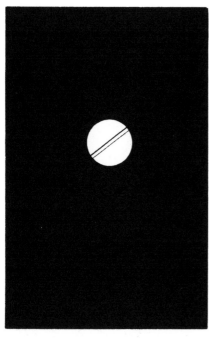

I don't want to do this, mom.

I know...

...but look at the bright side, at least you get out of school for a day!

Yeah, I guess.

How'd you meet Bob?

Mmm, I think I met him at volleyball.

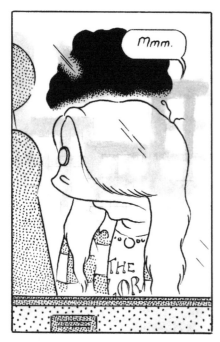
Mmm.

We're here for the Johnny B. Benefit. She's a performer.

BZZZ... Stacy?... We have an artist here, can you come out and show her to the back?

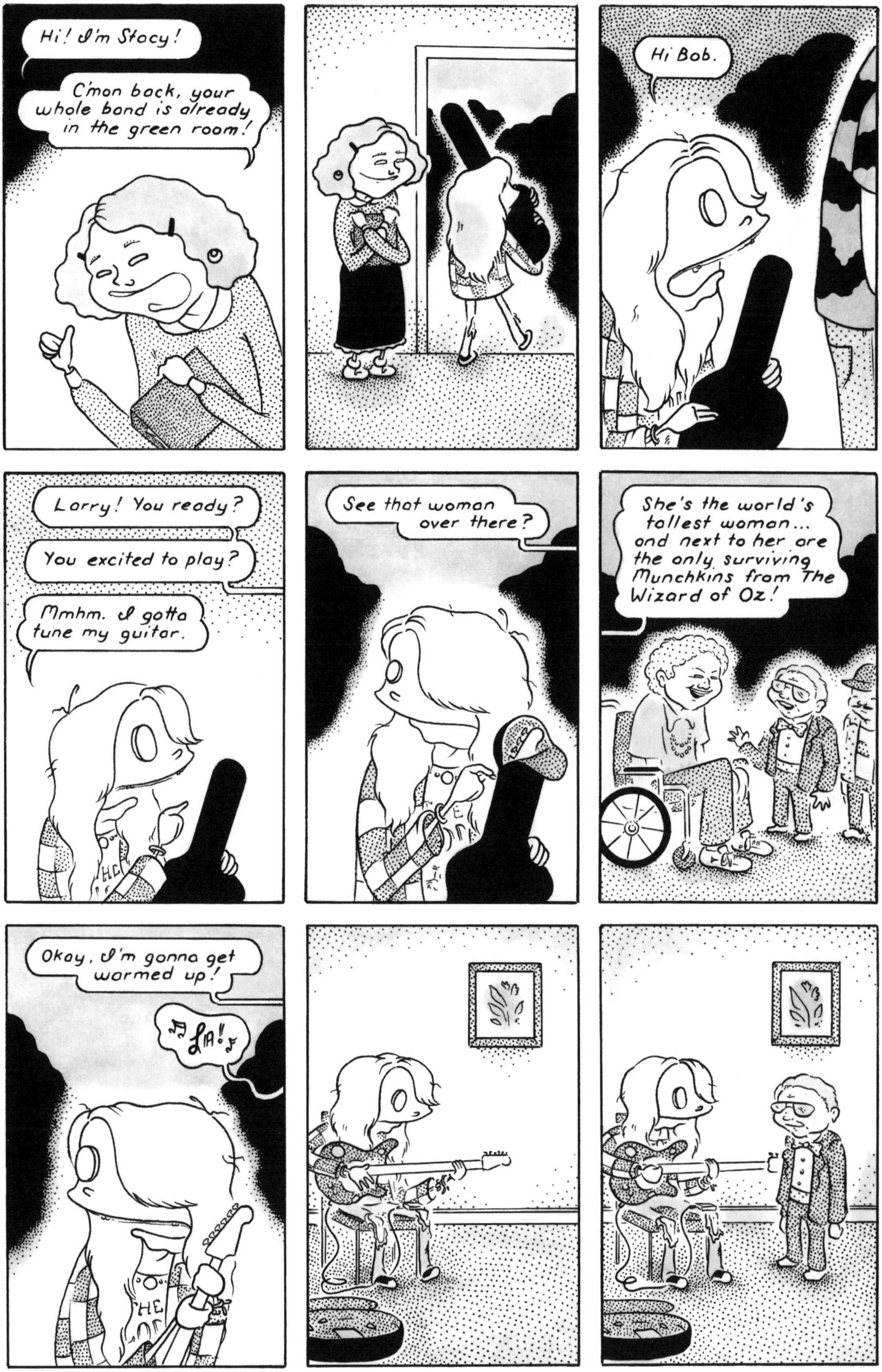
Hi! I'm Stacy!
C'mon back, your whole band is already in the green room!
Hi Bob.
Larry! You ready?
You excited to play?
Mmhm. I gotta tune my guitar.
See that woman over there?
She's the world's tallest woman... and next to her are the only surviving Munchkins from The Wizard of Oz!
Okay, I'm gonna get warmed up!
LA!

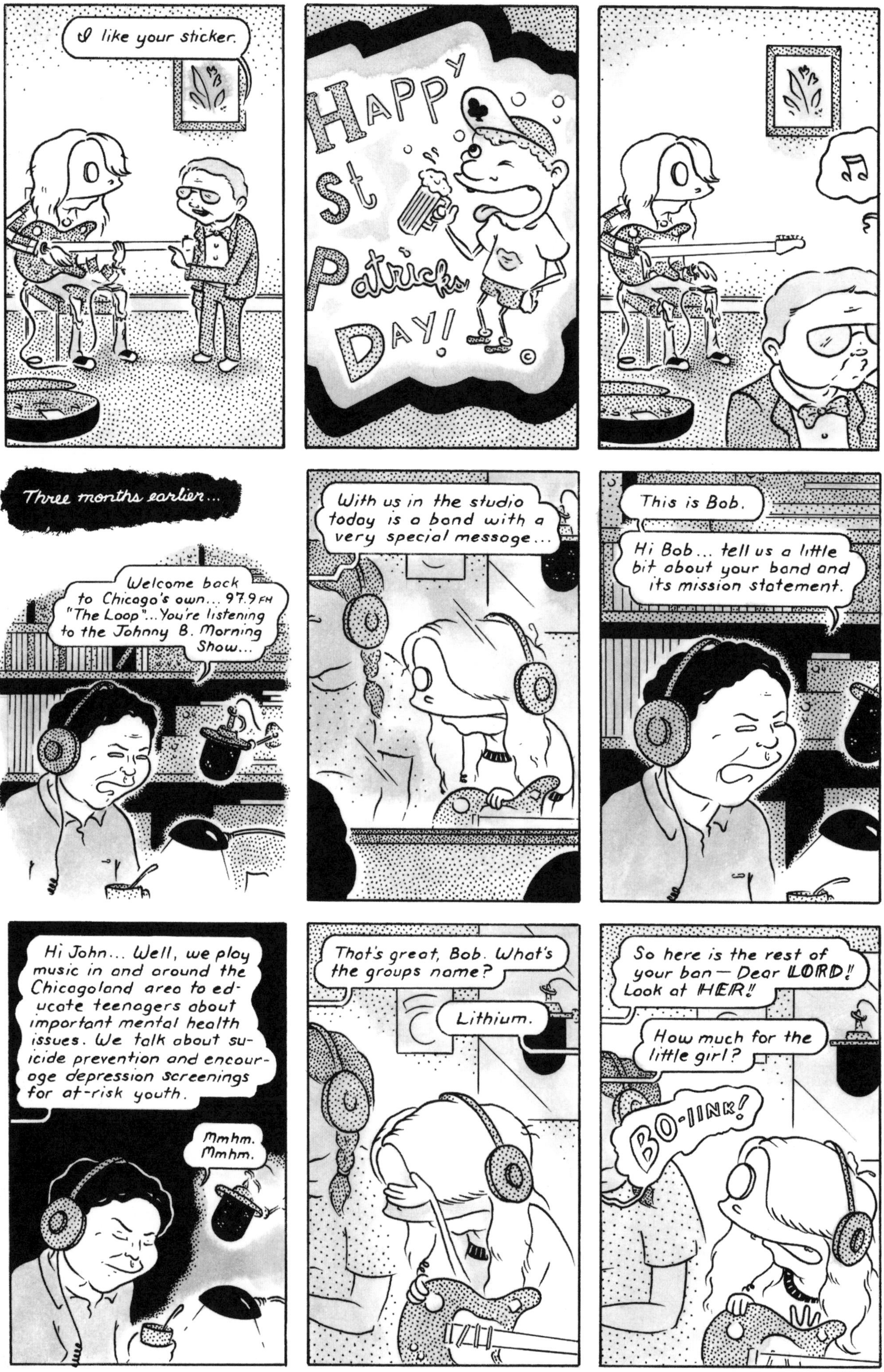
I like your sticker.
HAPPY St Patrick's DAY!
Three months earlier...
Welcome back to Chicago's own... 97.9 FM "The Loop"... You're listening to the Johnny B. Morning Show...
With us in the studio today is a band with a very special message...
This is Bob.
Hi Bob... tell us a little bit about your band and its mission statement.
Hi John... Well, we play music in and around the Chicagoland area to educate teenagers about important mental health issues. We talk about suicide prevention and encourage depression screenings for at-risk youth.
Mmhm. Mmhm.
That's great, Bob. What's the groups name?
Lithium.
So here is the rest of your ban— Dear LORD! Look at HER!
How much for the little girl?
BO-IINK!

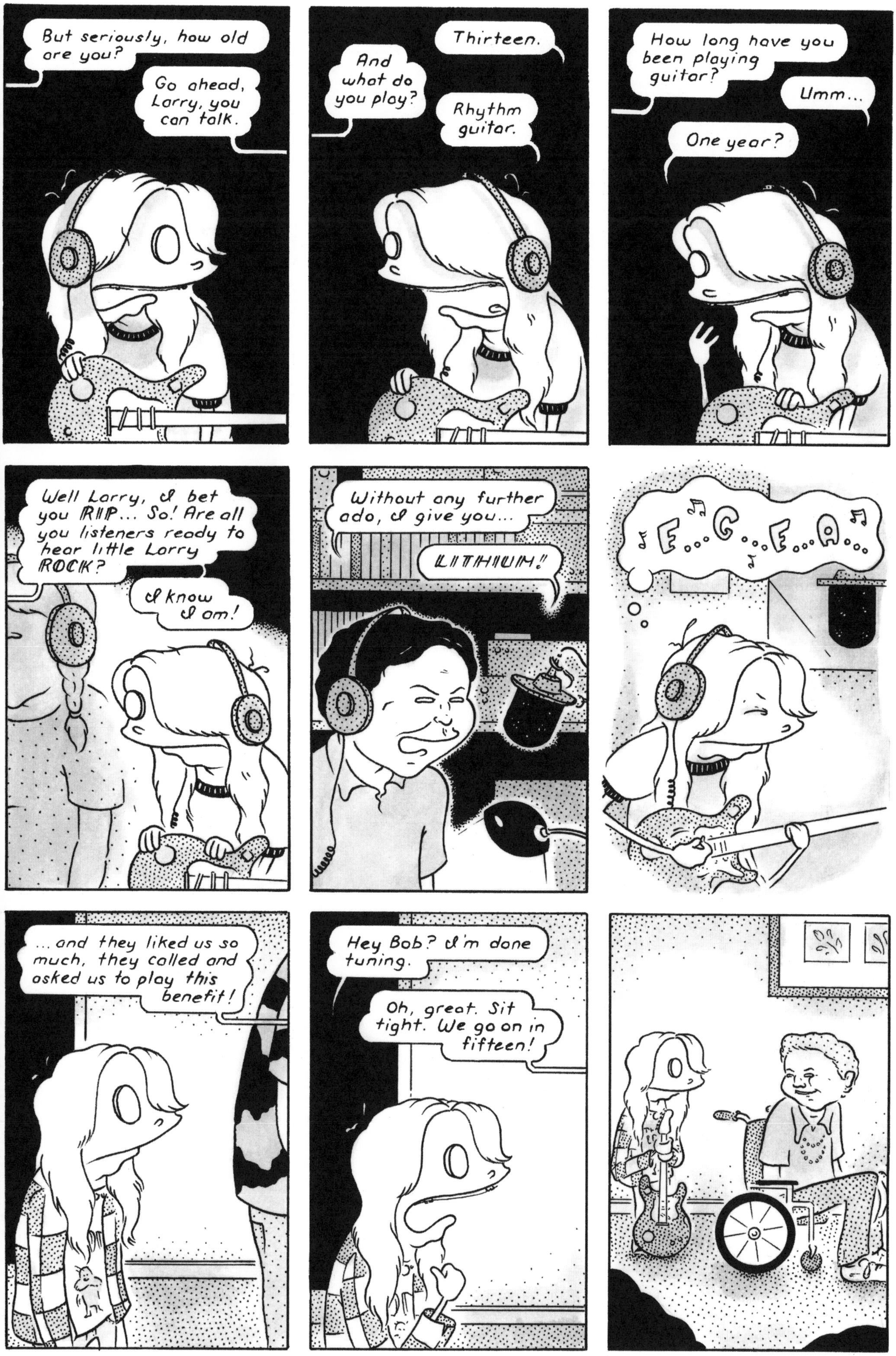
But seriously, how old are you?
Go ahead, Larry, you can talk.
Thirteen.
And what do you play?
Rhythm guitar.
How long have you been playing guitar?
Umm...
One year?
Well Larry, I bet you RIP... So! Are all you listeners ready to hear little Larry ROCK?
I know I am!
Without any further ado, I give you...
LITHIUM!
F...G...F...A...
...and they liked us so much, they called and asked us to play this benefit!
Hey Bob? I'm done tuning.
Oh, great. Sit tight. We go on in fifteen!

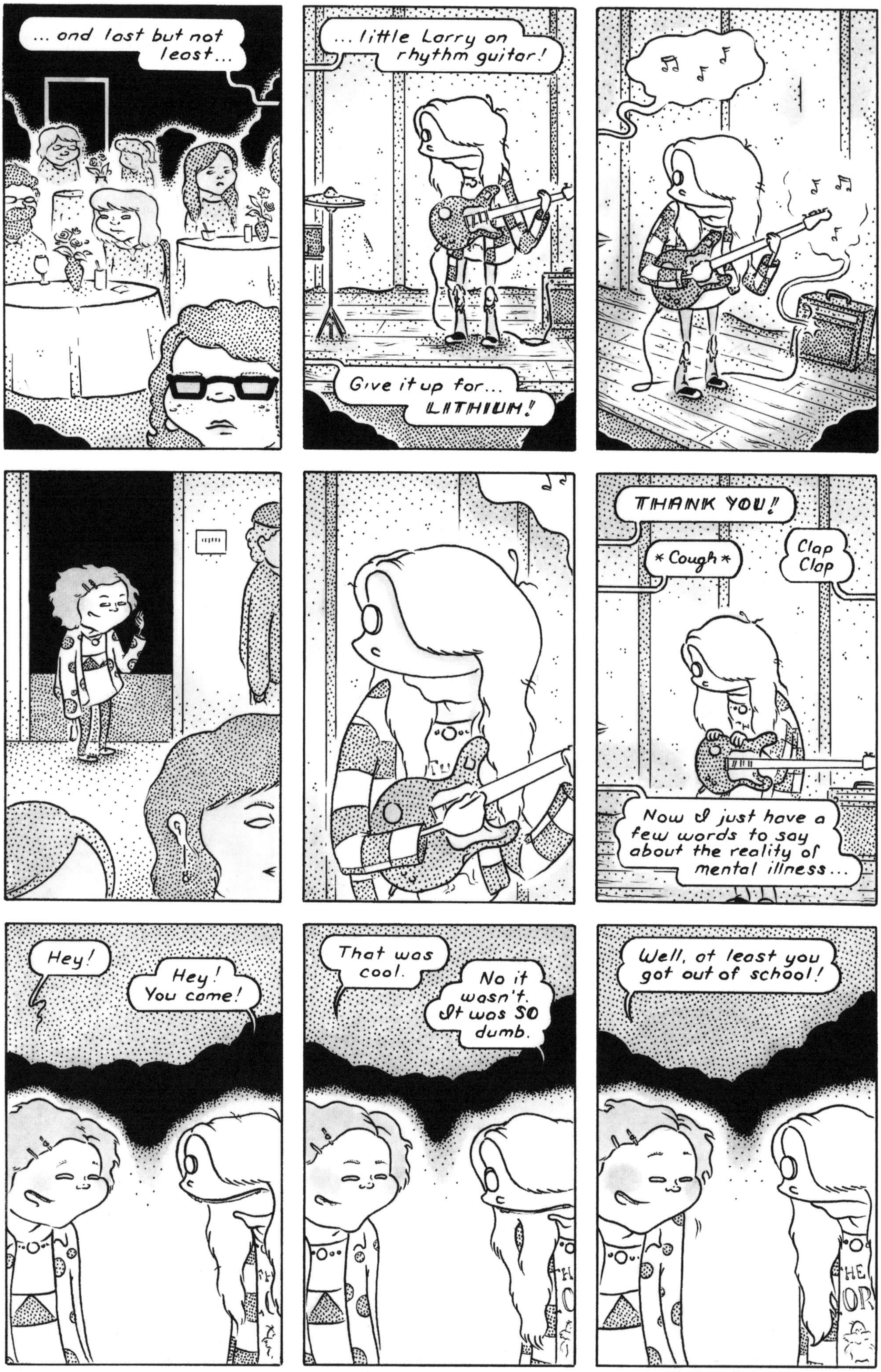
...and last but not least...
...little Larry on rhythm guitar!
Give it up for... LITHIUM!
THANK YOU!
Cough
Clap Clap
Now I just have a few words to say about the reality of mental illness...
Hey!
Hey! You came!
That was cool.
No it wasn't. It was SO dumb.
Well, at least you got out of school!

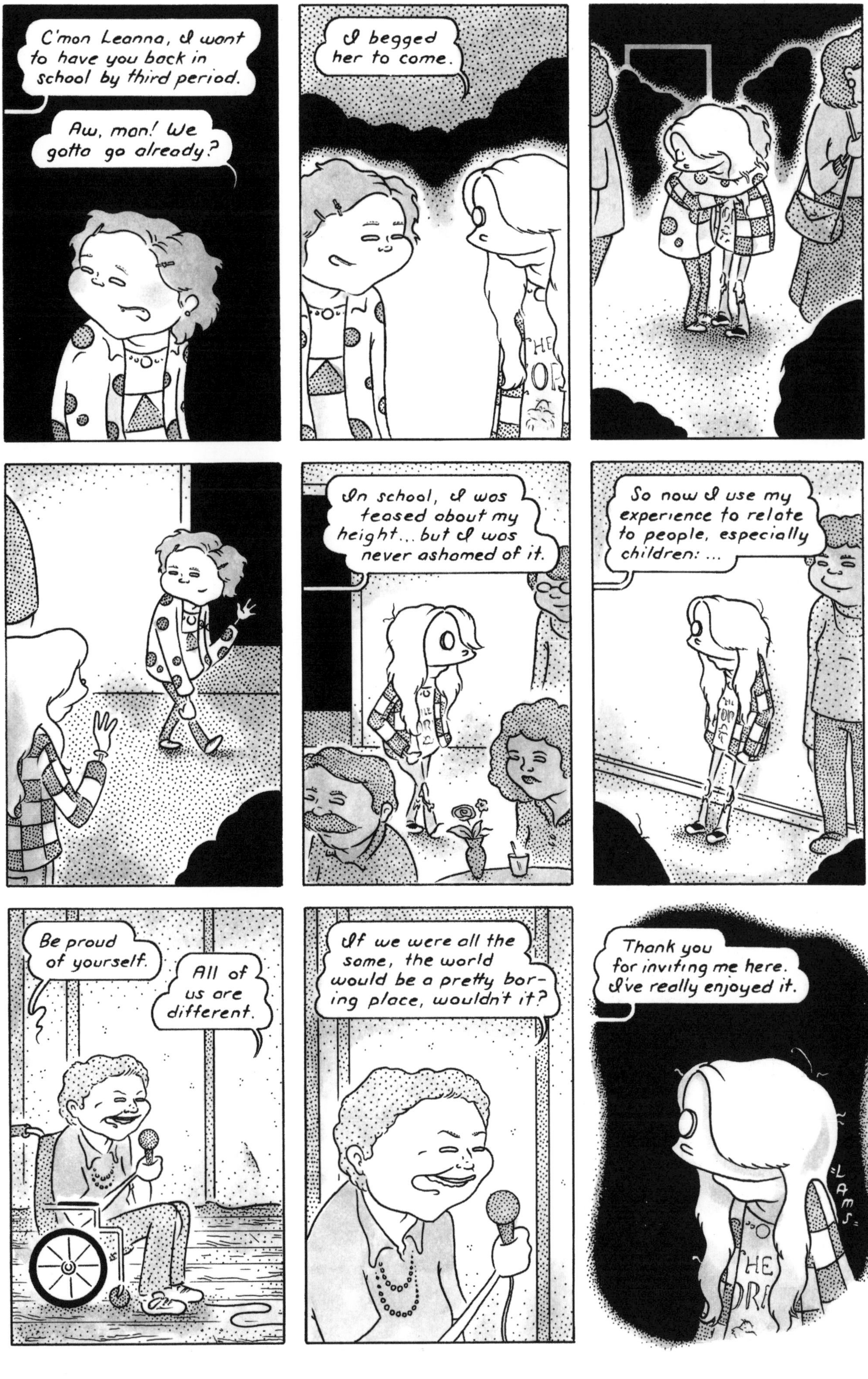
C'mon Leanna, I want to have you back in school by third period.
Aw, man! We gotta go already?
I begged her to come.
In school, I was teased about my height... but I was never ashamed of it.
So now I use my experience to relate to people, especially children: ...
Be proud of yourself.
All of us are different.
If we were all the same, the world would be a pretty boring place, wouldn't it?
Thank you for inviting me here. I've really enjoyed it.
LAMS

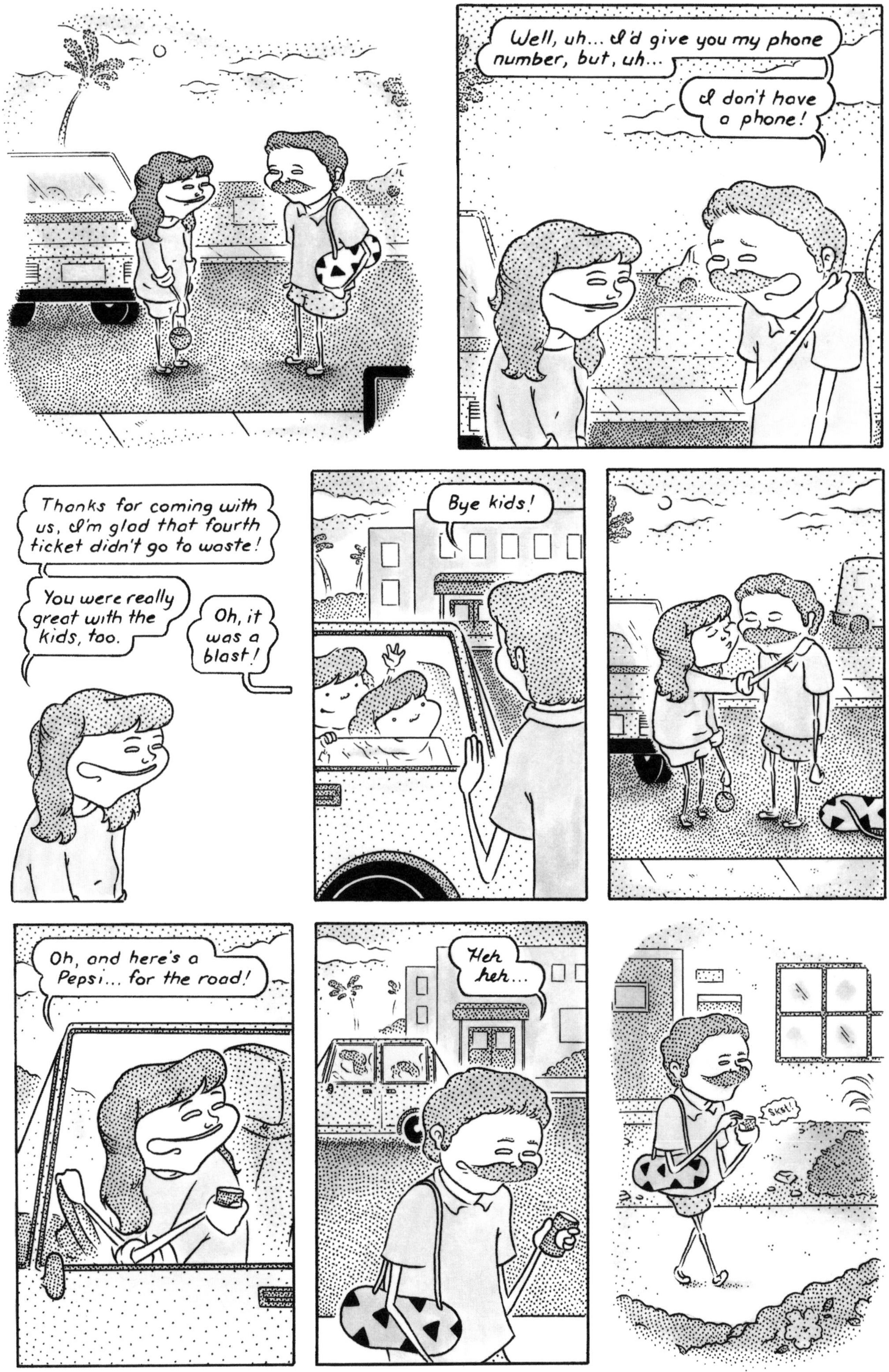
Well, uh... I'd give you my phone number, but, uh...
I don't have a phone!
Thanks for coming with us, I'm glad that fourth ticket didn't go to waste!
You were really great with the kids, too.
Oh, it was a blast!
Bye kids!
Oh, and here's a Pepsi... for the road!
Heh heh...
Skst!

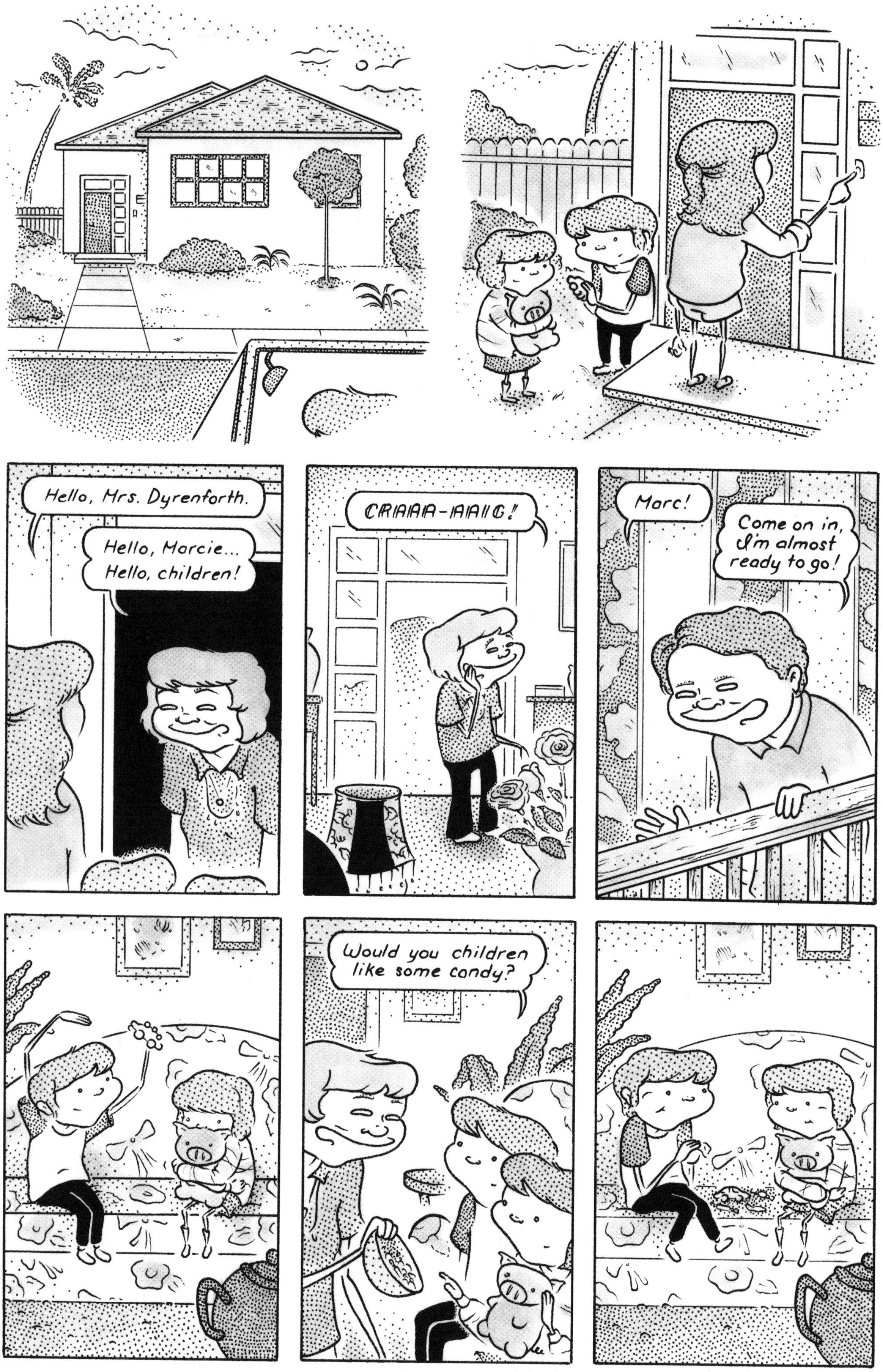
Hello, Mrs. Dyrenforth.
Hello, Marcie... Hello, children!
CRAAA-AAIG!
Marc!
Come on in, I'm almost ready to go!
Would you children like some candy?

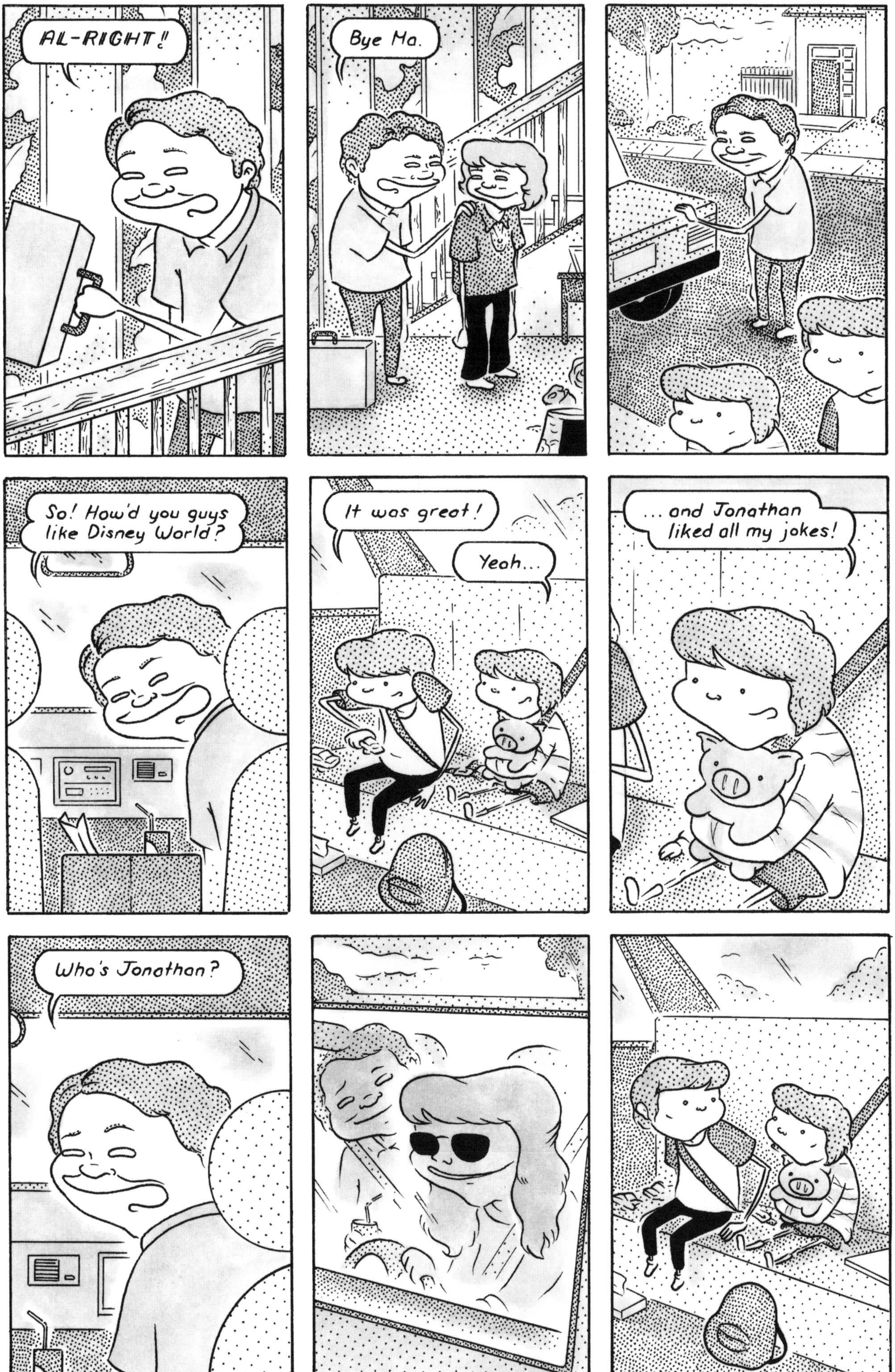
AL-RIGHT!!
Bye Ma.
So! How'd you guys like Disney World?
It was great!
Yeah...
...and Jonathan liked all my jokes!
Who's Jonathan?

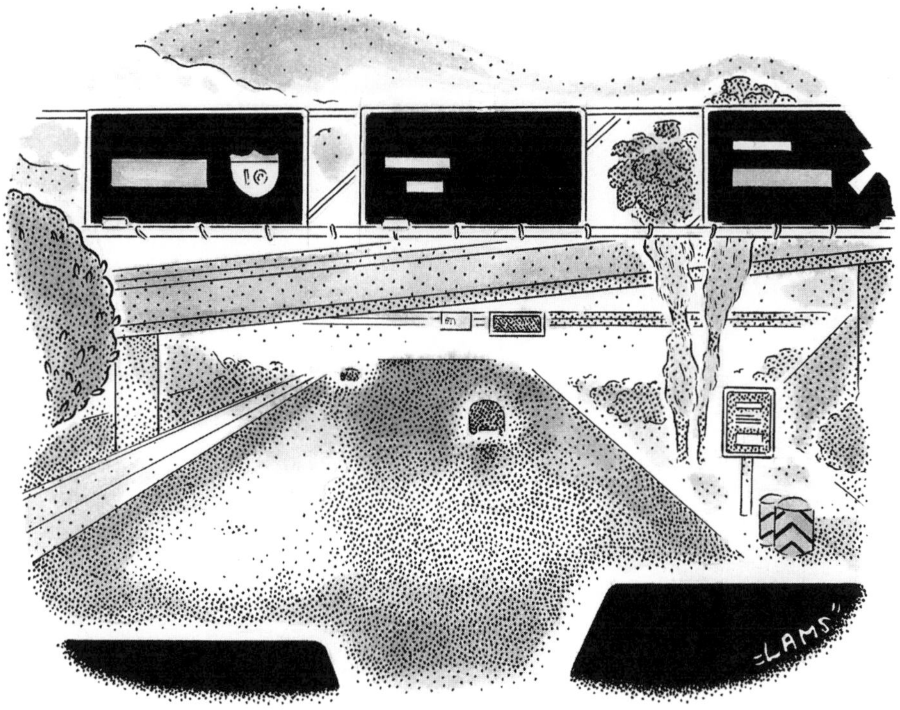
10
LAMS

a better

intoxication: the

subconscious

noodle

leslie stein

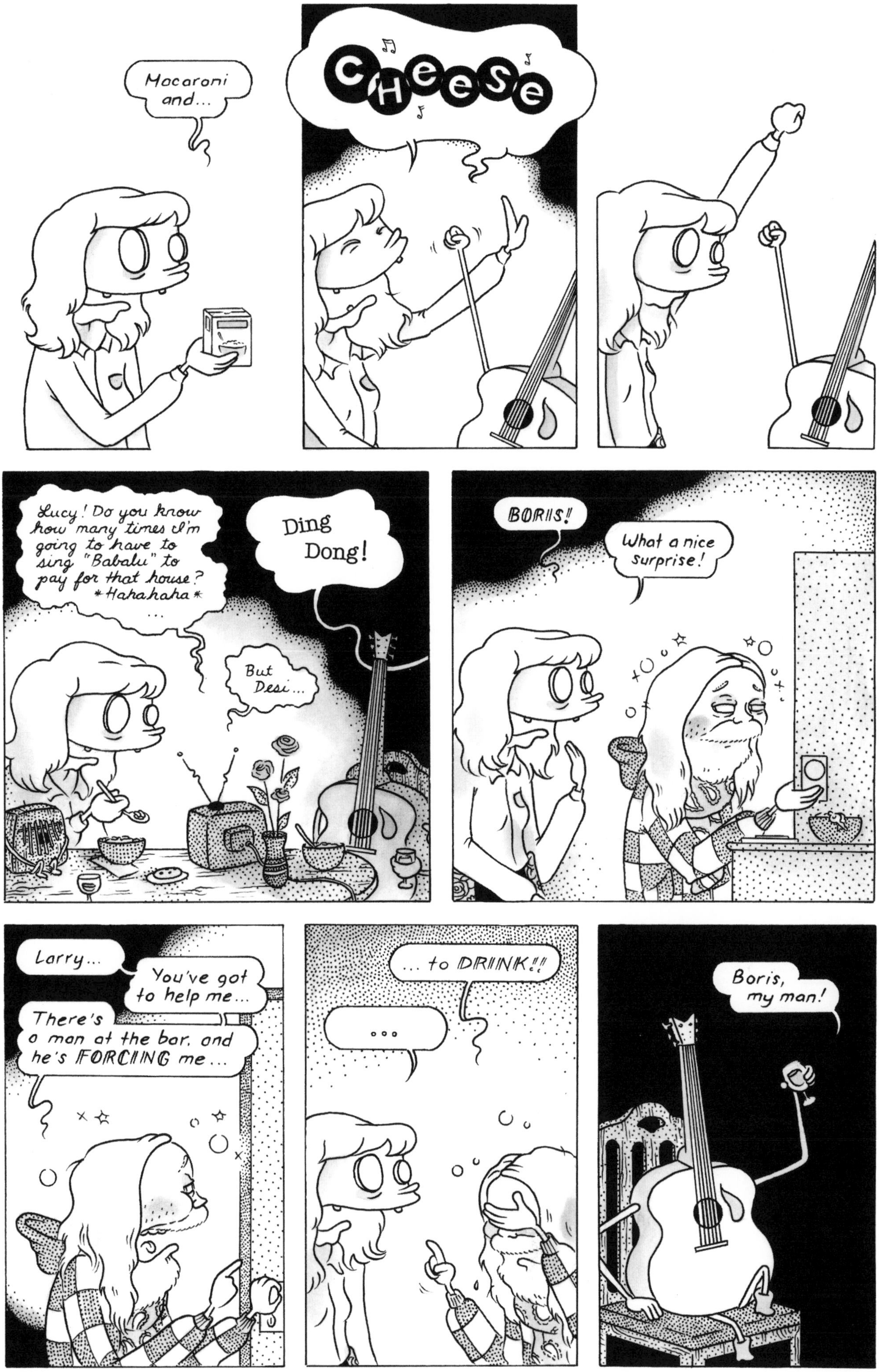

Macaroni and...
CHEESE
Lucy! Do you know how many times I'm going to have to sing "Babalu" to pay for that house? *Hahahaha* ...
But Desi...
Ding Dong!
BORIS!
What a nice surprise!
Larry...
You've got to help me...
There's a man at the bar, and he's FORCING me...
... to DRINK!!
...
Boris, my man!

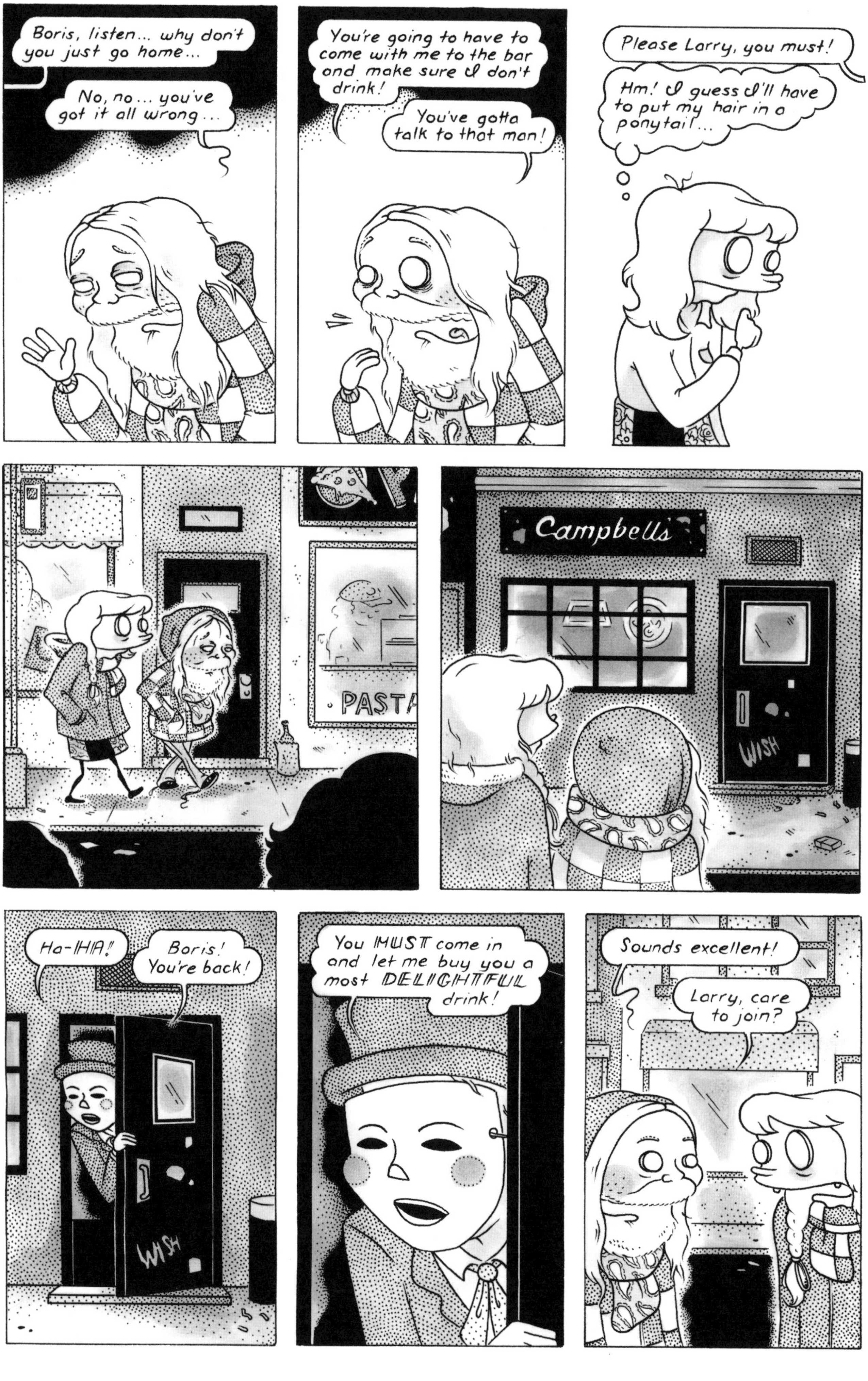
Boris, listen... why don't you just go home...
No, no... you've got it all wrong...
You're going to have to come with me to the bar and make sure I don't drink!
You've gotta talk to that man!
Please Larry, you must!
Hm! I guess I'll have to put my hair in a ponytail...
PASTA
Campbells
WISH
Ha-HA!
Boris! You're back!
WISH
You MUST come in and let me buy you a most DELIGHTFUL drink!
Sounds excellent!
Larry, care to join?

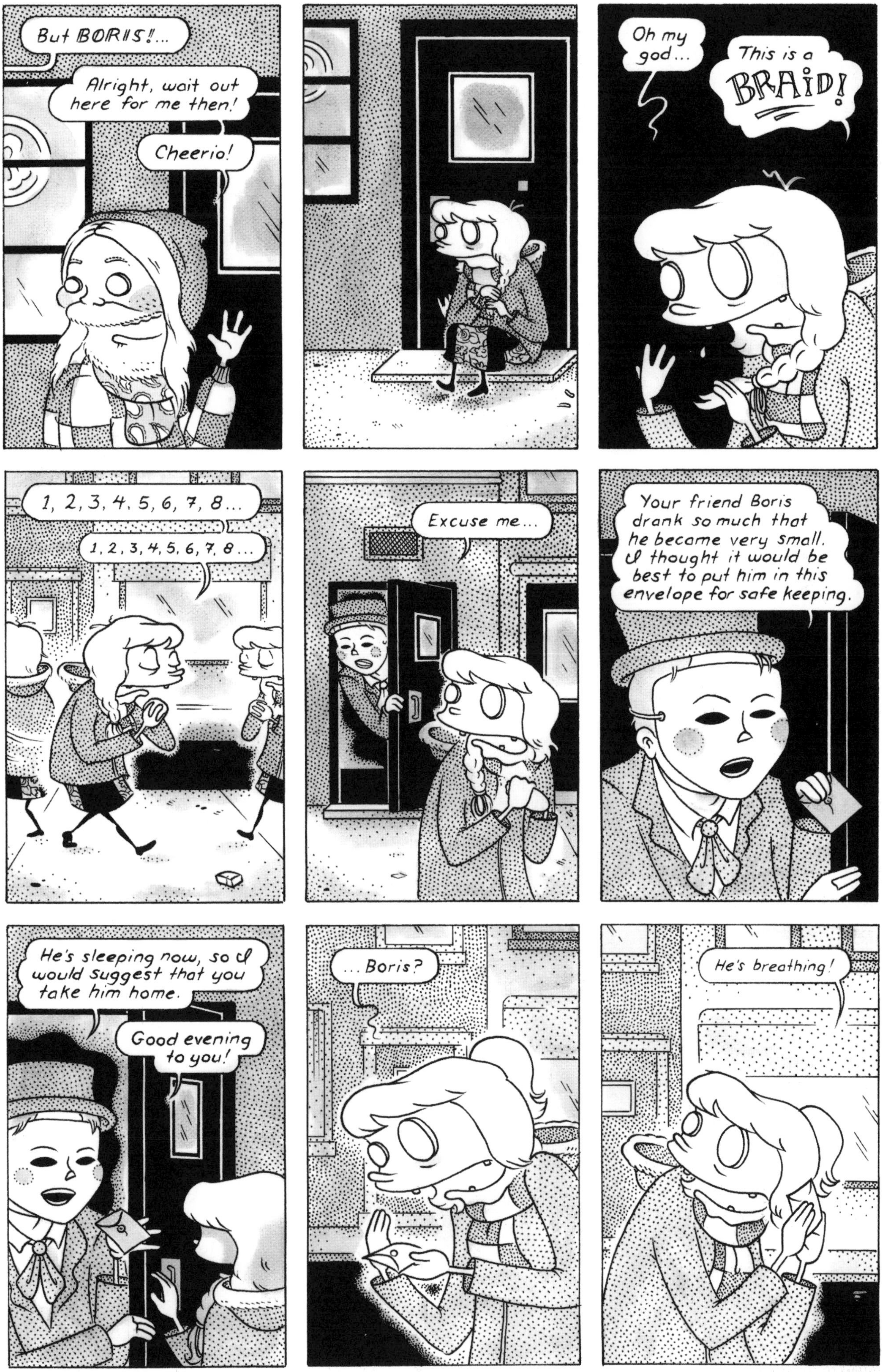
But BORIS!...
Alright, wait out here for me then!
Cheerio!
Oh my god...
This is a BRAID!
1, 2, 3, 4, 5, 6, 7, 8...
1, 2, 3, 4, 5, 6, 7, 8...
Excuse me...
Your friend Boris drank so much that he became very small. I thought it would be best to put him in this envelope for safe keeping.
He's sleeping now, so I would suggest that you take him home.
Good evening to you!
...Boris?
He's breathing!

Better put him in this gift box for the ride home... along with my spare change... aaand... a pocket of tissues!

DELI 231

♪

Marshy, ♪ I'm ho-ome!

Ha ha Ha ha Ha!

How'd it go?

Well, Boris drank so much that he got very small, so I have him in this envelope.

Mmm.

You know what? He's probably going to be really hungry when he wakes up.

I know! I'll make him some pasta!

This way, he'll have something to eat in the morning AND he'll be covered up...

There you go, Boris...

Boy, is HE going to be confused when he wakes up tomorrow!

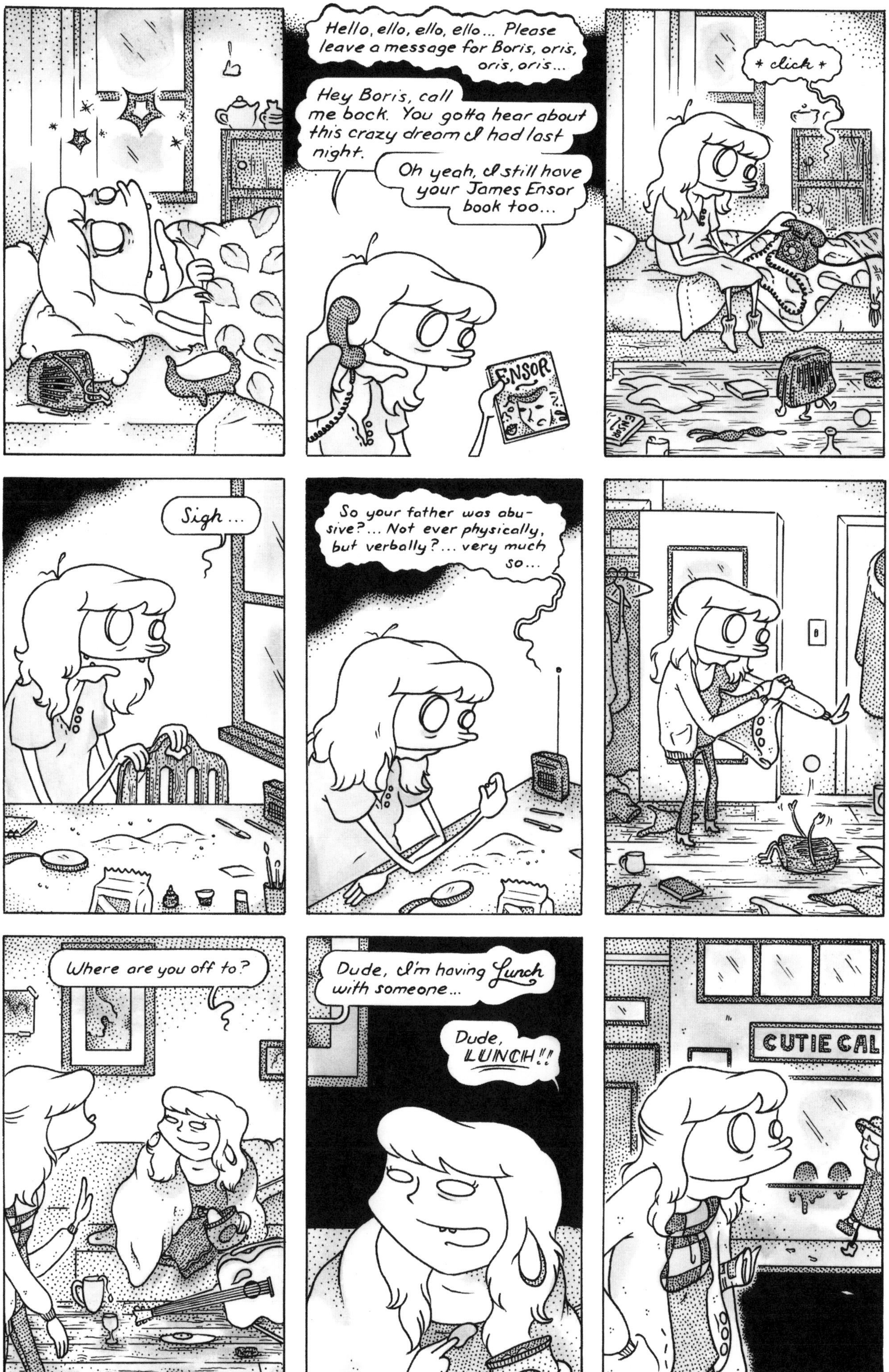
Hello, ello, ello, ello... Please leave a message for Boris, oris, oris, oris...
Hey Boris, call me back. You gotta hear about this crazy dream I had last night.
Oh yeah, I still have your James Ensor book too...
ENSOR
* click *
ENSOR
Sigh...
So your father was abusive?... Not ever physically, but verbally?... very much so...
Where are you off to?
Dude, I'm having Lunch with someone...
Dude, LUNCH!!
CUTIE CAL

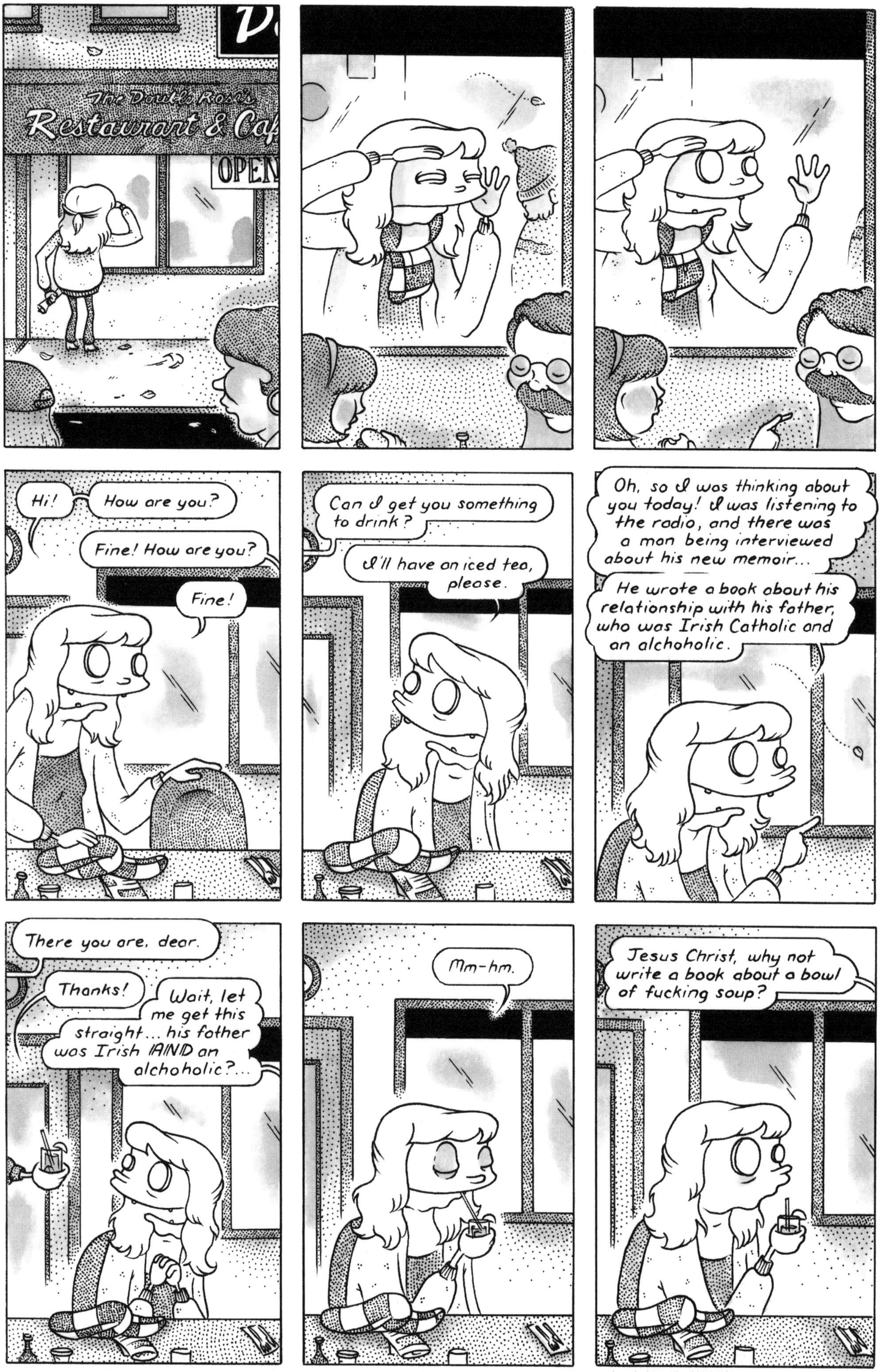
The Double Rose's
Restaurant & Caf
OPEN
Hi!
How are you?
Fine! How are you?
Fine!
Can I get you something to drink?
I'll have an iced tea, please.
Oh, so I was thinking about you today! I was listening to the radio, and there was a man being interviewed about his new memoir...
He wrote a book about his relationship with his father, who was Irish Catholic and an alchoholic.
There you are, dear.
Thanks!
Wait, let me get this straight... his father was Irish AND an alchoholic?...
Mm-hm.
Jesus Christ, why not write a book about a bowl of fucking soup?

soup

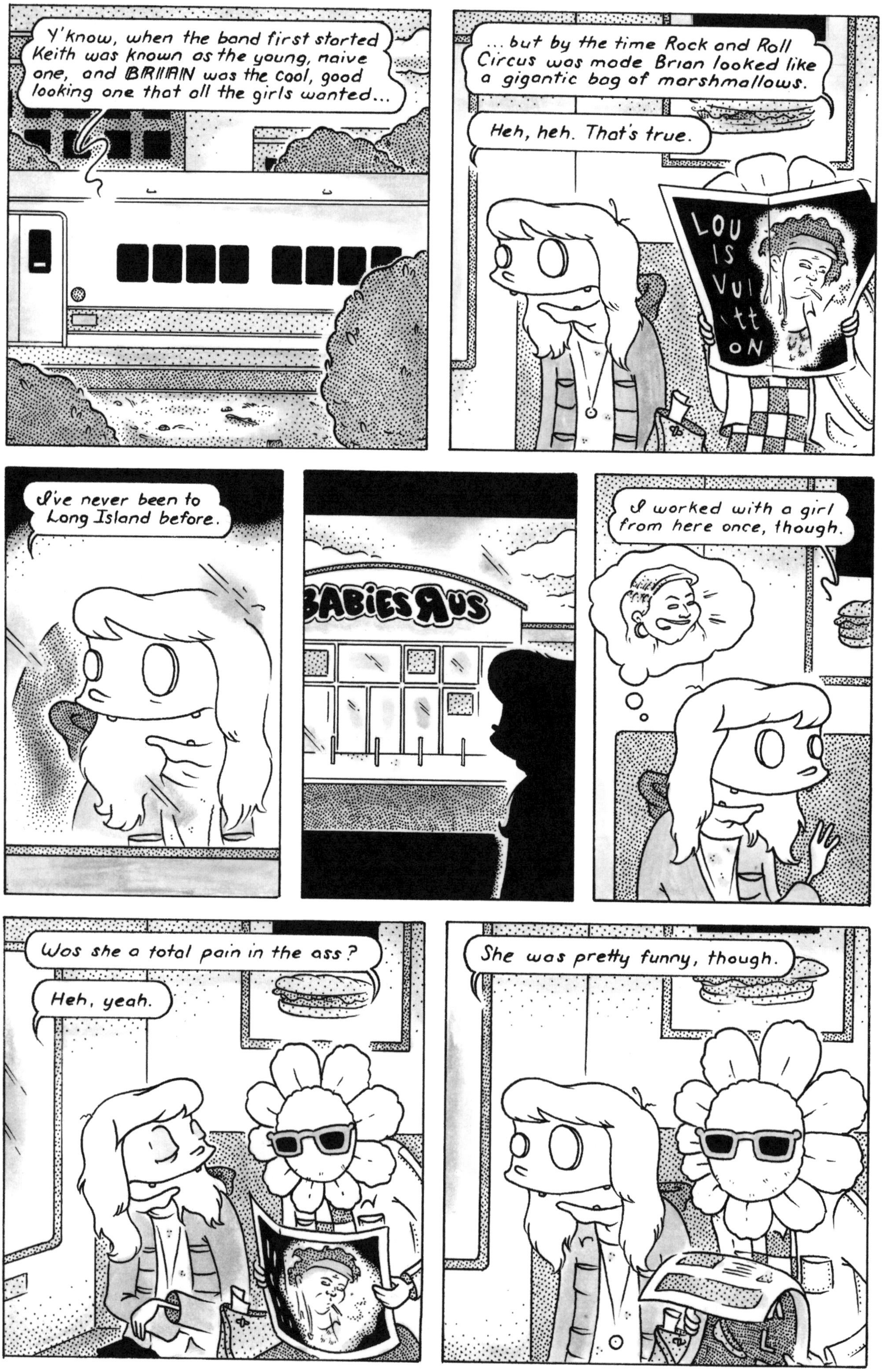
Y'know, when the band first started Keith was known as the young, naive one, and BRIAN was the cool, good looking one that all the girls wanted...
...but by the time Rock and Roll Circus was made Brian looked like a gigantic bag of marshmallows.
Heh, heh. That's true.
LOUIS VUITTON
I've never been to Long Island before.
BABIES R US
I worked with a girl from here once, though.
Was she a total pain in the ass?
Heh, yeah.
She was pretty funny, though.

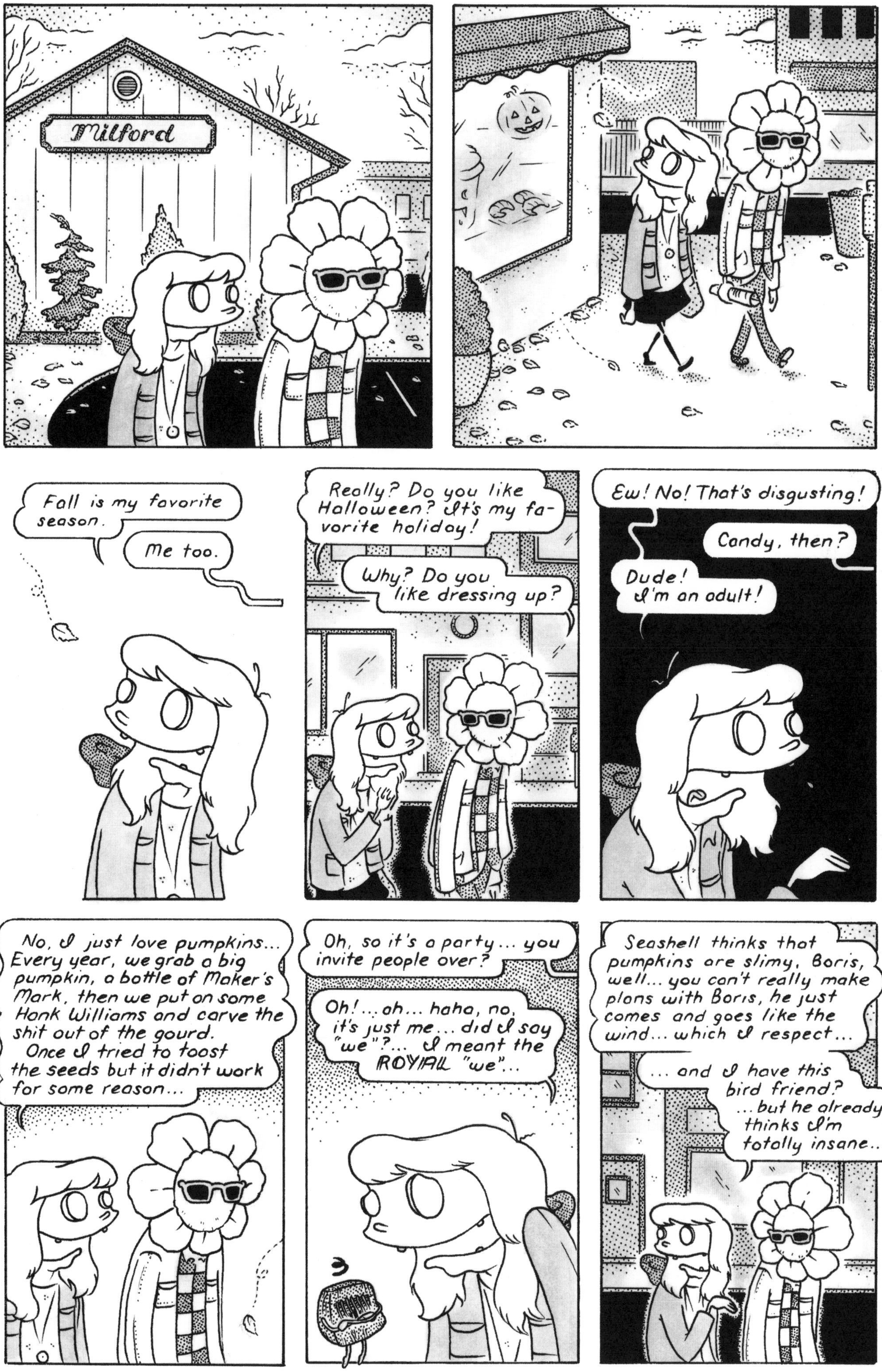
Milford
Fall is my favorite season.
Me too.
Really? Do you like Halloween? It's my favorite holiday!
Why? Do you like dressing up?
Ew! No! That's disgusting!
Candy, then?
Dude! I'm an adult!
No, I just love pumpkins... Every year, we grab a big pumpkin, a bottle of Maker's Mark, then we put on some Hank Williams and carve the shit out of the gourd. Once I tried to toast the seeds but it didn't work for some reason...
Oh, so it's a party... you invite people over?
Oh!... oh... haha, no, it's just me... did I say "we"?... I meant the ROYAL "we"...
Seashell thinks that pumpkins are slimy, Boris, well... you can't really make plans with Boris, he just comes and goes like the wind... which I respect...
... and I have this bird friend? ...but he already thinks I'm totally insane...

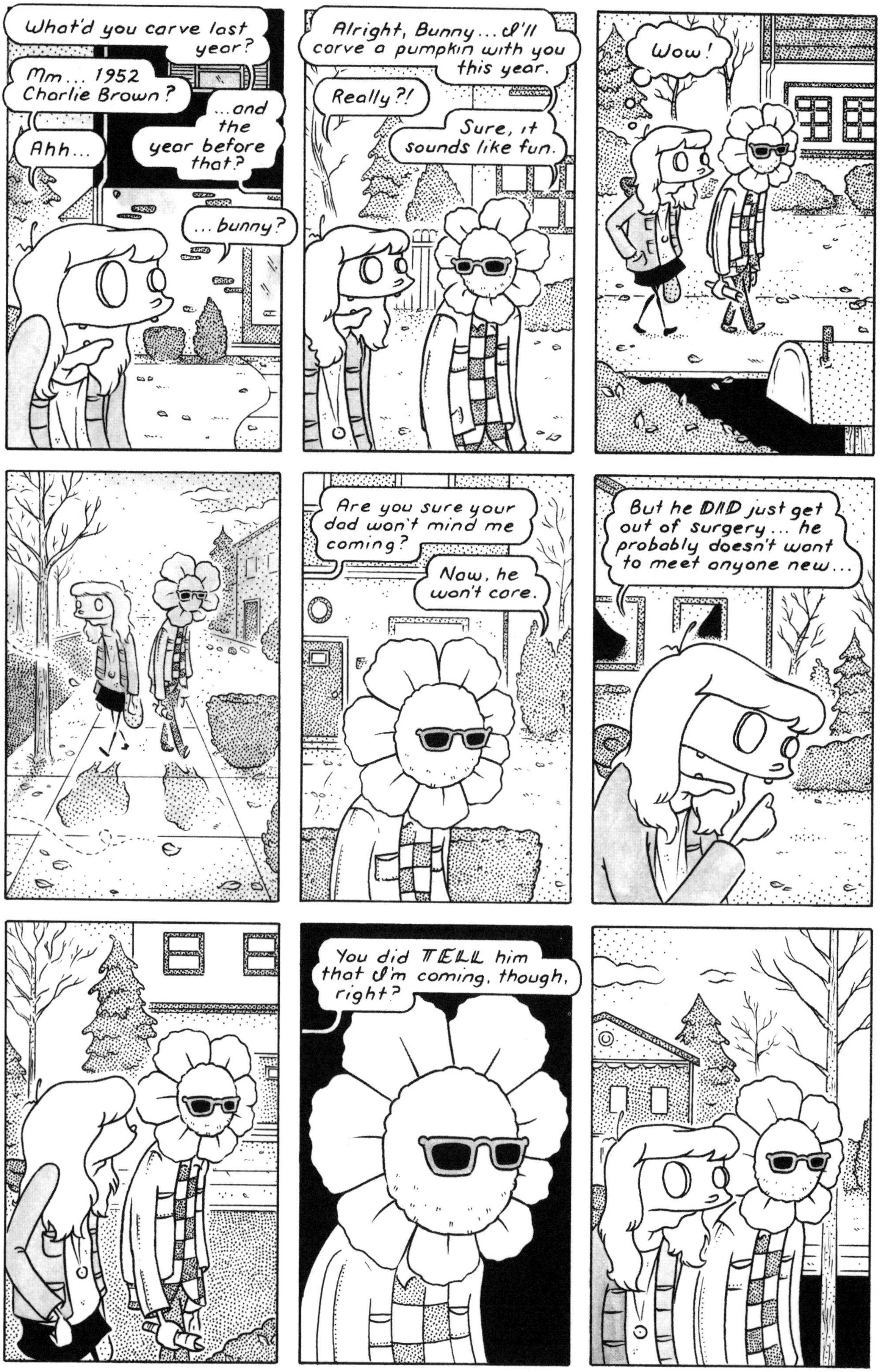
What'd you carve last year?
Mm... 1952 Charlie Brown?
Ahh...
...and the year before that?
...bunny?
Alright, Bunny... I'll carve a pumpkin with you this year.
Really?!
Sure, it sounds like fun.
Wow!
Are you sure your dad won't mind me coming?
Naw, he won't care.
But he DID just get out of surgery... he probably doesn't want to meet anyone new...
You did TELL him that I'm coming, though, right?

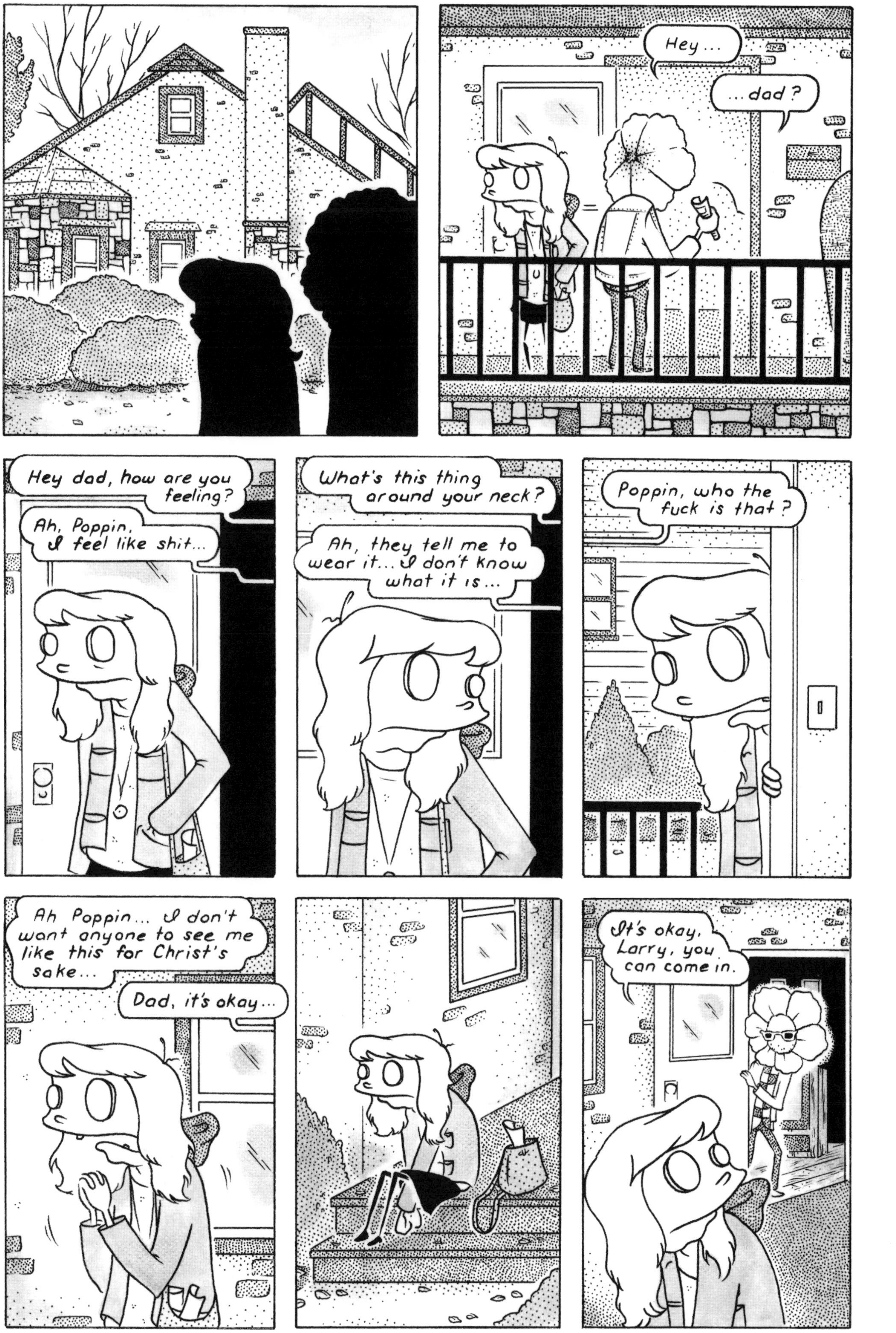
Hey...
...dad?
Hey dad, how are you feeling?
Ah, Poppin, I feel like shit...
What's this thing around your neck?
Ah, they tell me to wear it... I don't know what it is...
Poppin, who the fuck is that?
Ah Poppin... I don't want anyone to see me like this for Christ's sake...
Dad, it's okay...
It's okay, Larry, you can come in.

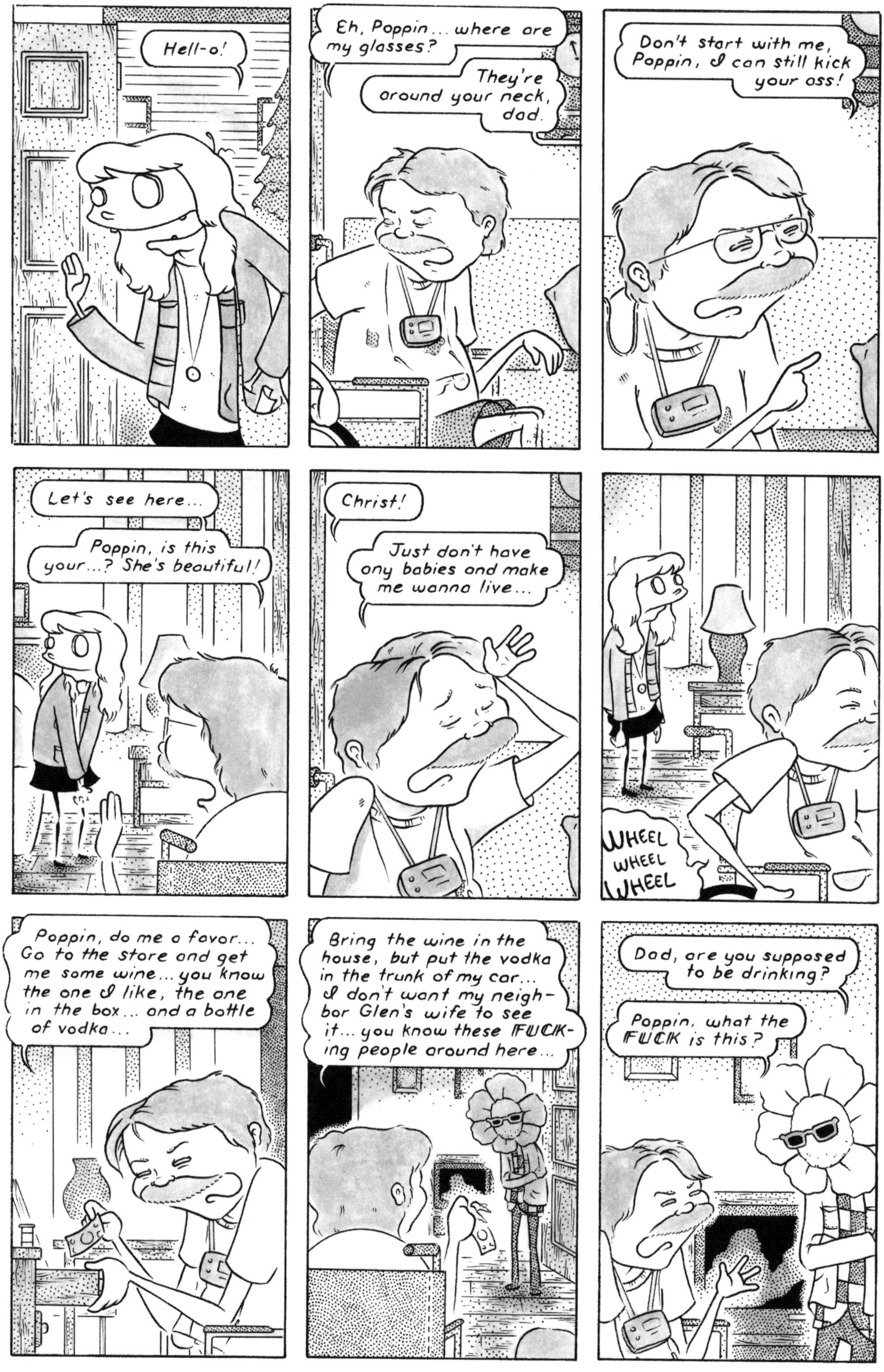

Hell-o!
Eh, Poppin... where are my glasses?
They're around your neck, dad.
Don't start with me, Poppin, I can still kick your ass!
Let's see here...
Poppin, is this your...? She's beautiful!
Christ!
Just don't have any babies and make me wanna live...
WHEEL WHEEL WHEEL
Poppin, do me a favor... Go to the store and get me some wine... you know the one I like, the one in the box... and a bottle of vodka...
Bring the wine in the house, but put the vodka in the trunk of my car... I don't want my neighbor Glen's wife to see it... you know these FUCKing people around here...
Dad, are you supposed to be drinking?
Poppin, what the FUCK is this?

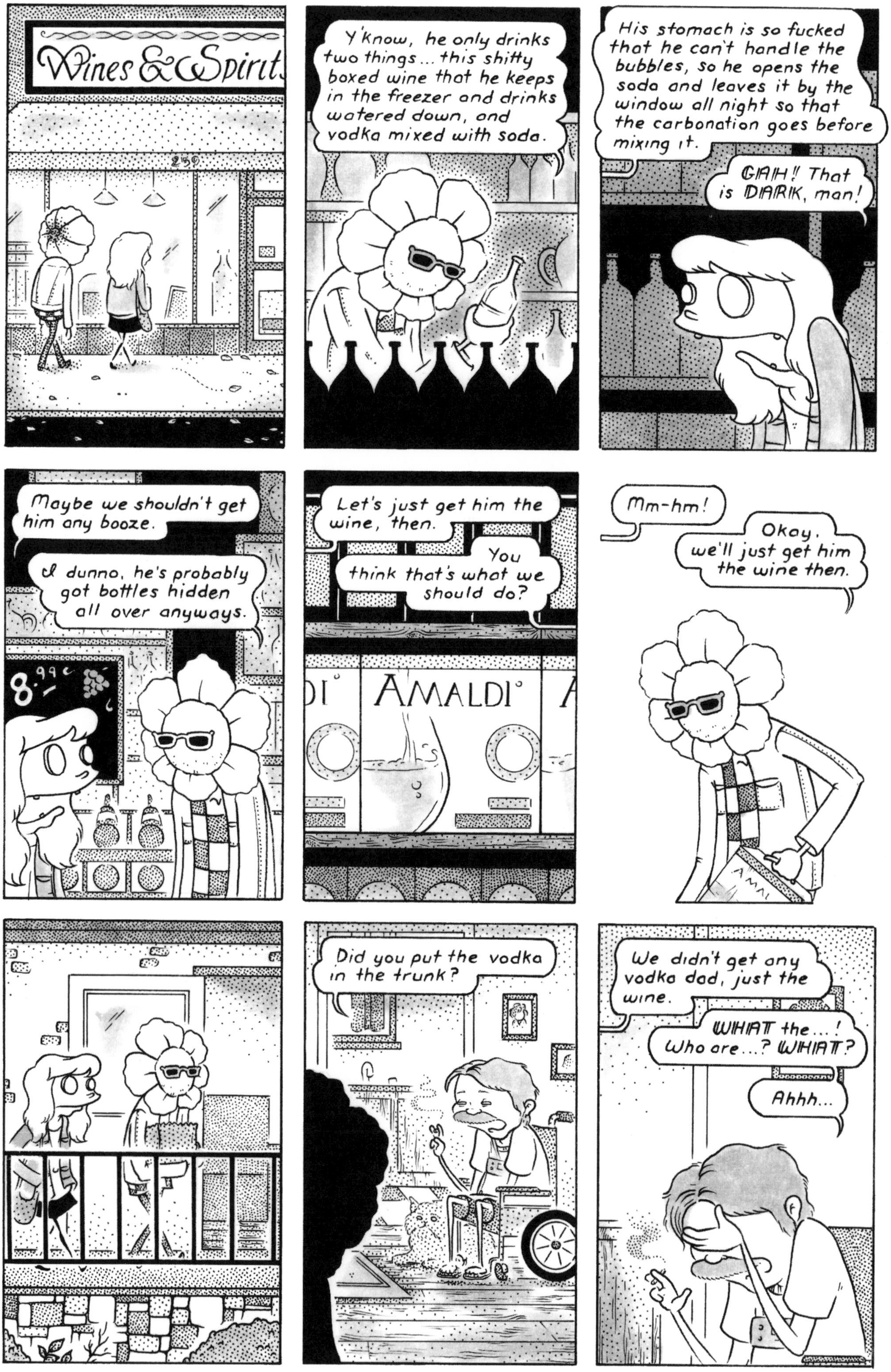
Wines & Spirits
259
Y'know, he only drinks two things... this shitty boxed wine that he keeps in the freezer and drinks watered down, and vodka mixed with soda.
His stomach is so fucked that he can't handle the bubbles, so he opens the soda and leaves it by the window all night so that the carbonation goes before mixing it.
GAH!! That is DARK, man!
Maybe we shouldn't get him any booze.
I dunno, he's probably got bottles hidden all over anyways.
8.99¢
Let's just get him the wine, then.
You think that's what we should do?
AMALDI
Mm-hm!
Okay, we'll just get him the wine then.
Did you put the vodka in the trunk?
We didn't get any vodka dad, just the wine.
WHAT the...! Who are...? WHAT?
Ahhh...

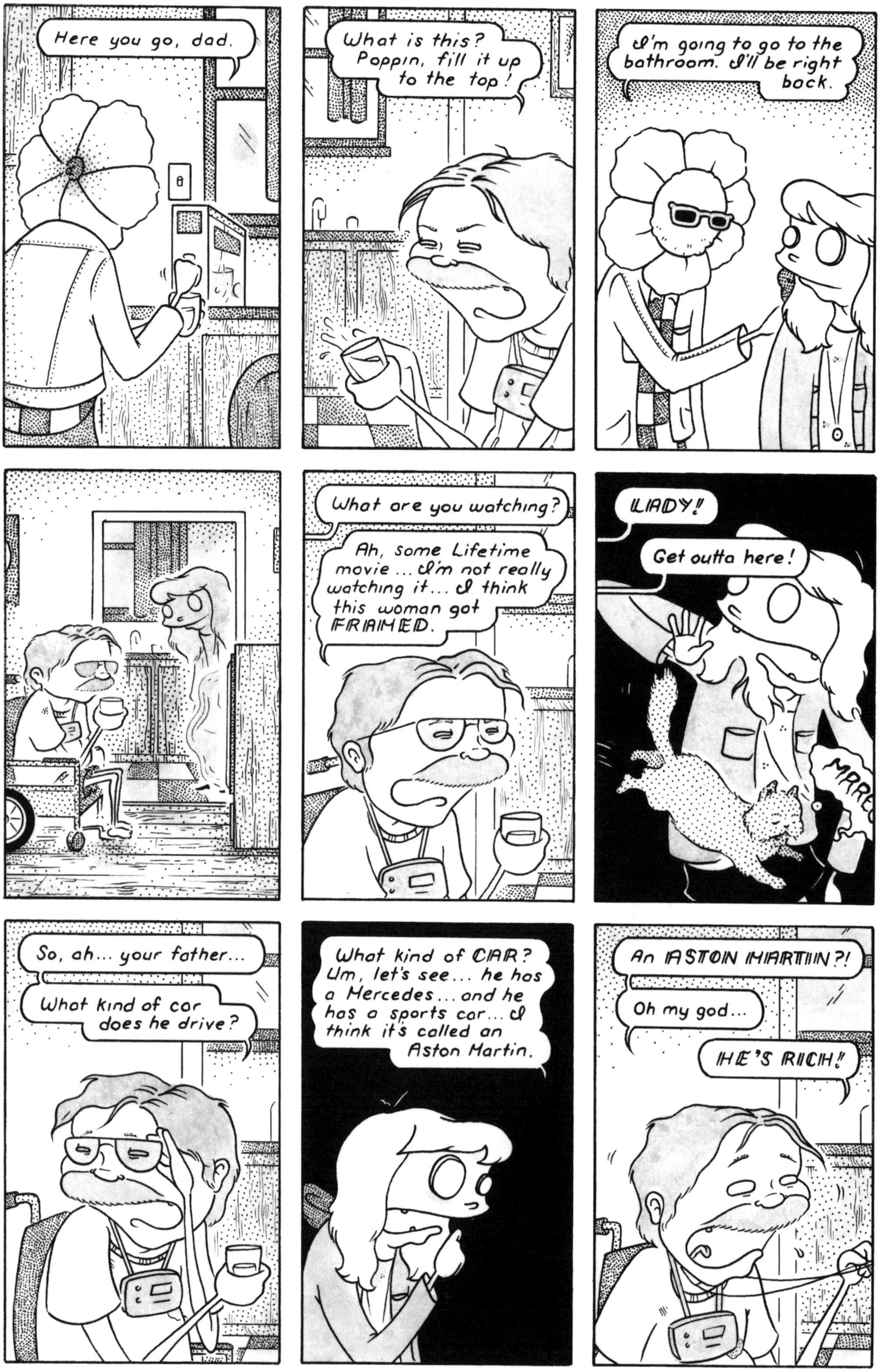
Here you go, dad.
What is this? Poppin, fill it up to the top!
I'm going to go to the bathroom. I'll be right back.
What are you watching?
Ah, some Lifetime movie ... I'm not really watching it... I think this woman got FRAMED.
LADY!
Get outta here!
MRRR
So, ah... your father...
What kind of car does he drive?
What kind of CAR? Um, let's see... he has a Mercedes... and he has a sports car... I think it's called an Aston Martin.
An ASTON MARTIN?!
Oh my god...
HE'S RICH!

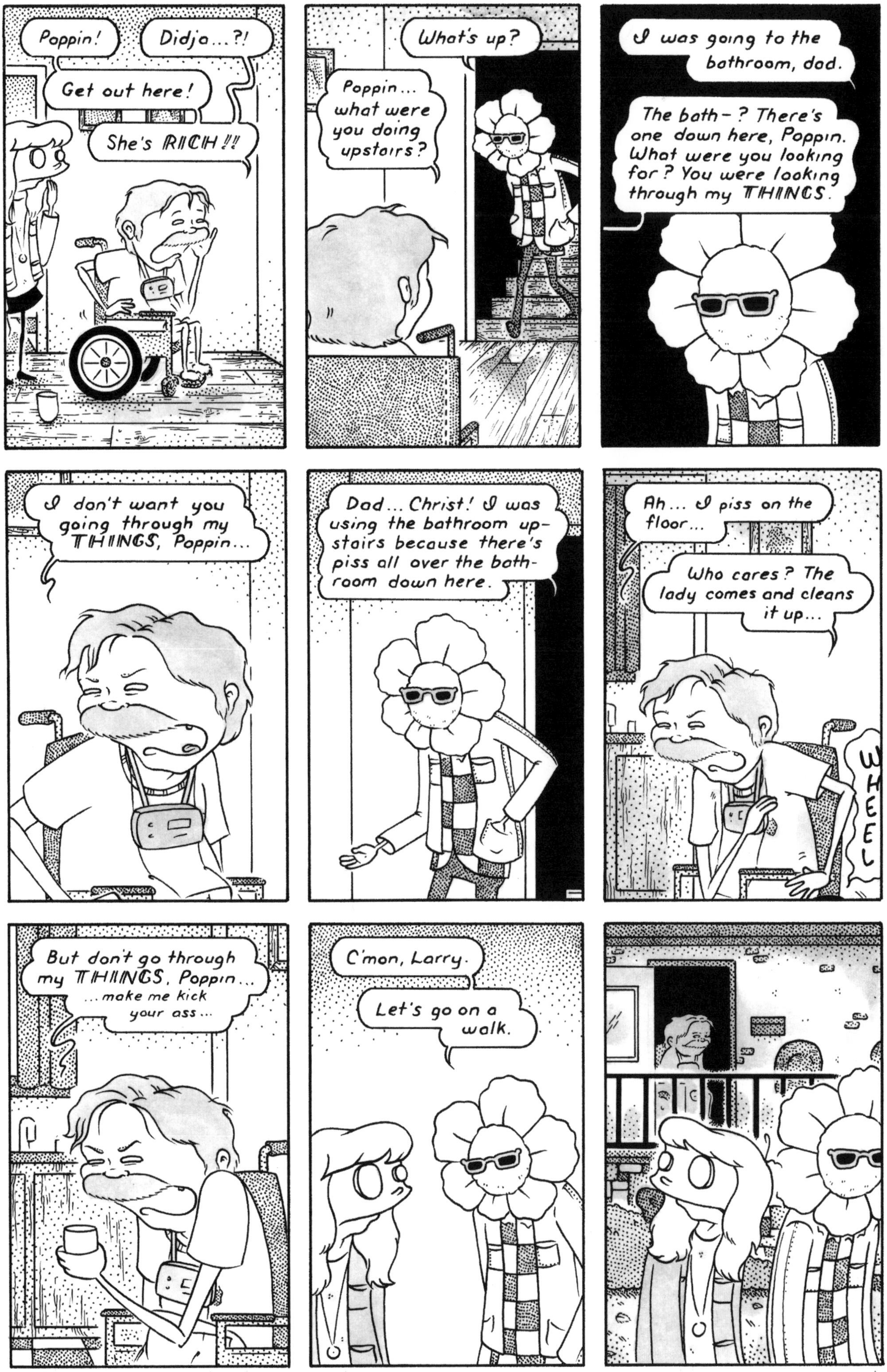
Poppin!
Didja...?!
Get out here!
She's RICH!!!
What's up?
Poppin... what were you doing upstairs?
I was going to the bathroom, dad.
The bath-? There's one down here, Poppin. What were you looking for? You were looking through my THINGS.
I don't want you going through my THINGS, Poppin...
Dad... Christ! I was using the bathroom upstairs because there's piss all over the bathroom down here.
Ah... I piss on the floor...
Who cares? The lady comes and cleans it up...
WHEEL
But don't go through my THINGS, Poppin...
...make me kick your ass...
C'mon, Larry.
Let's go on a walk.

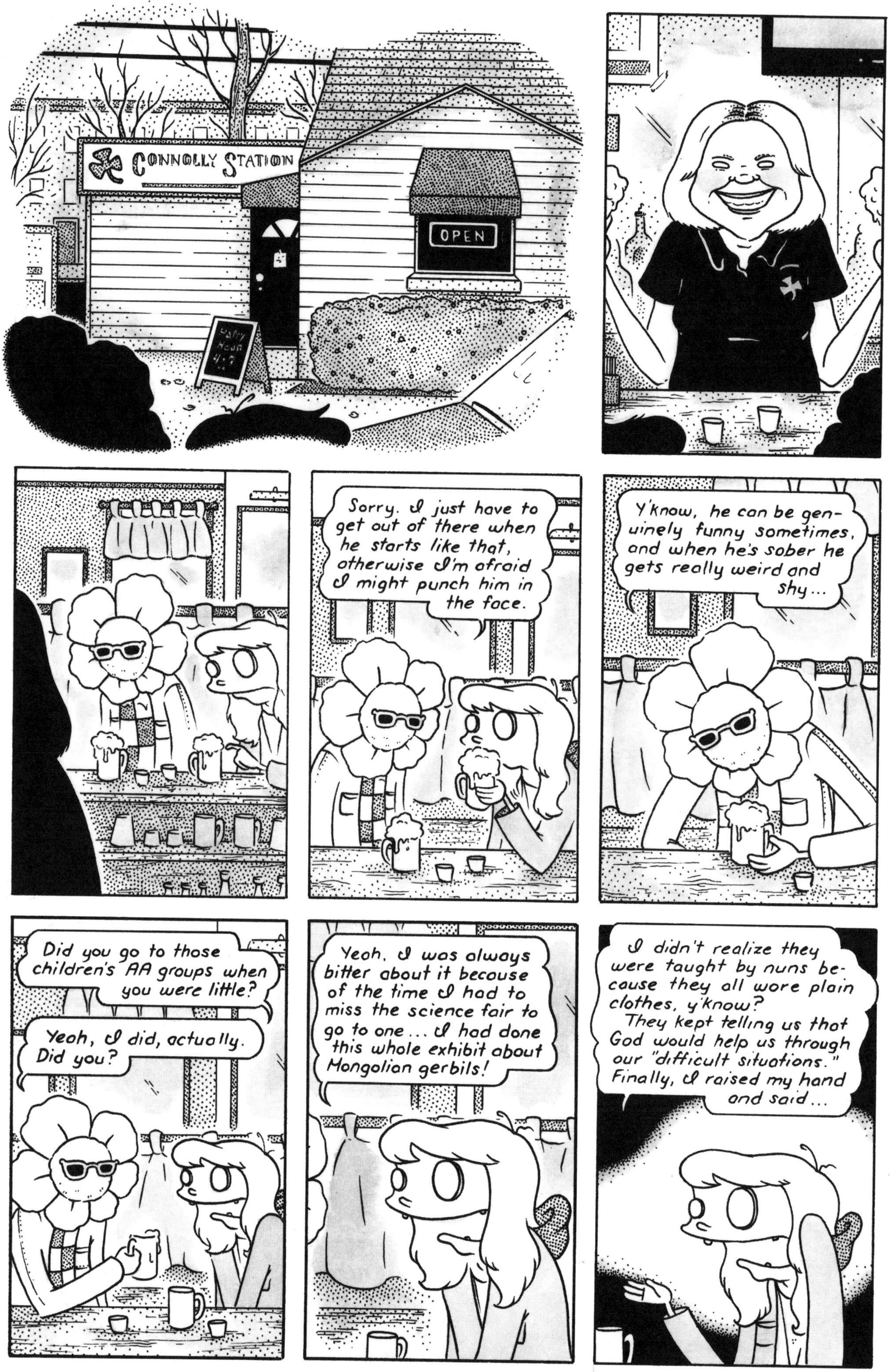
CONNOLLY STATION
OPEN
Sorry. I just have to get out of there when he starts like that, otherwise I'm afraid I might punch him in the face.
Y'know, he can be genuinely funny sometimes, and when he's sober he gets really weird and shy...
Did you go to those children's AA groups when you were little?
Yeah, I did, actually. Did you?
Yeah. I was always bitter about it because of the time I had to miss the science fair to go to one... I had done this whole exhibit about Mongolian gerbils!
I didn't realize they were taught by nuns because they all wore plain clothes, y'know? They kept telling us that God would help us through our "difficult situations." Finally, I raised my hand and said...

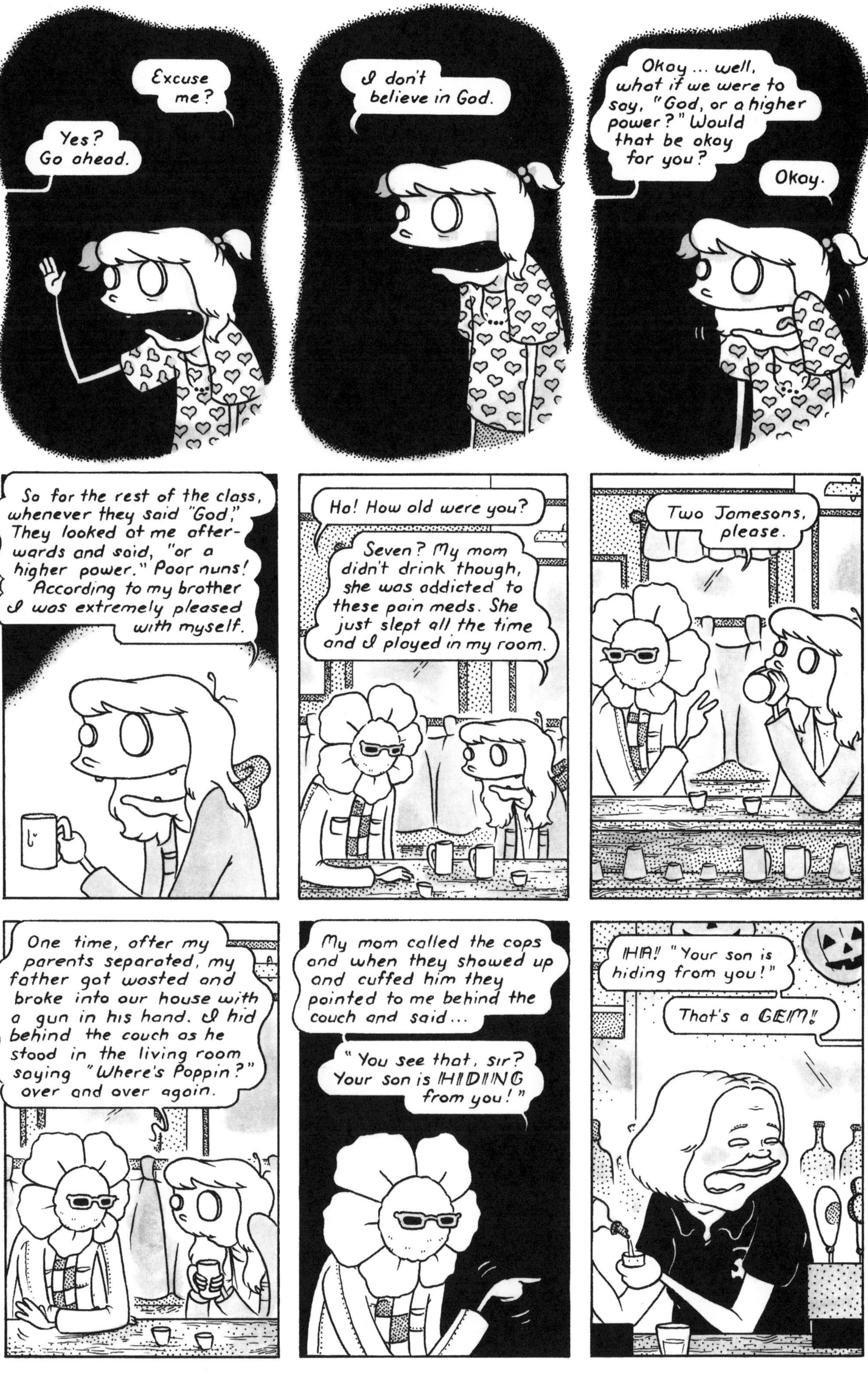
Excuse me?
Yes? Go ahead.
I don't believe in God.
Okay ... well, what if we were to say, "God, or a higher power?" Would that be okay for you?
Okay.
So for the rest of the class, whenever they said "God," They looked at me afterwards and said, "or a higher power." Poor nuns! According to my brother I was extremely pleased with myself.
Ha! How old were you?
Seven? My mom didn't drink though, she was addicted to these pain meds. She just slept all the time and I played in my room.
Two Jamesons, please.
One time, after my parents separated, my father got wasted and broke into our house with a gun in his hand. I hid behind the couch as he stood in the living room saying "Where's Poppin?" over and over again.
My mom called the cops and when they showed up and cuffed him they pointed to me behind the couch and said...
"You see that, sir? Your son is HIDING from you!"
HA! "Your son is hiding from you!"
That's a GEM!

These internet jukeboxes are weird.

Oh my god! See if they have The MOVE!!!

The Move! I can't believe that's your favorite band.

It's a matter of PRINCIPLE. The Move had perfect craftmanship, were totally hilarious, and they were completely underrated!

THUD!

WOAH!!

KNOCK KNOCK KNOCK

JIMBO!!

He locked us out.

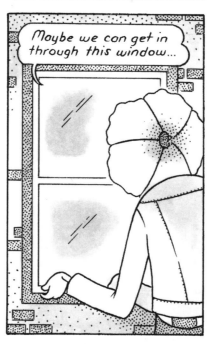

Maybe we can get in through this window...

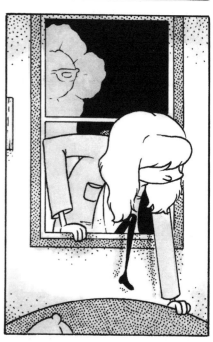

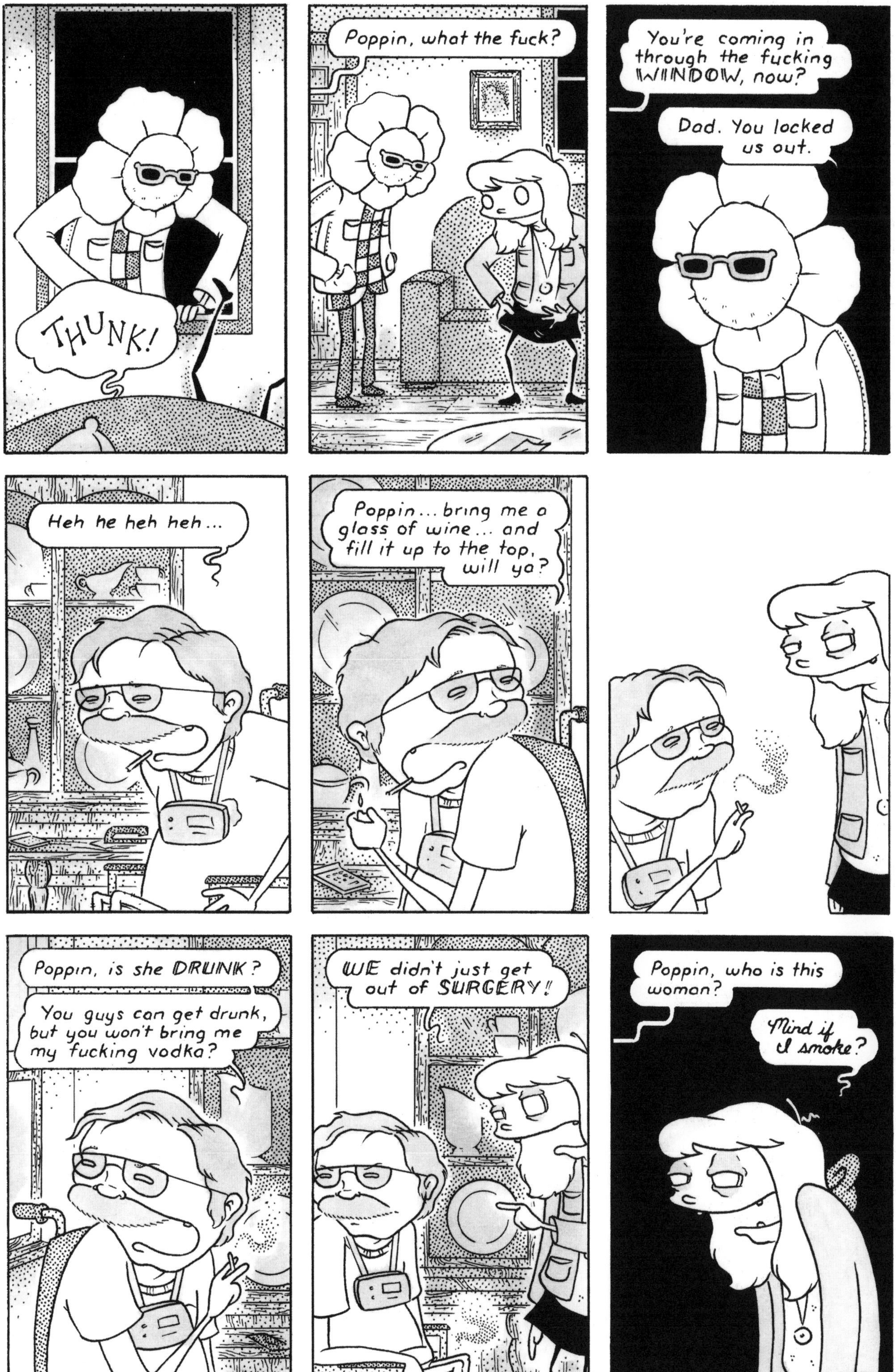
THUNK!
Poppin, what the fuck?
You're coming in through the fucking WINDOW, now?
Dad. You locked us out.
Heh he heh heh...
Poppin... bring me a glass of wine... and fill it up to the top, will ya?
Poppin, is she DRUNK?
You guys can get drunk, but you won't bring me my fucking vodka?
WE didn't just get out of SURGERY!
Poppin, who is this woman?
Mind if I smoke?

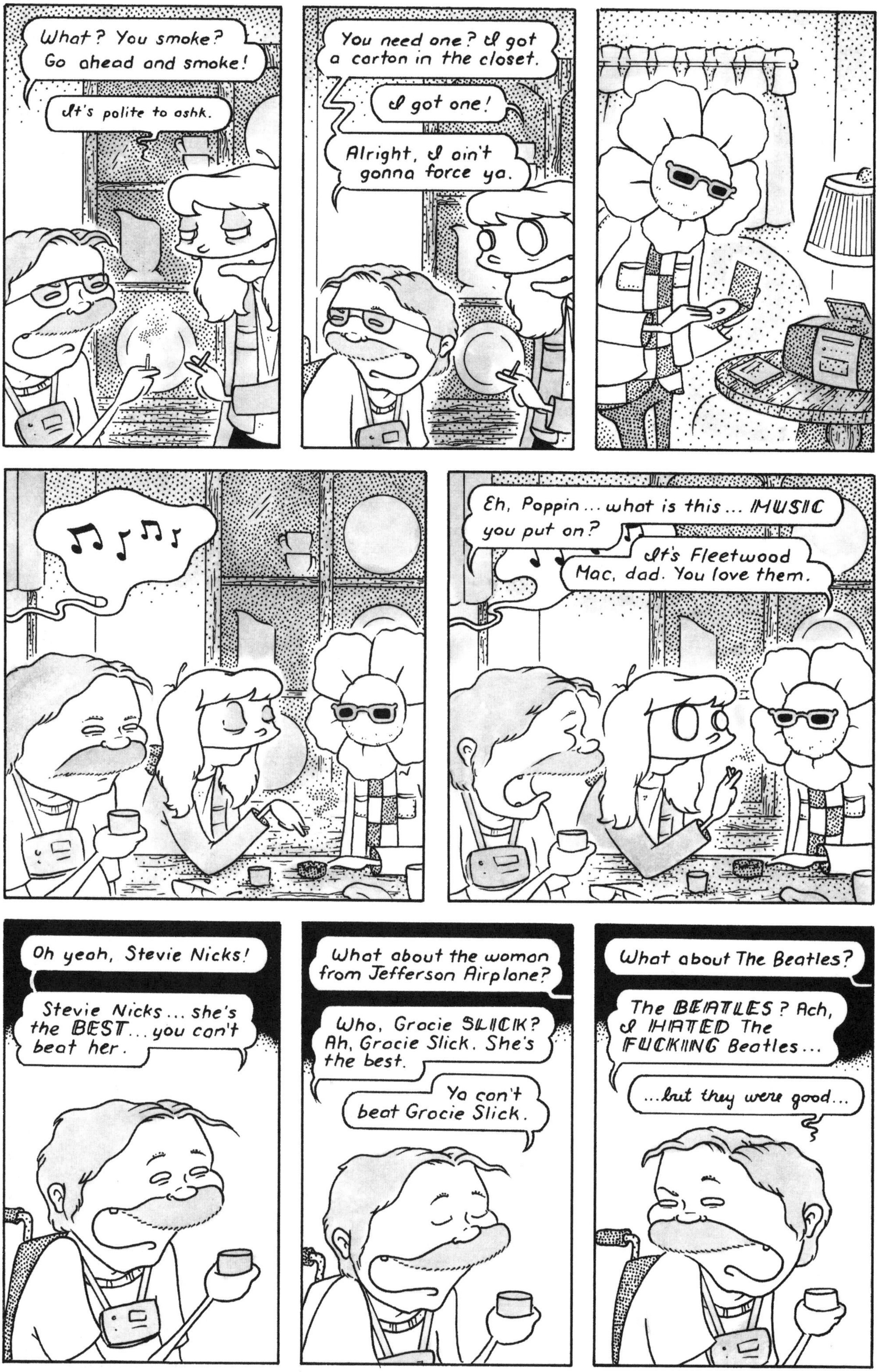

What? You smoke? Go ahead and smoke!
It's polite to ashk.
You need one? I got a carton in the closet.
I got one!
Alright, I ain't gonna force ya.
Eh, Poppin... what is this... MUSIC you put on?
It's Fleetwood Mac, dad. You love them.
Oh yeah, Stevie Nicks!
Stevie Nicks... she's the BEST... you can't beat her.
What about the woman from Jefferson Airplane?
Who, Gracie SLICK? Ah, Gracie Slick. She's the best.
Ya can't beat Gracie Slick.
What about The Beatles?
The BEATLES? Ach, I HATED The FUCKING Beatles...
...but they were good...

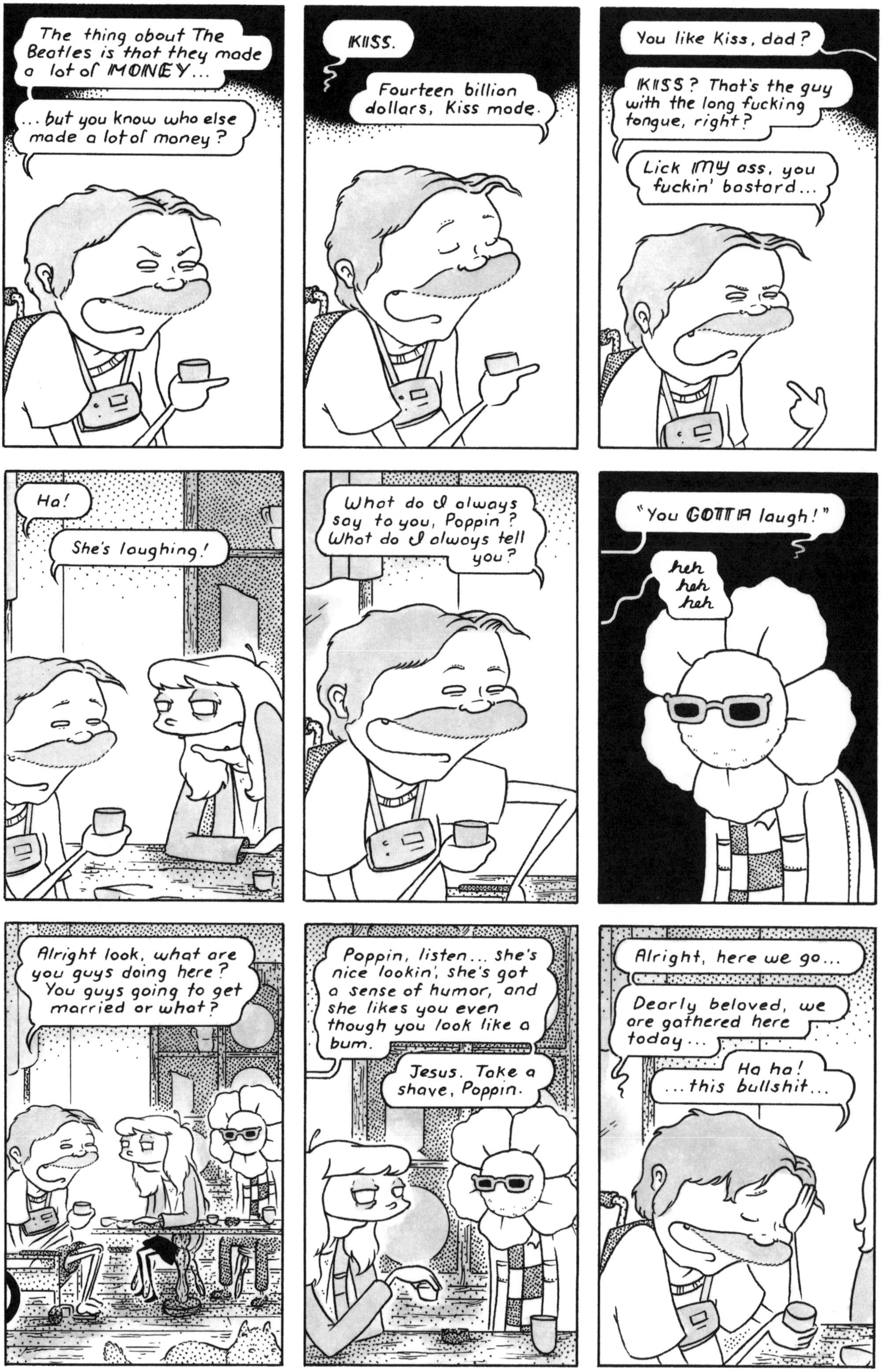
The thing about The Beatles is that they made a lot of MONEY...
...but you know who else made a lot of money?
KISS.
Fourteen billion dollars, Kiss mode.
You like Kiss, dad?
KISS? That's the guy with the long fucking tongue, right?
Lick MY ass, you fuckin' bastard...
Ha!
She's laughing!
What do I always say to you, Poppin? What do I always tell you?
"You GOTTA laugh!"
heh heh heh
Alright look, what are you guys doing here? You guys going to get married or what?
Poppin, listen... she's nice lookin', she's got a sense of humor, and she likes you even though you look like a bum.
Jesus. Take a shave, Poppin.
Alright, here we go...
Dearly beloved, we are gathered here today...
Ha ha! ...this bullshit...

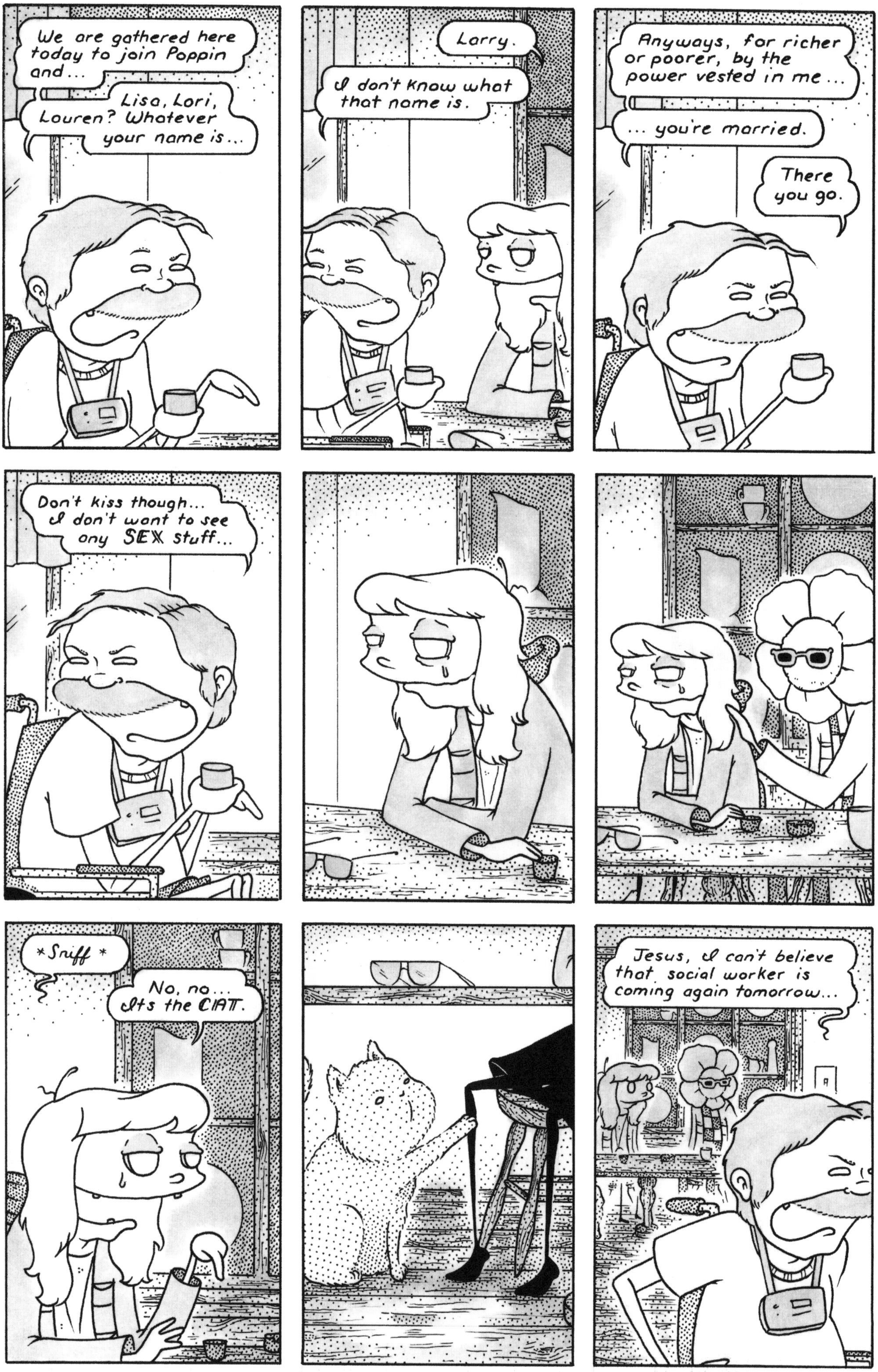
We are gathered here today to join Poppin and...
Lisa, Lori, Louren? Whatever your name is...
Larry.
I don't know what that name is.
Anyways, for richer or poorer, by the power vested in me...
... you're married.
There you go.
Don't kiss though... I don't want to see any SEX stuff...
Sniff
No, no... Its the CAT.
Jesus, I can't believe that social worker is coming again tomorrow...

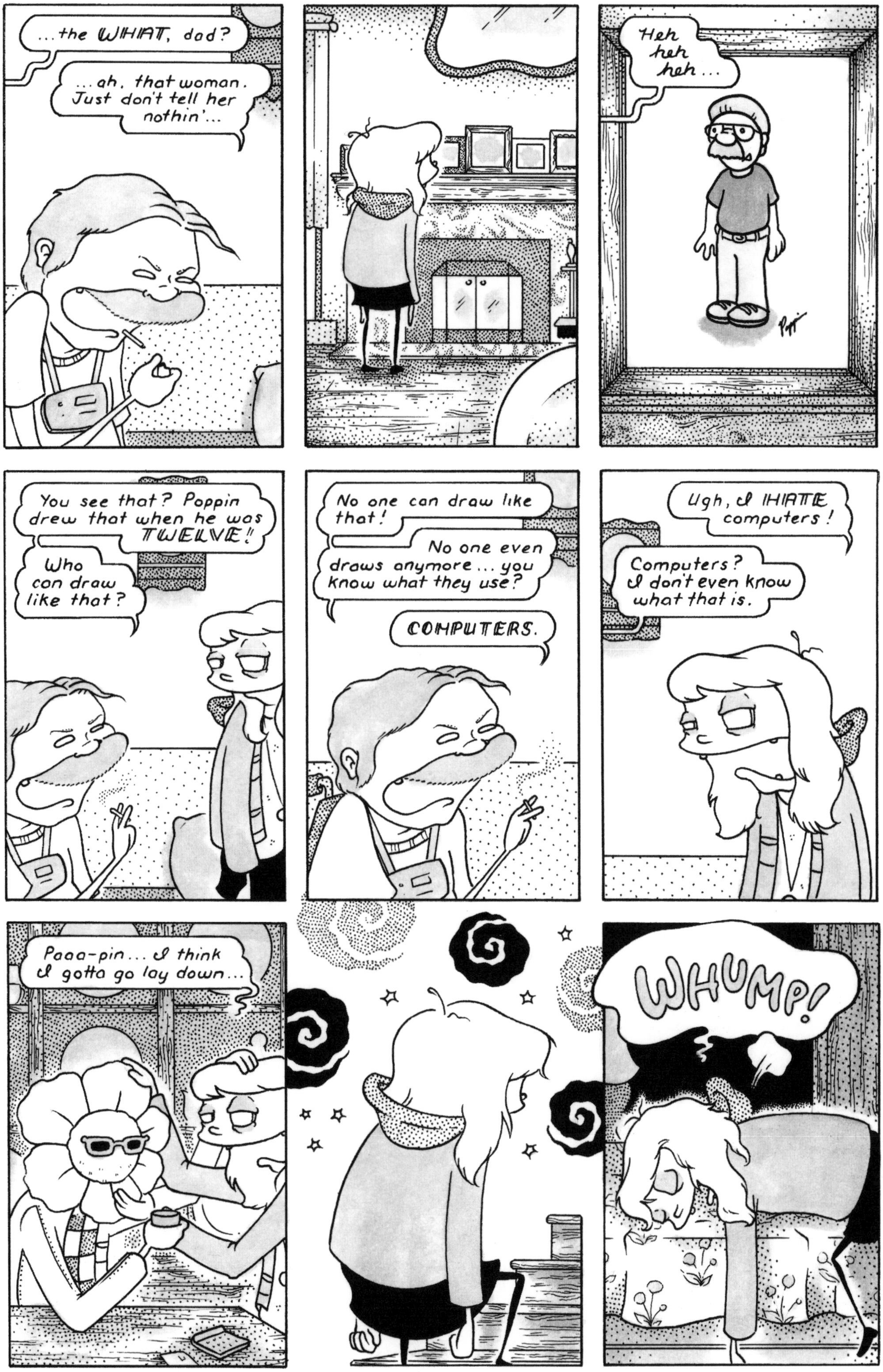
...the WHAT, dad?
...ah, that woman. Just don't tell her nothin'...
Heh heh heh...
Poppin
You see that? Poppin drew that when he was TWELVE!
Who can draw like that?
No one can draw like that!
No one even draws anymore... you know what they use?
COMPUTERS.
Ugh, I HATE computers!
Computers? I don't even know what that is.
Paaa-pin... I think I gotta go lay down...
WHUMP!

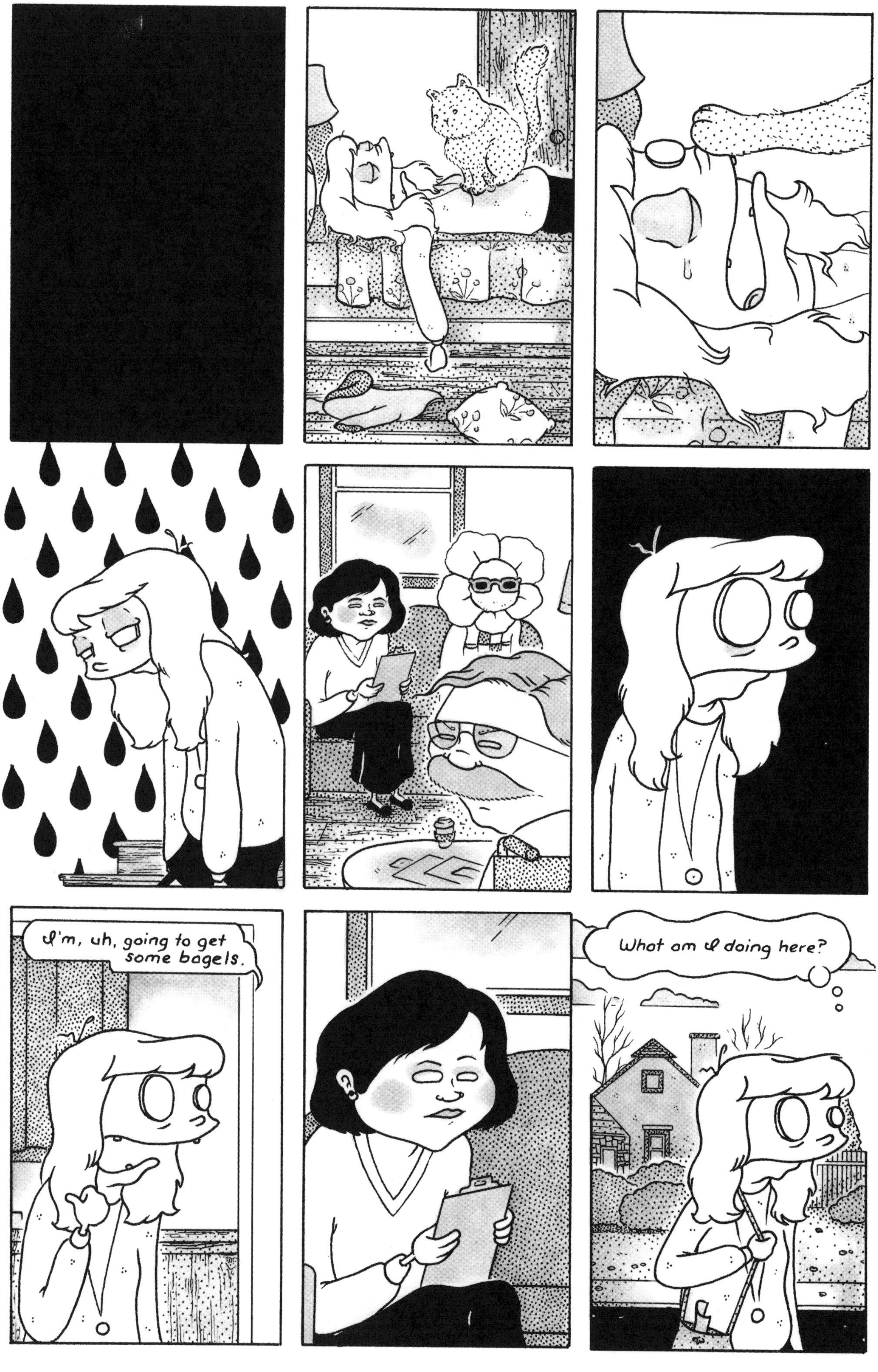
I'm, uh, going to get some bagels.
What am I doing here?

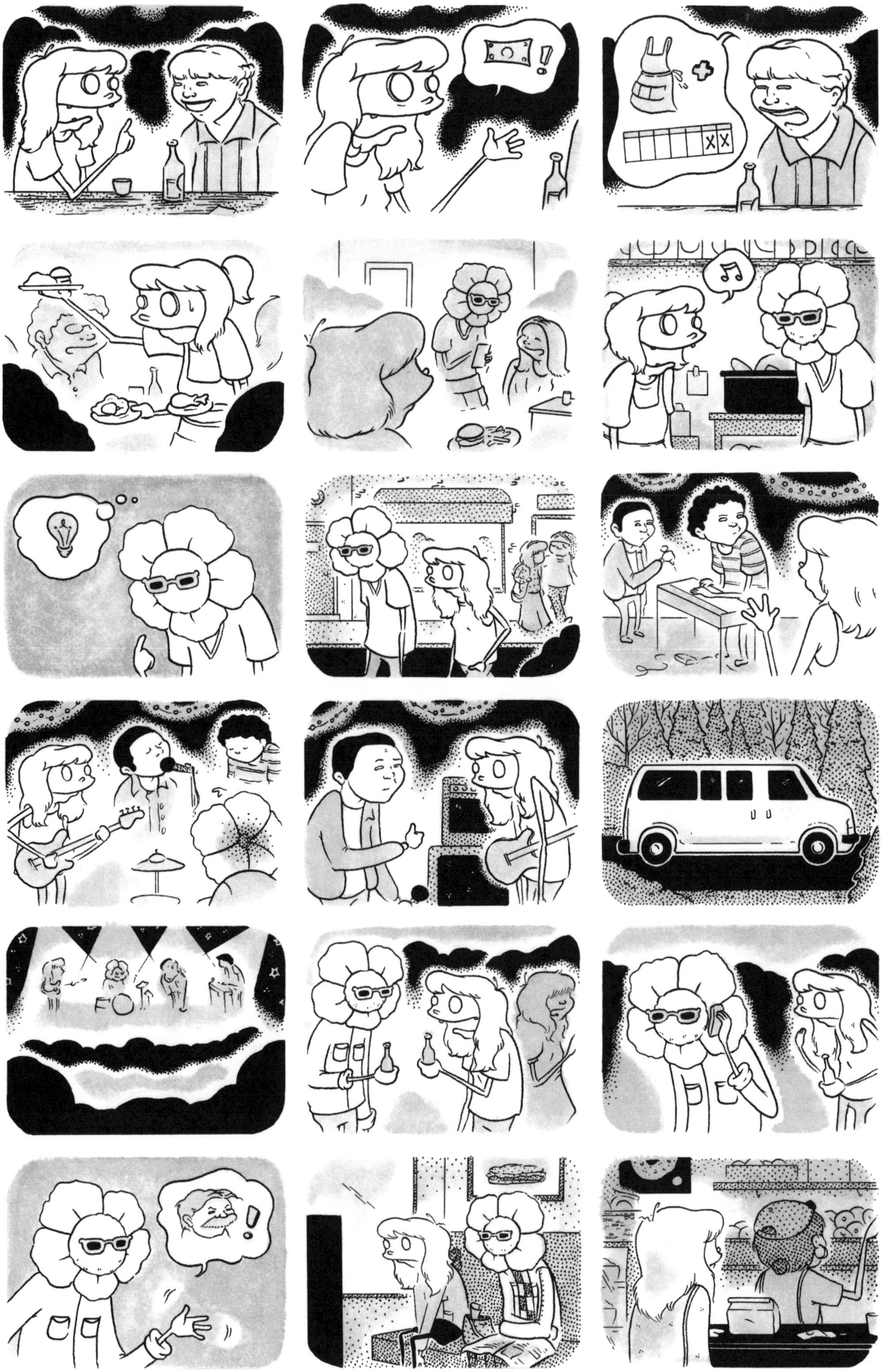

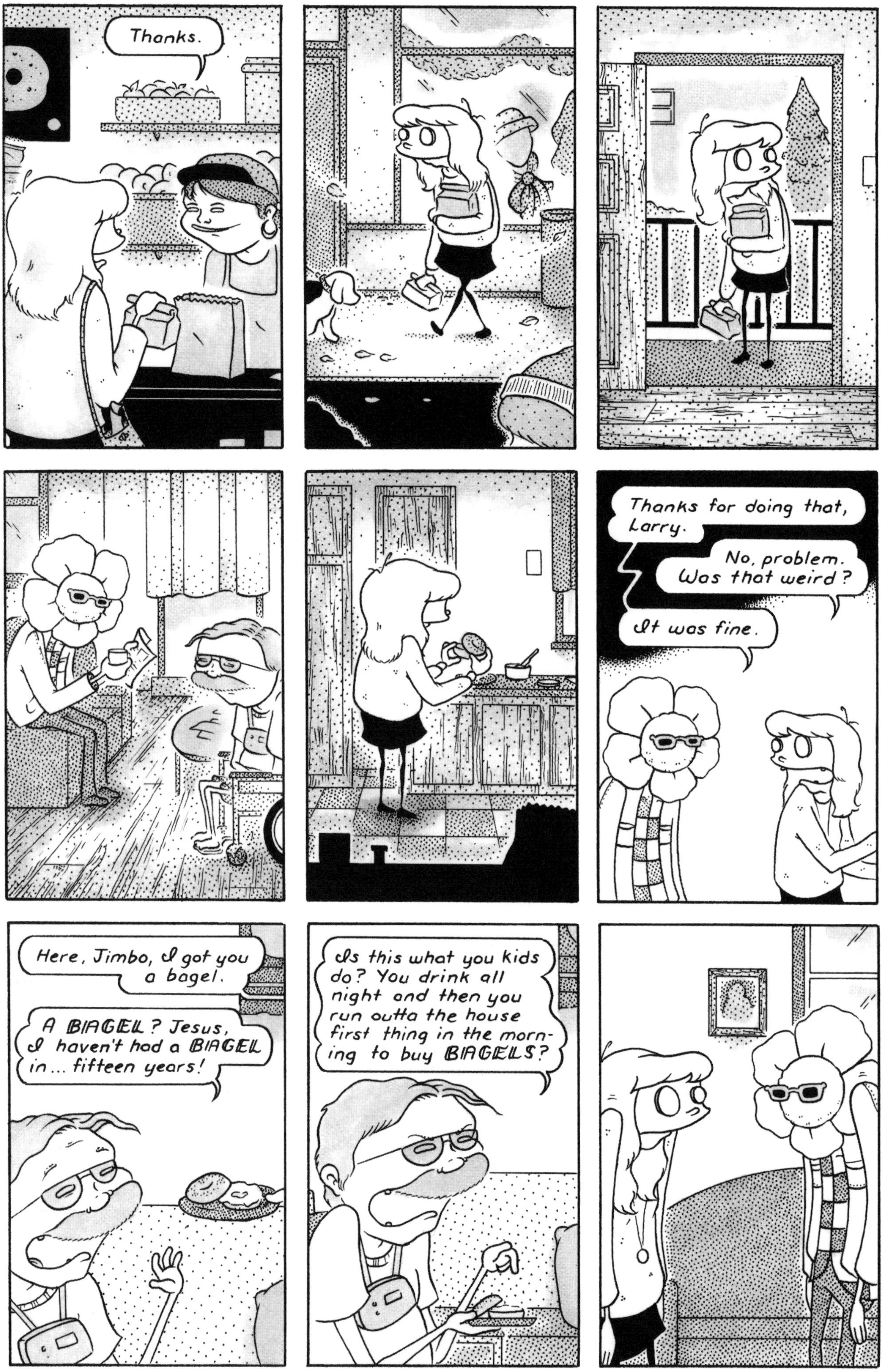
Thanks.
Thanks for doing that, Larry.
No, problem. Was that weird?
It was fine.
Here, Jimbo, I got you a bagel.
A BAGEL? Jesus, I haven't had a BAGEL in... fifteen years!
Is this what you kids do? You drink all night and then you run outta the house first thing in the morning to buy BAGELS?

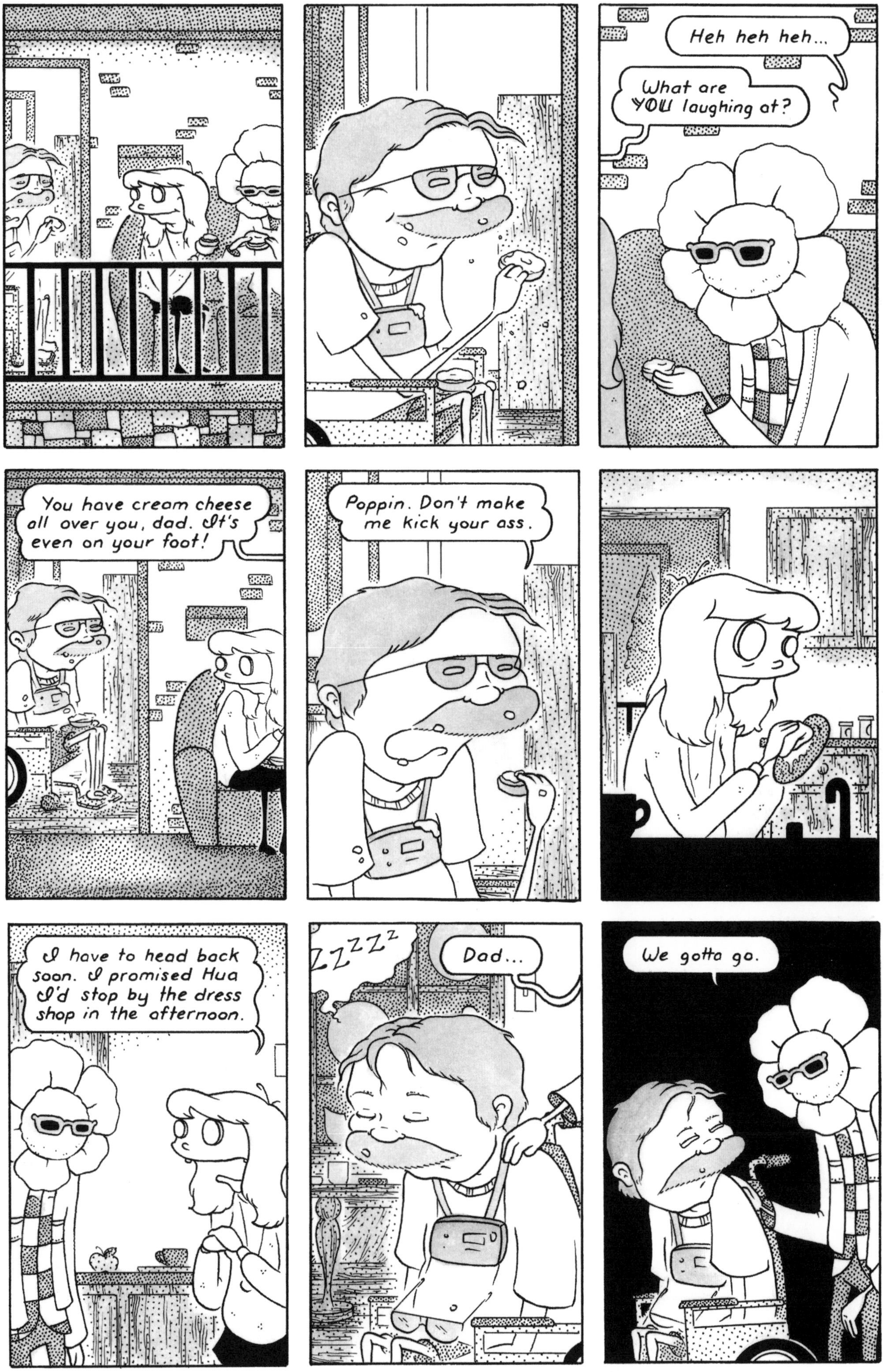
Heh heh heh...
What are YOU laughing at?
You have cream cheese all over you, dad. It's even on your foot!
Poppin. Don't make me kick your ass.
I have to head back soon. I promised Hua I'd stop by the dress shop in the afternoon.
ZZZZZ
Dad...
We gotta go.

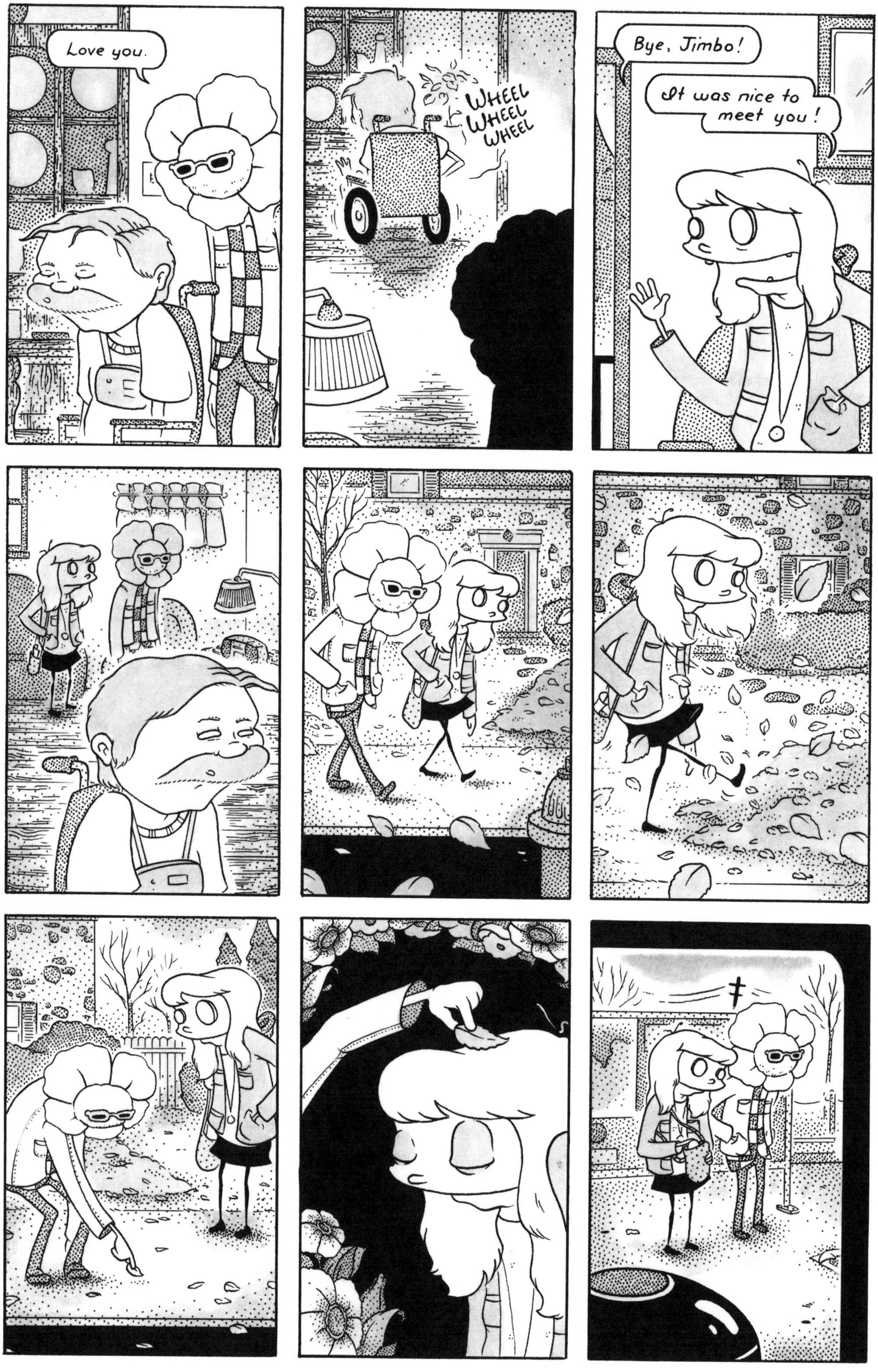
Love you.
WHEEL
WHEEL
WHEEL
Bye, Jimbo!
It was nice to meet you!

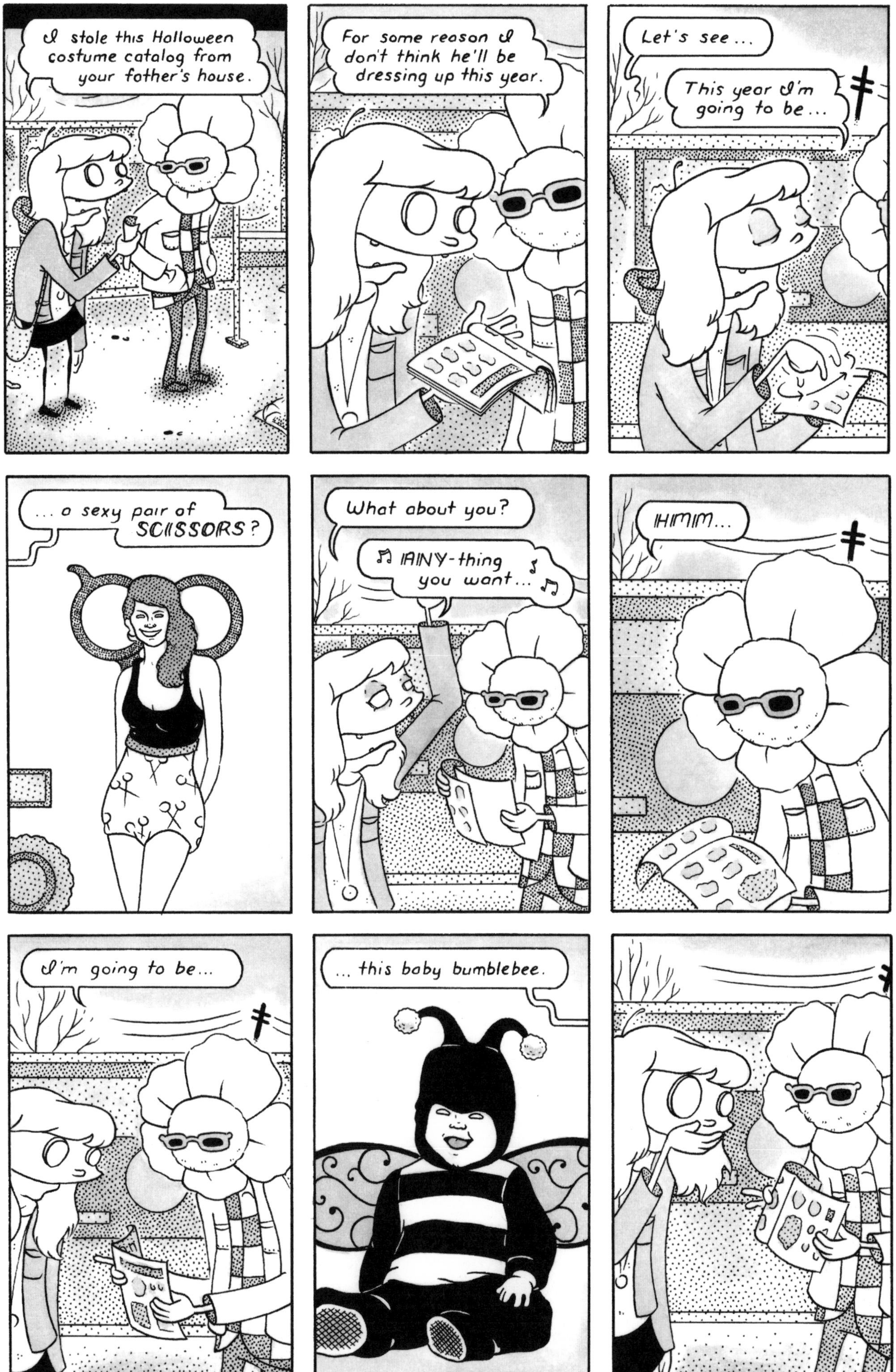
I stole this Halloween costume catalog from your father's house.
For some reason I don't think he'll be dressing up this year.
Let's see...
This year I'm going to be...
... a sexy pair of SCISSORS?
What about you?
ANY-thing you want...
HMM...
I'm going to be...
... this baby bumblebee.

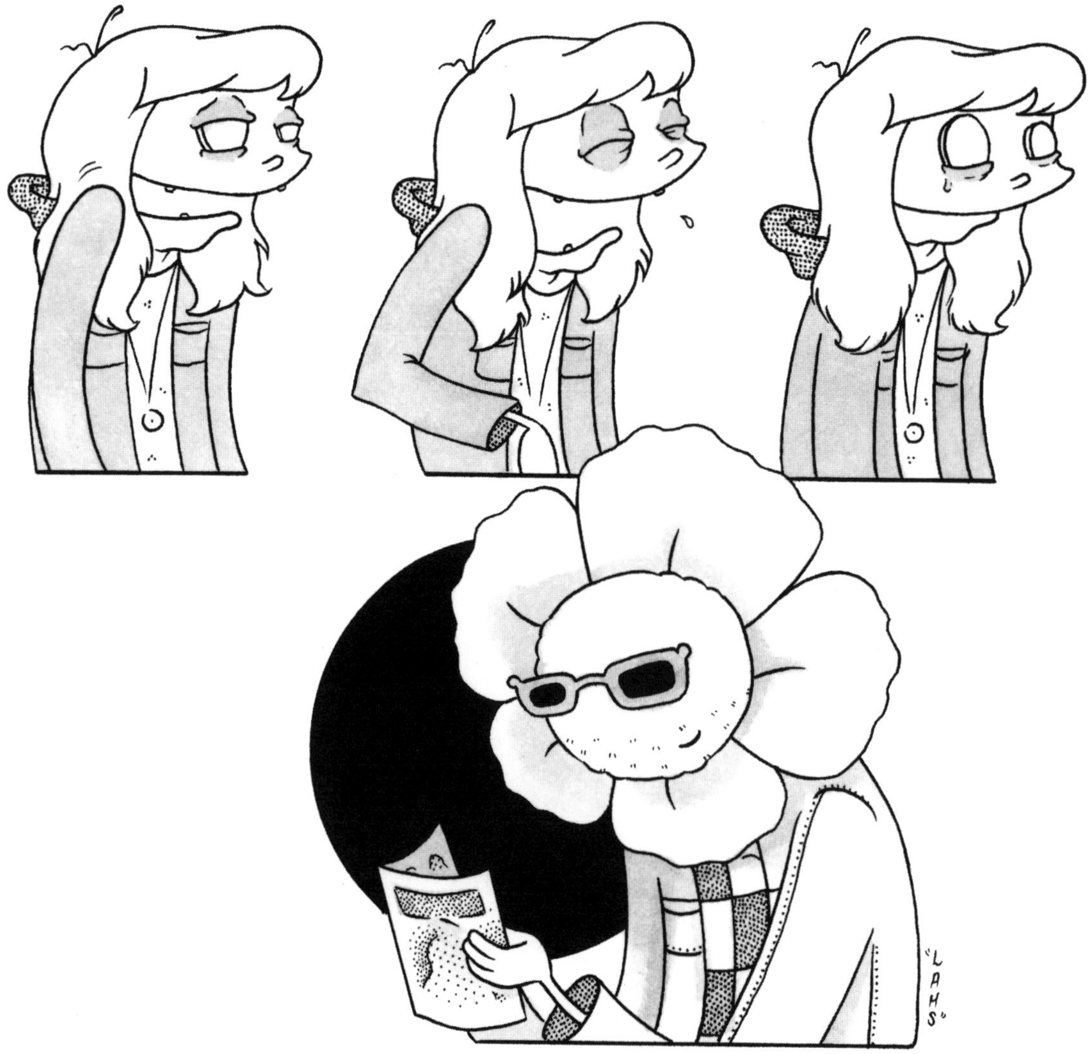
"LAHS"

Who are You?

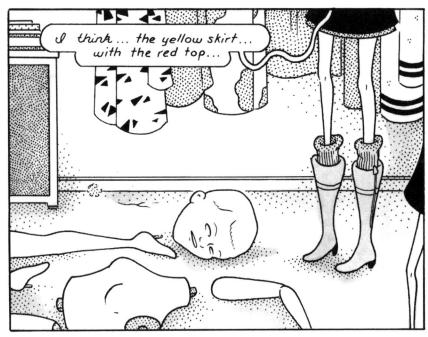

I think ... the yellow skirt... with the red top...

It's spring-y, it's bright. People will notice the colors when they walk by.

Thanks, Yael.

I'm no good at this.

What, you aren't selling shit?

Dude, I'm not selling SHIT.

Most of these clothes? They're defective, some even have holes in them, so if I DO sell something I have to give a big discount.

The worst part is that I've been working here for two years, and Hua won't raise my hourly rate, only my commission, which would be fine if I could manage to actually SELL something...

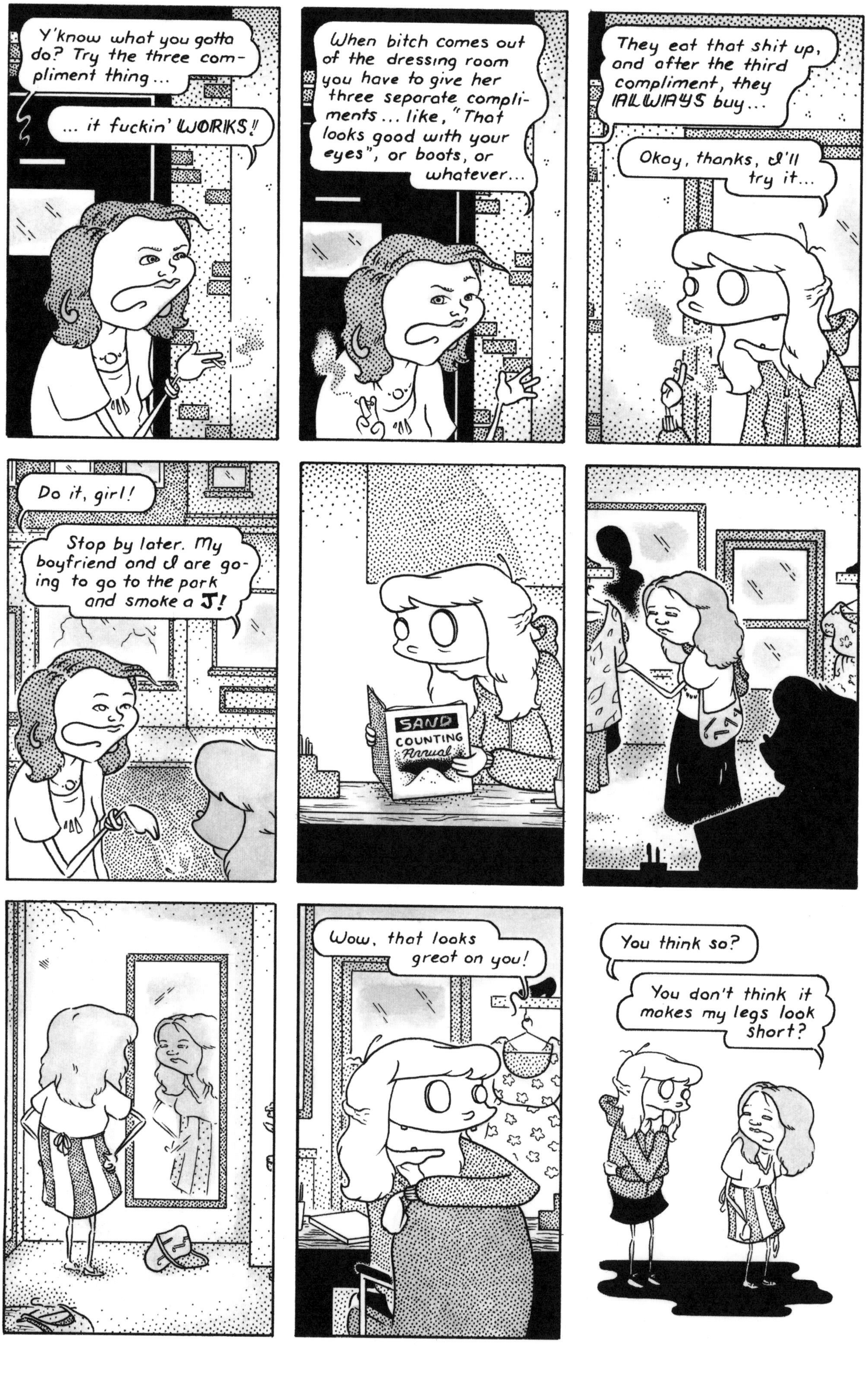
Y'know what you gotta do? Try the three compliment thing...
... it fuckin' WORKS!!
When bitch comes out of the dressing room you have to give her three separate compliments... like, "That looks good with your eyes", or boots, or whatever...
They eat that shit up, and after the third compliment, they ALWAYS buy...
Okay, thanks, I'll try it...
Do it, girl!
Stop by later. My boyfriend and I are going to go to the park and smoke a J!
SAND COUNTING Annual
Wow, that looks great on you!
You think so?
You don't think it makes my legs look short?

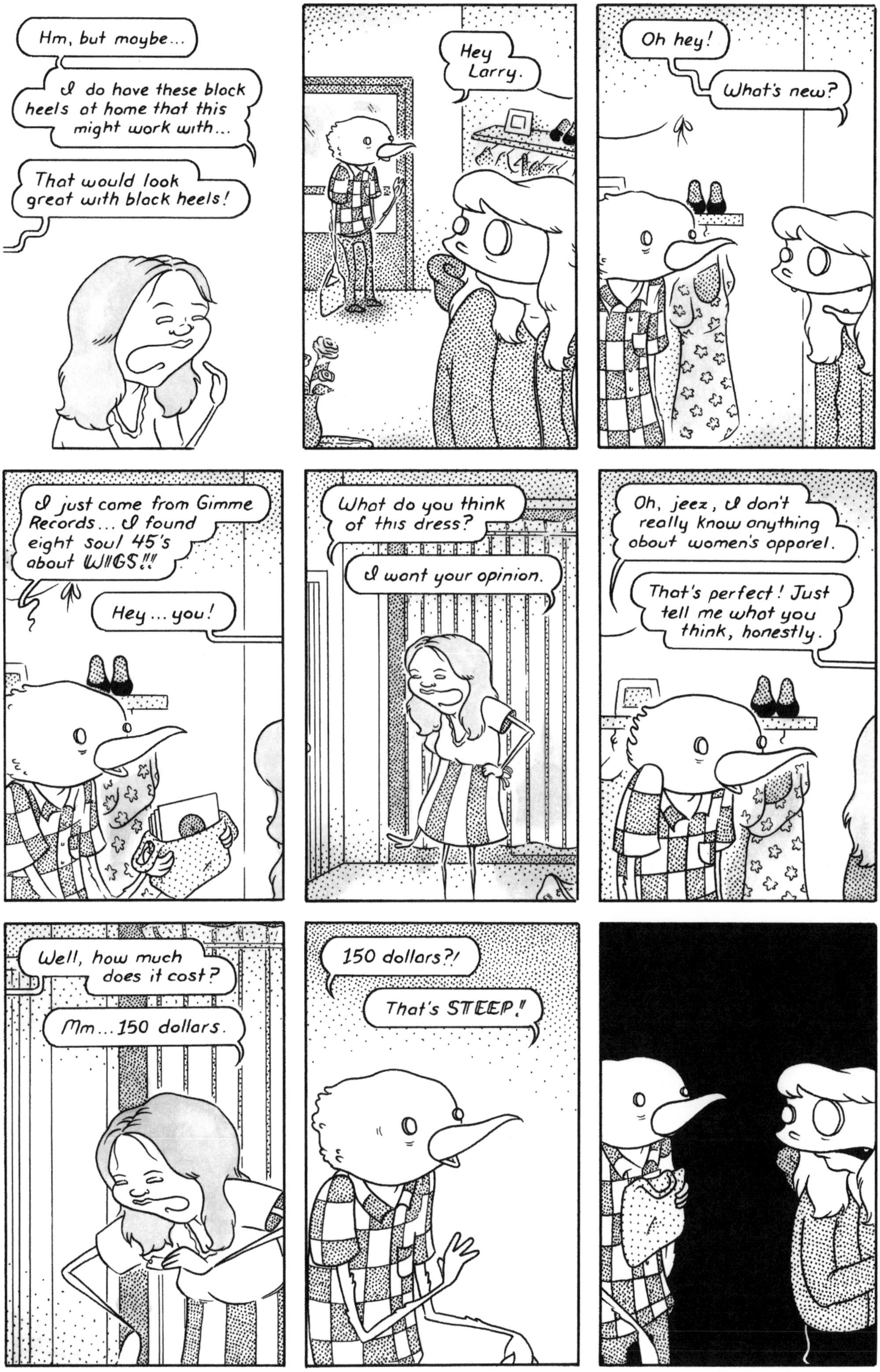
Hm, but maybe...
I do have these black heels at home that this might work with...
That would look great with black heels!
Hey Larry.
Oh hey!
What's new?
I just came from Gimme Records... I found eight soul 45's about WIGS!!!
Hey... you!
What do you think of this dress?
I want your opinion.
Oh, jeez, I don't really know anything about women's apparel.
That's perfect! Just tell me what you think, honestly.
Well, how much does it cost?
Mm... 150 dollars.
150 dollars?!
That's STEEP!

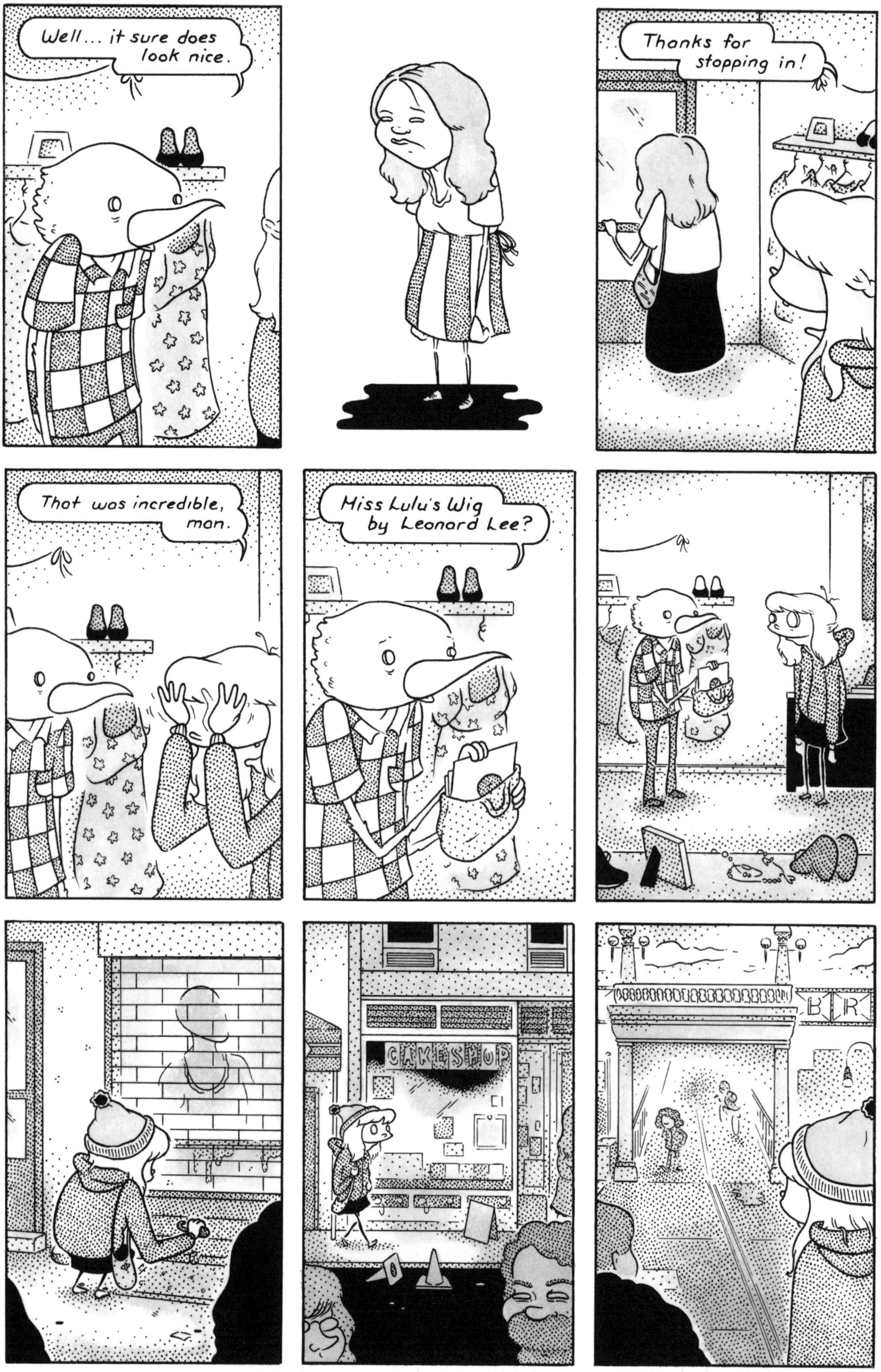
Well... it sure does look nice.
Thanks for stopping in!
That was incredible, man.
Miss Lulu's Wig by Leonard Lee?
CAKESHOP
B R

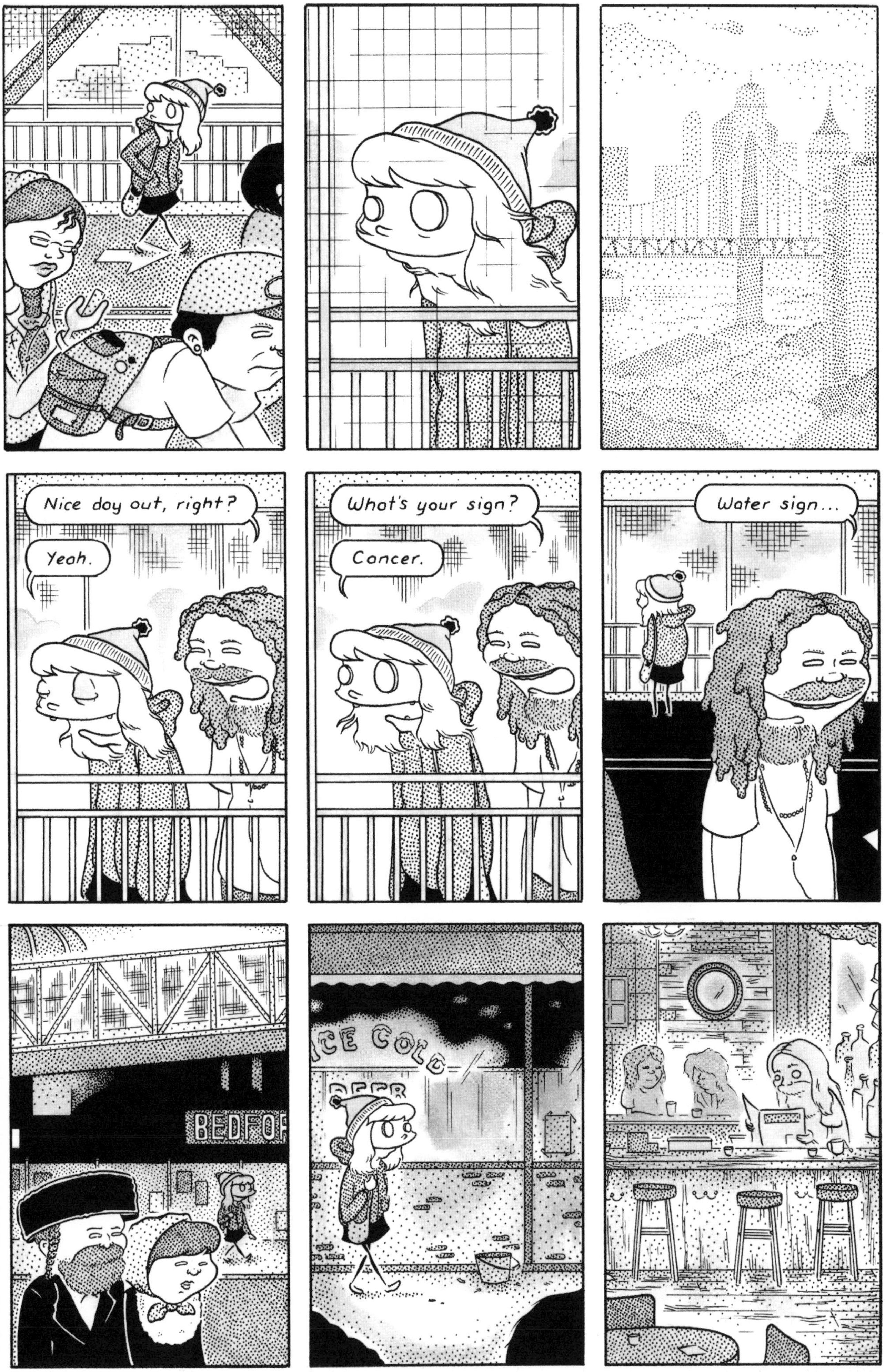
Nice day out, right?
Yeah.
What's your sign?
Cancer.
Water sign...
BEDFOR

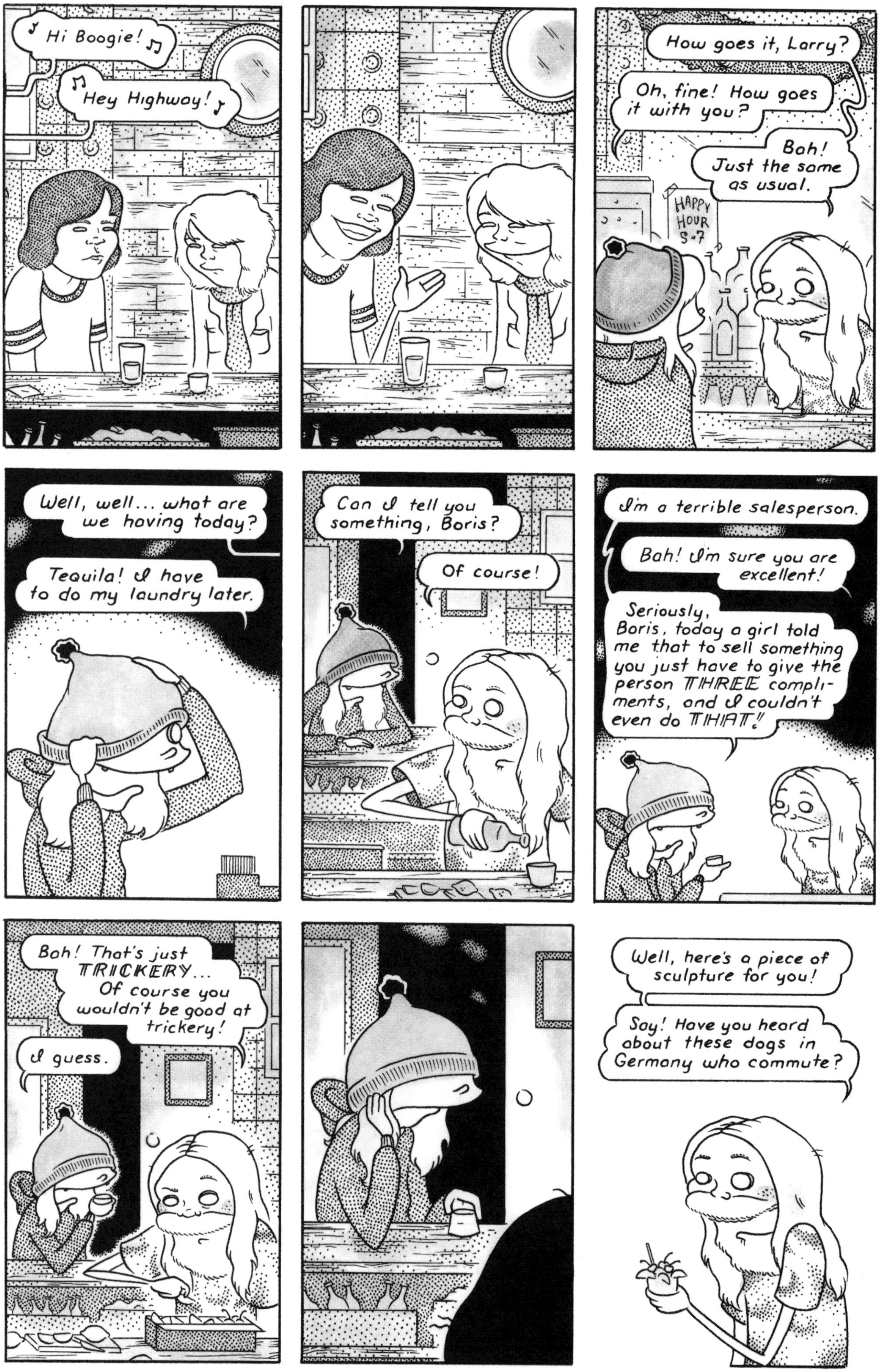
Hi Boogie!
Hey Highway!
How goes it, Larry?
Oh, fine! How goes it with you?
Boh! Just the same as usual.
HAPPY HOUR 5-7
Well, well... what are we having today?
Tequila! I have to do my laundry later.
Can I tell you something, Boris?
Of course!
I'm a terrible salesperson.
Bah! I'm sure you are excellent!
Seriously, Boris, today a girl told me that to sell something you just have to give the person THREE compliments, and I couldn't even do THAT!
Boh! That's just TRICKERY... Of course you wouldn't be good at trickery!
I guess.
Well, here's a piece of sculpture for you!
Say! Have you heard about these dogs in Germany who commute?

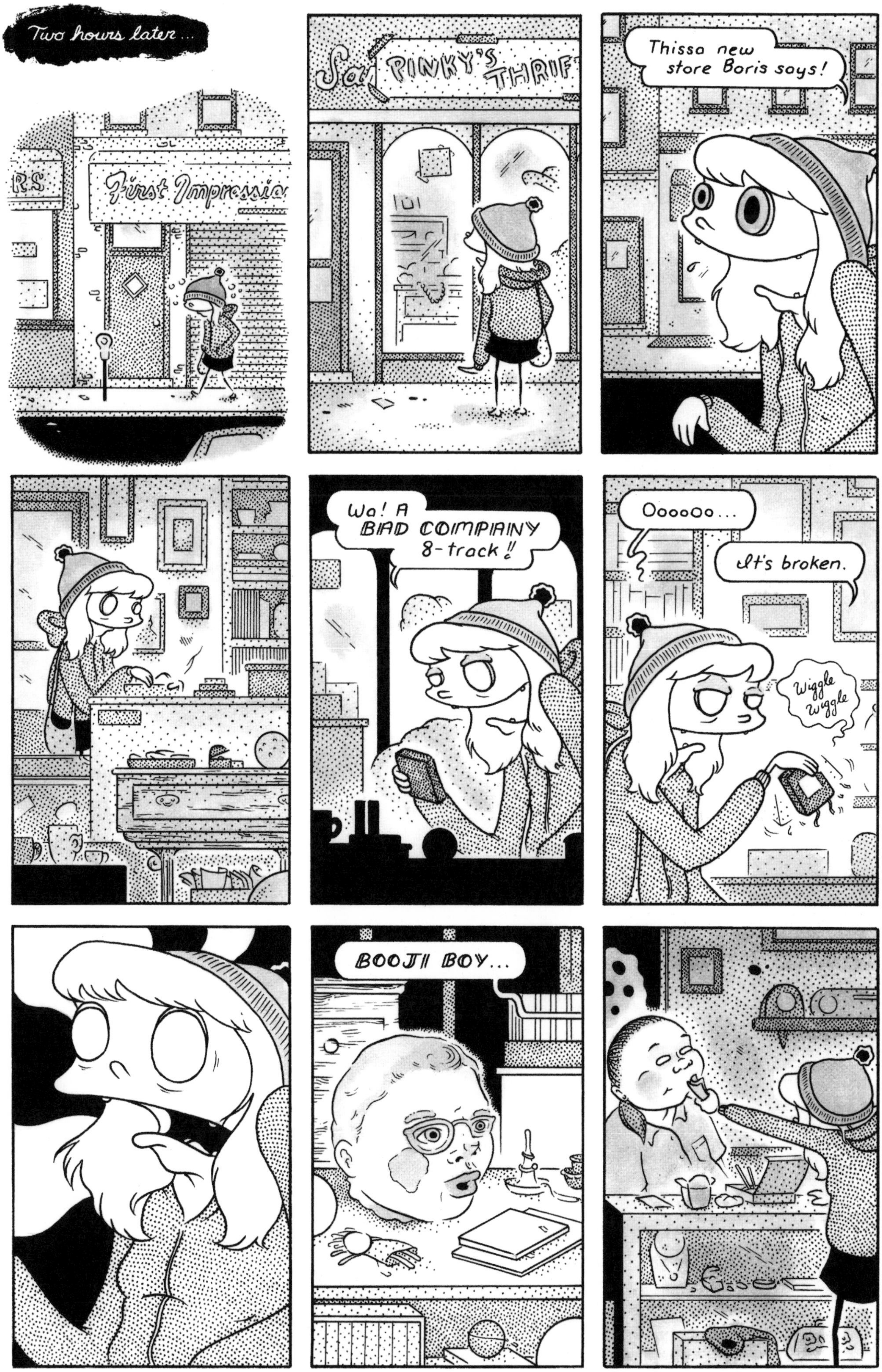

Two hours later...
First Impressio
R.S.
Sa PINKY'S THRIF
Thisso new store Boris soys!
Wa! A BAD COMPANY 8-track!!
Oooooo...
It's broken.
Wiggle wiggle
BOOJI BOY...

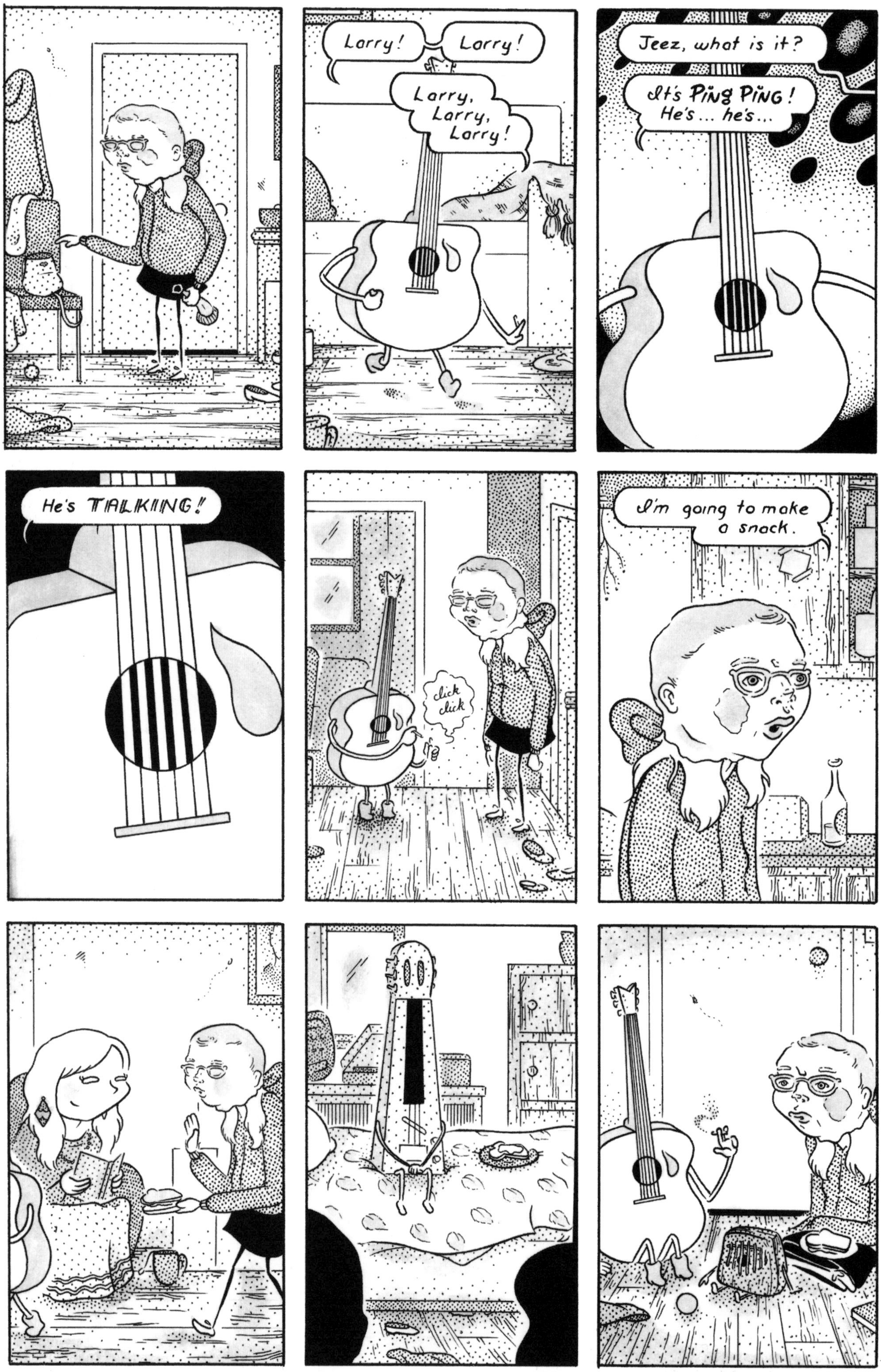
Larry!
Larry!
Larry, Larry, Larry!
Jeez, what is it?
It's PING PING! He's... he's...
He's TALKING!
click click
I'm going to make a snack.

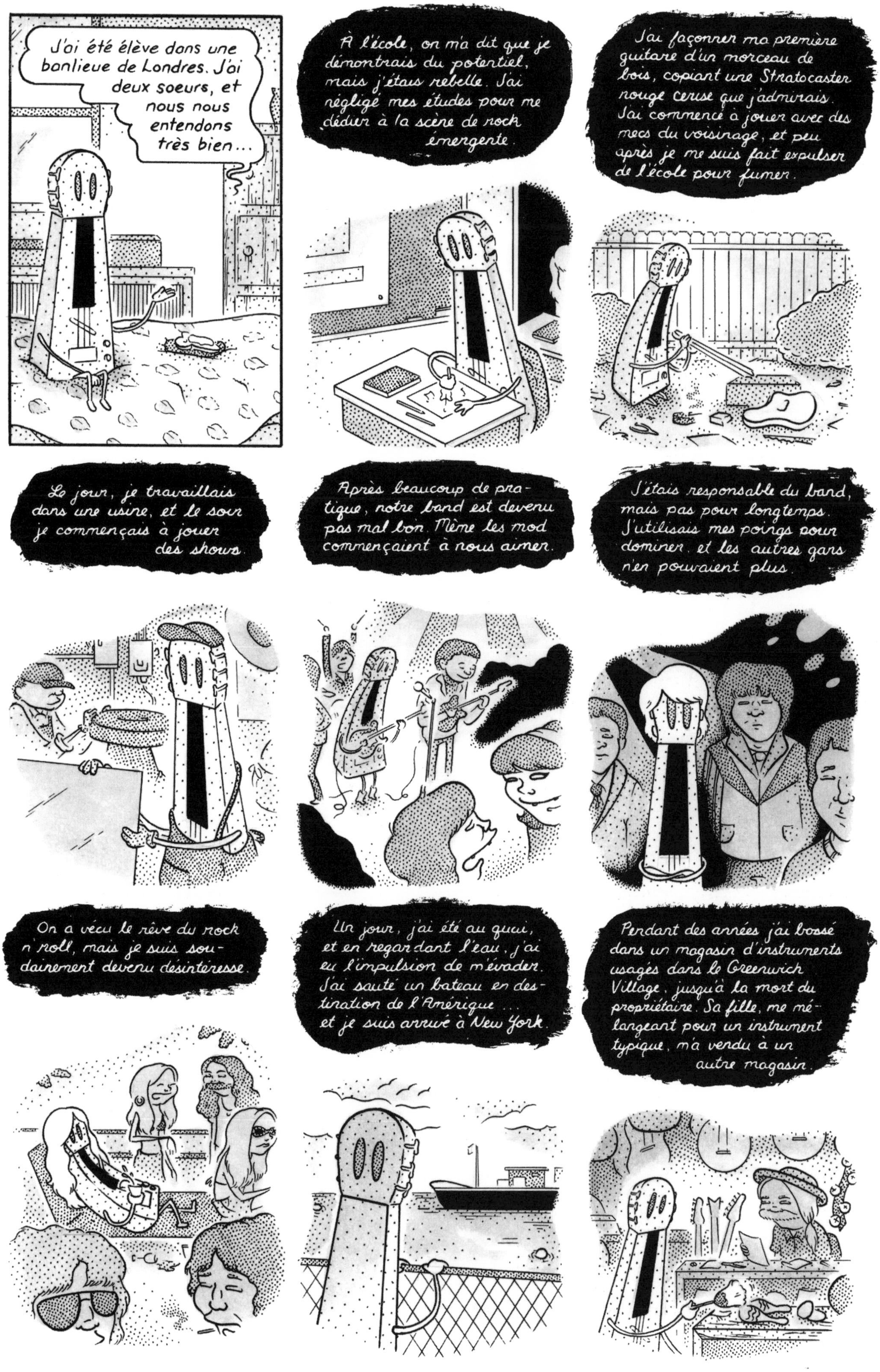
J'ai été élève dans une banlieue de Londres. J'ai deux soeurs, et nous nous entendons très bien...
À l'école, on m'a dit que je démontrais du potentiel, mais j'étais rebelle. J'ai négligé mes études pour me dédier à la scène de rock émergente.
J'ai façonner ma première guitare d'un morceau de bois, copiant une Stratocaster rouge cerise que j'admirais. J'ai commencé à jouer avec des mecs du voisinage, et peu après je me suis fait expulser de l'école pour fumer.
Le jour, je travaillais dans une usine, et le soir je commençais à jouer des shows.
Après beaucoup de pratique, notre band est devenu pas mal bon. Même les mod commençaient à nous aimer.
J'étais responsable du band, mais pas pour longtemps. J'utilisais mes poings pour dominer, et les autres gars n'en pouvaient plus.
On a vécu le rêve du rock n'roll, mais je suis soudainement devenu désintéressé.
Un jour, j'ai été au quai, et en regardant l'eau, j'ai eu l'impulsion de m'évader. J'ai sauté un bateau en destination de l'Amérique... et je suis arrivé à New York.
Pendant des années j'ai bossé dans un magasin d'instruments usagés dans le Greenwich Village, jusqu'à la mort du propriétaire. Sa fille, me mélangeant pour un instrument typique, m'a vendu à un autre magasin.

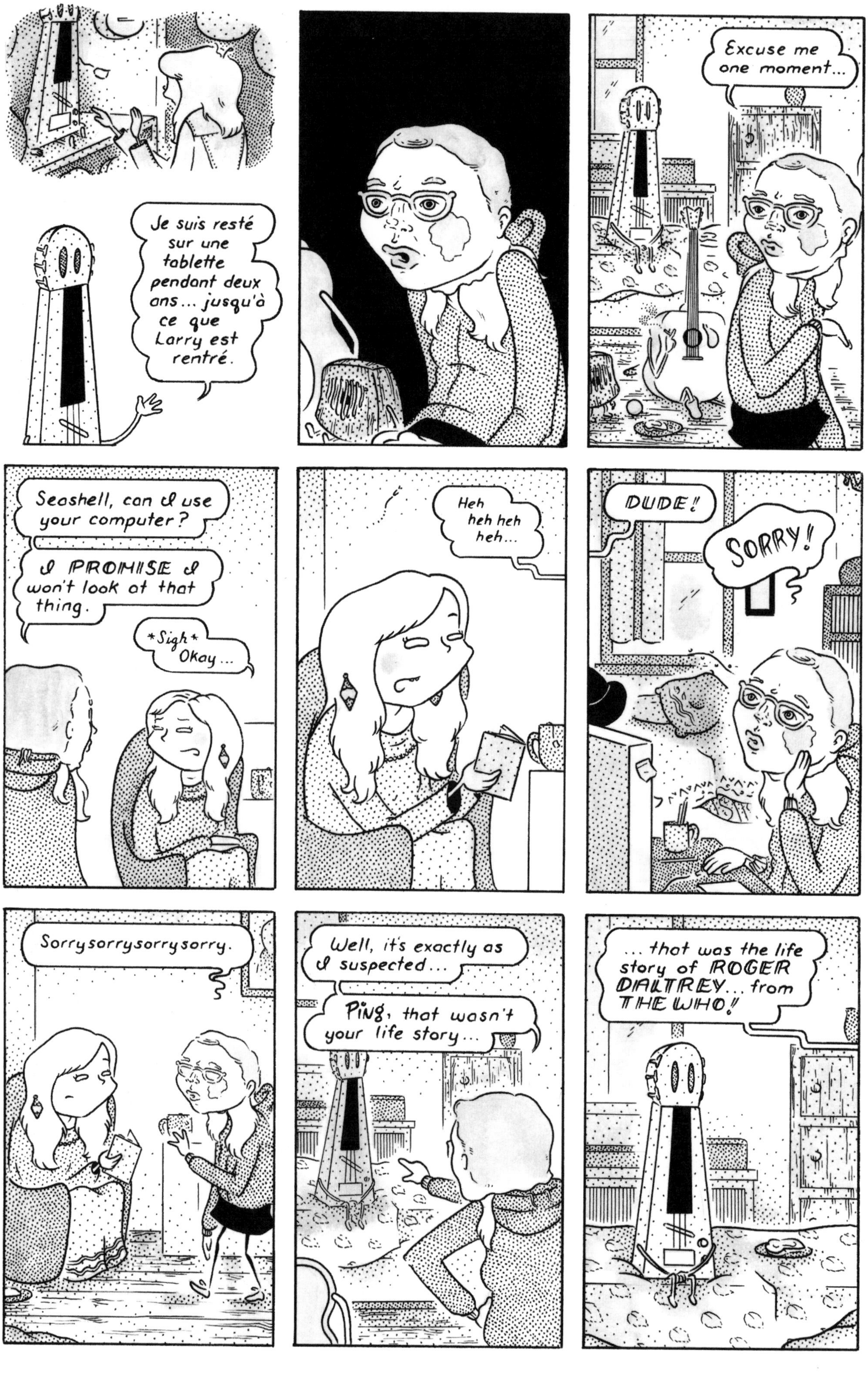

Je suis resté sur une tablette pendant deux ans... jusqu'à ce que Larry est rentré.
Excuse me one moment...
Seashell, can I use your computer?
I PROMISE I won't look at that thing.
Sigh Okay...
Heh heh heh heh...
DUDE!
SORRY!
Sorrysorrysorrysorry.
Well, it's exactly as I suspected...
Ping, that wasn't your life story...
... that was the life story of ROGER DALTREY... from THE WHO!

SLAM

Don't worry, Mim.
He'll probably be back.

PAL
PAL

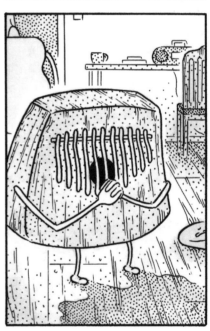

Well, this isn't going
to happen.

I guess
I'll call it a night.

What do you want
me to read, Lar?

Ah! A
classic!

Preheat oven to 425
degrees. Place one
crust in a nine-inch pie
pan. Mix together sugar,
flour, and cinnamon. Mix
lightly through the berries...

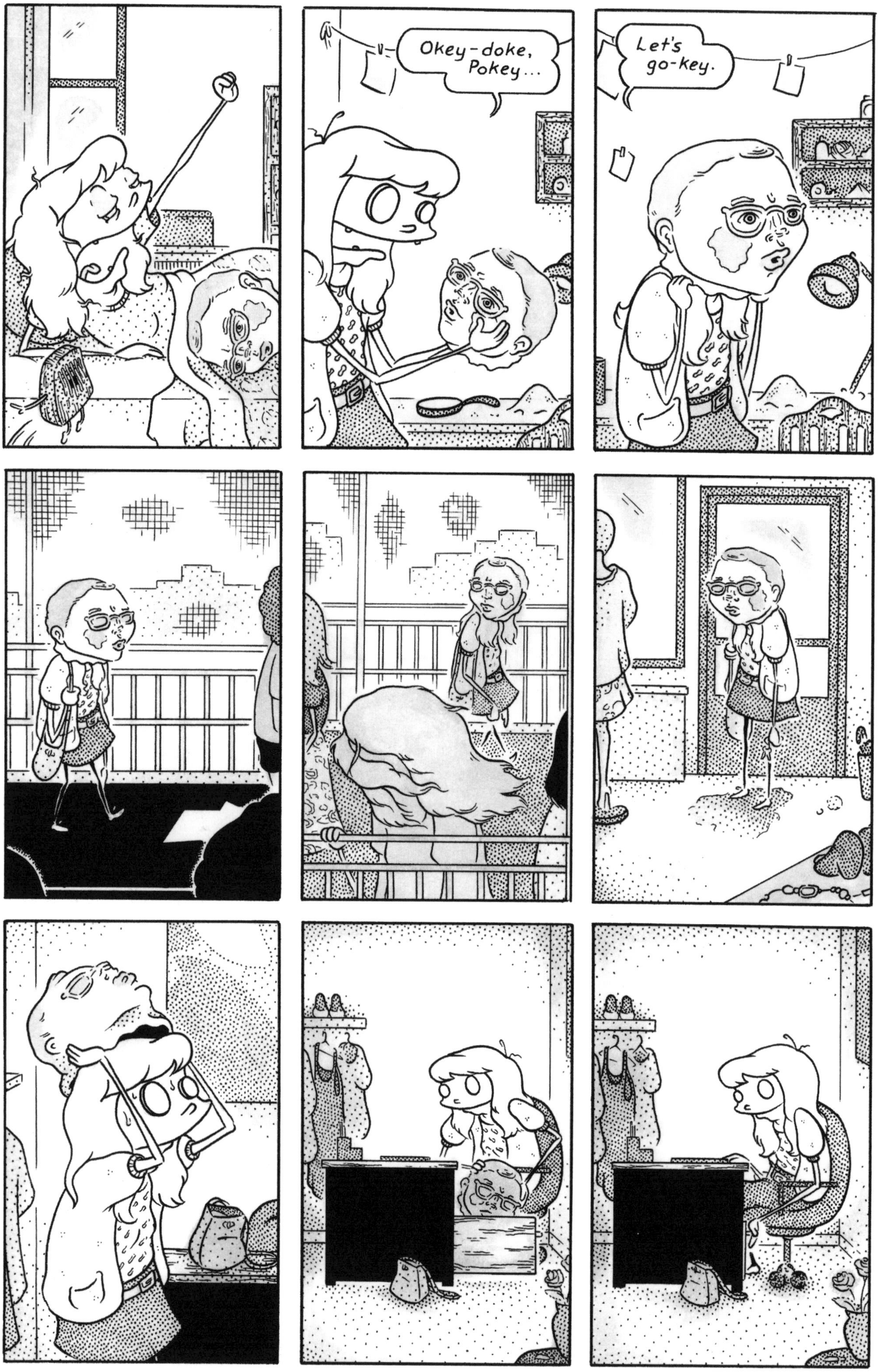
Okey-doke, Pokey...
Let's go-key.

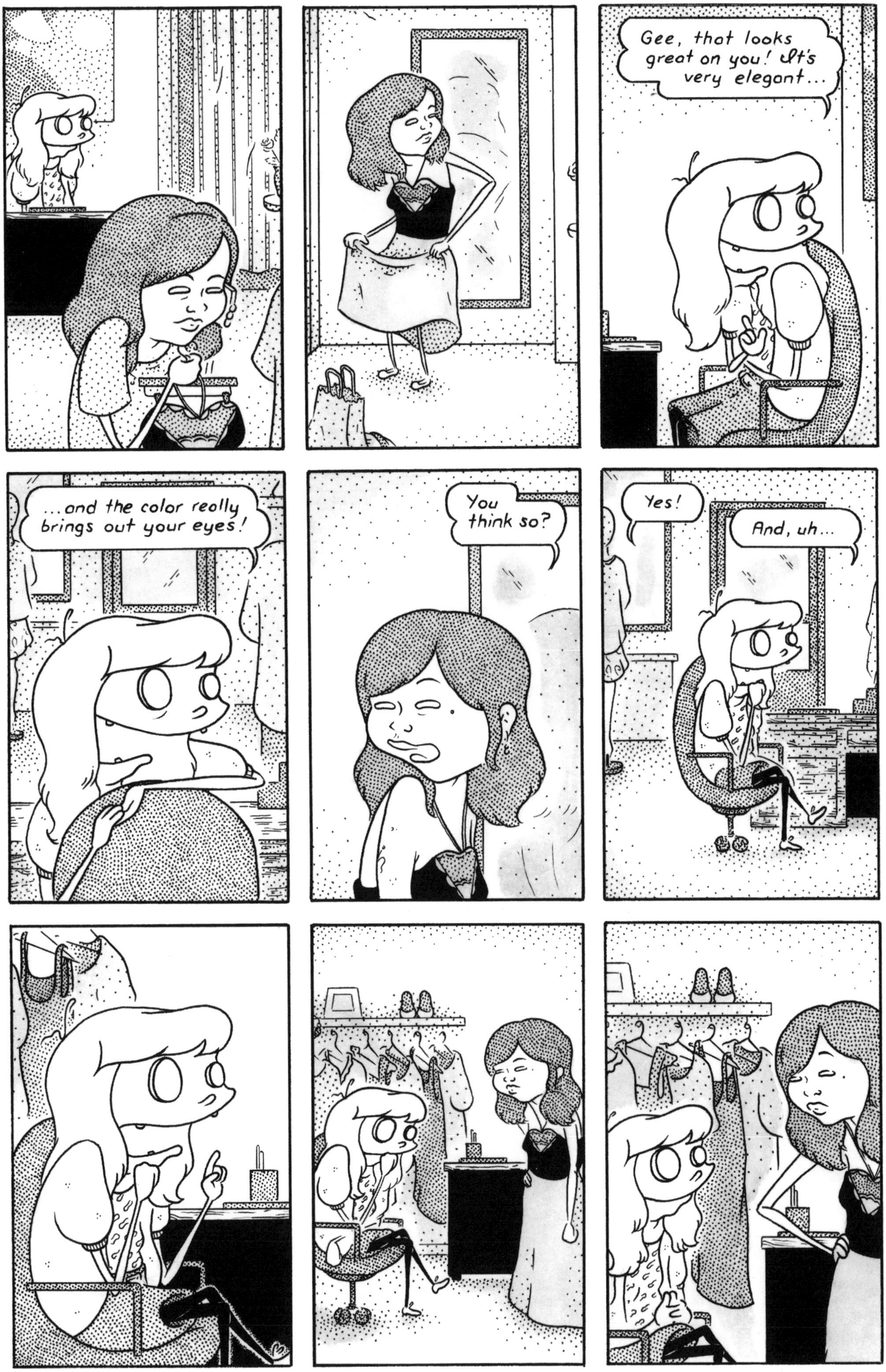
Gee, that looks great on you! It's very elegant...
...and the color really brings out your eyes!
You think so?
Yes!
And, uh...

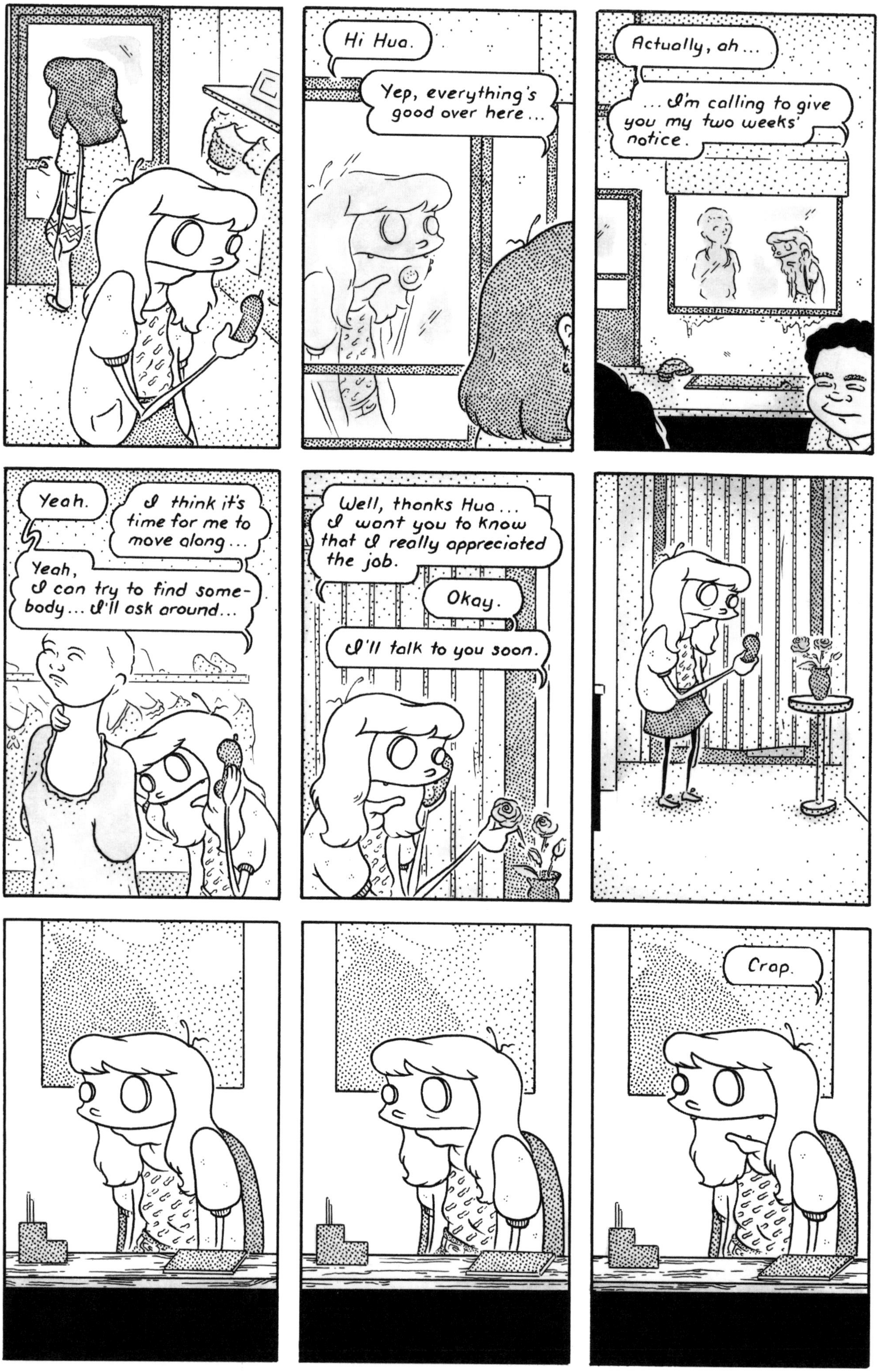
Hi Hua.
Yep, everything's good over here...
Actually, ah...
...I'm calling to give you my two weeks' notice.
Yeah.
I think it's time for me to move along...
Yeah, I can try to find somebody... I'll ask around...
Well, thanks Hua... I want you to know that I really appreciated the job.
Okay.
I'll talk to you soon.
Crap.

Theodore Dreiser

BORN in Indiana in 1871, Dreiser is considered one of the great American naturalist writers. His first novel, Sister Carrie, tells the story of a young country girl who ends up in two large cities, Chicago and New York, hoping to realize her version of the American dream.

Booji Boy is

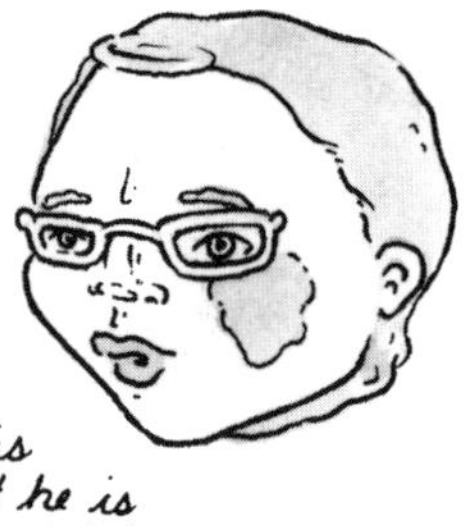

a fictional character created by the band DEVO in the early 1970s. Mark Mothersbaugh portrayed him on stage, symbolizing the regression of western culture: de-evolution.

Although he is very kind to his audience, he looks forward to the day all "normal" humans go extinct. It is said that the mask is not a true representation of Booji Boy and that he is in fact a good-looking German with poor eyesight.

Leslie Stein lives in
Brooklyn, New York.